Timely Assistance

Jessie Boucherett (1825-1905)

Timely Assistance

The Work of the Society for Promoting the Training of Women
1859 – 2009

by
Anne Bridger
Ellen Jordan

SOCIETY for
PROMOTING
the TRAINING
of WOMEN

The Society for Promoting the Training of Women
The Secretary
The Old Dairy
Appledore
Ashford
Kent
TN26 2AJ

email: sec.sptw@btinternet.com

ISBN 978 0 9562449 0 1

Produced by MRM Associates Ltd, Reading

Contents

Timely Assistance

The apprentice as a rule, is to repay the sum advanced for her premium out of her earnings, but as this can only be done by small instalments, it will be some time before the Society can be repaid; it is hoped that after a few years timely assistance may often be rendered to promising girls at a very moderate cost to the fund, and such assistance, it is believed, will on every account be preferable to the ordinary mode of giving money to necessitous women for the temporary relief of distress. *(Annual Report 1867)*

Acknowledgements

Our thanks go to the Mistress and Fellows of Girton College for permission to reproduce the images from the Girton College Collection; to the University of Sydney Library for those from the London Illustrated News; to the City of London Metropolitan Archives for the photographs of Berners Street; and to the Hagley Museum and Library, Manuscripts and Archives Department, for the photographs of the Remington Typewriters (courtesy of Marjorie McNinch, Reference Archivist). We are also grateful to the families of Lord and Lady Monteagle, of Lady Crowther, and of Mrs Golding for permission to use their images.

Abbreviations

AM	Annual Meeting
AR	Annual Report of the SPEW
C&GL	City and Guilds of London Archive. Guildhall Library: Ms. 21, 872/10
CF	Correspondence File, SPTW Archive
CI	Card Index, SPTW Archive
EWJ	*English Woman's Journal:*
EWR	*Englishwomen's Review*
FF	Financial File, SPTW Archive
GCPP	Girton College, Parkes Papers
GCIP	SPTW Archive at Girton College
GCM	Minutes of the General Committee of the SPEW
LSE	Archives at the London School of Economics
MCM	Minutes of the Managing Committee of the SPEW
Minutes	The Society's 20th Century Minute Books
PP	Parliamentary Papers
POST	Post Office Archives, Mount Pleasant

CHAPTER 1

"Bringing social position and influence to their aid": The founding of the SPEW

Nearly two years ago, Miss Boucherett and a few ladies, feeling deeply the helpless and necessitous condition of the great number of women obliged to resort to non-domestic industry as a means of subsistence, consulted together as the best way in which they might bring social position and influence to their aid.
(First Annual Report of the SPEW, 1860)

In November 1859 the *Times* newspaper announced the founding of the Society for Promoting the Employment of Women, and published the following comment:

> We sincerely hope that a new system may be instituted at once, and that we may no longer see women who, like men, must needs turn often to labor for their bread, condemned, unlike men, to the ranks of one miserable and hopeless calling, or left with the single alternative of becoming, according to their positions, either distressed needlewomen or distressed governesses (*The Times* 8.11.1859).

The "distressed needlewomen" and "distressed governesses" were familiar objects of pity to the audience the *Times* addressed. In 1841 a society called the Governesses' Benevolent Institution had been founded to help governesses in distress and uncovered unsuspected levels of poverty among them, while in 1843 the Report to Parliament of the Commissioners on the Employment of Children had revealed the very poor conditions offered to young women apprenticed to dressmakers. The press and various charities kept concern alive and in the mid-1850s the journalist Anna Jameson published the text of two drawing room lectures (Jameson, 1855; Jameson, 1856) which prompted an animated discussion in the serious press of the problems of women in these occupations (Jordan, 1999a).

Barbara Bodichon
1827-1891
(Girton College Collection)

A PROBLEM AND A SOLUTION

A variety of explanations and suggestions for reform grew out of this debate, but the one that prompted the founding of the Society for Promoting the Employment of Women was that put forward by two young admirers of Anna Jameson, Barbara Leigh Smith (soon to become Madame Bodichon) and Bessie Rayner Parkes (later Madame Belloc). They argued that the core of the problem lay in the very limited range of occupations regarded as feminine. Only teaching and dressmaking were open to the women who considered themselves too genteel for domestic service and factory work, and in consequence these occupations were "overstocked", too many women were pursuing too few positions. Employers could make exorbitant demands on the employee's time and drive down her wages, and so she could make very little provision for illness and old age. (Hirsch 1998: 184-90) The solution they proposed was that women must move into a wider range of occupations. Barbara Leigh Smith put the case in 1857 in a pamphlet entitled *Women and Work*:

> There is no way of aiding governesses or needlewomen but by opening more ways of gaining livelihoods for women ... apprentice 10,000 to watchmakers, train 10,000 for teachers of the young; make 10,000 good accountants; put 10,000 more to be nurses under deaconesses trained by Florence Nightingale; put some thousands in the electric telegraph offices over all the country; educate 1000 lecturers for mechanics-institutions; 1000 readers to read the best books to the working people; train up 10,000 to manage washing machines, sewing machines, &c. Then the distressed needle-women would vanish; the decayed gentlewomen and broken down governesses would no longer exist. (Smith 1857: 16-17)

This was not a solution that appeared axiomatic to her contemporaries and the proposal drew a certain amount of ridicule. There was a widely-held and as yet unchallenged assumption that the current division between men's work and women's work was "natural" and divinely appointed, and that interfering with it was foolhardy or even sacrilegious. The two friends believed this created what Anna Jameson had called in her first lecture, "a 'Chinese wall of prejudices:' prejudices religious, social, professional", and felt that one way to break it down was to found a journal that would focus on the need for change. Thus in March 1858 the first number of the *English Woman's*

Journal appeared. Though the Journal also dealt with such "women's rights" issues as divorce and married women's property, it tried to keep the question of women's work before its readership. In fact the occupations dealt with suggest that these pioneers were themselves having difficulty thinking outside the conventional framework and usually described work where there were already some female trail-blazers – telegraphs, clerical work, wood-engraving, nursing, medicine – the most daring suggestion being that women should sell life insurance.

Nevertheless the editors were soon "literally deluged" with requests for help from the kind of women whose plight they were revealing, help which they had no means of offering, though they attempted to meet the need by establishing a register where women in search of work and those

Bessie Rayner Parkes
1829-1925
(Girton College Collection)

with work to offer could make contact. (Parkes 1860: 114) Just as significantly for the future, they established a central meeting place for those concerned with the "woman question" by opening a reading room for women in the same house as the *Journal's* office in 14a Princes Street, just north of Oxford Street, and attracted seventy subscribers in the first year. (GCPP XI 33) Twenty years later Jessie Boucherett, the founder of the Society for Promoting the Employment of Women, wrote that "from this small office and humble reading-room have grown almost all the great women's movements of the present day. They have long passed into other hands and become a shop, but I shall always regard the place as classic ground" (Boucherett, 1884: 97).

Furthermore, their efforts kept the topic alive, and prompted the female journalist Harriet Martineau to write an article on the subject, "Female Industry", for the *Edinburgh Review* in which a passage occurred that was from 1865 until 1940 (when paper rationing caused a change in format) printed on the title page of the Annual Reports of the Society for Promoting the Employment of Women and, after the name change (see Chapter 4), the Society for Promoting the Training of Women:

> The tale is plain enough – from whatever mouth it comes. So far from our countrywomen being all maintained, as a matter of course by us, 'the breadwinners', three millions out of six adult Englishwomen work for subsistence; and two out of the three in independence. With this new condition of affairs, new duties and new views must be accepted (Martineau 1859:336)

Jessie Boucherett
1825-1905
(Girton College Collection)

This passage was read soon after its publication by a thirty-four year old woman, unmarried and of substantial private means, named Jessie Boucherett (1825-1905) and it changed not only her own life but that of many thousands, perhaps millions, of women since. Although Jessie Boucherett was probably in London for the Season when she read the article, her home was a country house in North Willingham, Lincolnshire, where her family was prominent in local politics and philanthropic activities. She herself was strongly interested in public affairs and appears to have devoted a good deal of her time to reading the serious press and thinking about the issues being discussed at the time.

She had already encountered a copy or two of the *English Woman's Journal*, but the full impact of its message does not seem to have reached her until she read the article in the *Edinburgh Review*. "It must," she wrote twenty-five years later, "have had a wide effect, and inspired many with a desire to assist women to earn their livelihood. It gave me the idea of establishing a society, the object of which should be to introduce women into new employments." (Boucherett 1884: 97) Her first step was to make contact with the editors of the *English Woman's Journal*.

According to an account written by one of her supporters towards the end of her life,

> She lost no time in repairing to the office of the journal, where she expected to find some rather dowdy old lady. But instead a handsome young woman dressed in admirable taste, was seated at the table. It was Miss Parkes; in a few minutes another young lady, also beautifully dressed, came in, of radiant beauty, with masses of golden hair. Such is the description given by Jessie Boucherett, long years after, of her first meeting with Barbara Leigh Smith and Bessie Parkes. (Blackburn, 1902: 50)

Jessie Boucherett's earlier accounts of this meeting, however, suggest that her reception was somewhat chilly. Bessie Parkes's first reaction, she recalled, was a refusal to join her in this project "on the ground that it was a rash enterprize, and that on account of the Journal she did not wish her name to be connected with an undertaking which might fail". Nevertheless Bessie Parkes invited her to attend a meeting of the *Journal*'s supporters to be held in the reading room attached to the Journal's office. (SPTW 4/1) Jessie Boucherett later wrote:

> On that evening, so memorable to me, I found some twenty ladies seated round the very primitive apartment which then formed the Reading Room. After some other business had been discussed, I was presented to the meeting by Miss Parkes, who in a few words explained my object. For a moment there was a general silence, and no one moved; then a lady came forward, expressed her approbation of the plan, and promised her assistance. An appointment was made for the following day, and I retired. (Boucherett, 1864)

This helper was the poet Adelaide Procter (author of the very popular "The Lost Chord"), and Jessie Boucherett always regarded her (she died of TB in 1864) as the joint founder of the Society for Promoting the Employment of Women:

> At the end of three weeks the public seeming deaf to our appeals, I grew discouraged and should have given up the project in despair, had she not encouraged me to persevere. At length we excited some little attention. Lord Raynham, now Marquis Townshend, Mrs. Bayne, and a few others joined us. Something like a committee was formed; we assumed the name of the "Society for Promoting the Employment of Women;" a prospectus was printed. (Boucherett, 1864)

The Committee first met on July 7, 1859 (SPTW 2/1, 1860). As can be seen from the page of the Prospectus reproduced here, it consisted of twelve women and four men. A number of the women listed were to have a long association with the Society: Mrs Bayne and Mrs Locke King remained on the Committee until 1884 when both died and each was then replaced by her daughter; Lady Elizabeth Cust was a Committee member until 1878, became a Patroness in 1880, and was still sufficiently interested to address the Annual Meeting in 1908; the Assistant Secretary, Sarah Lewin (1812-1898), was employed by the Society until she retired in 1889. Bessie Parkes had by this time changed her mind and joined the Society,[1] as had another recruit to the group surrounding the *Journal*, Emily Faithfull. The Society does not, however, seem to have shared the rooms of the *Journal*, but to have established a separate office around the corner at 26 Great Castle Street. (*AR* 1860)

ESTABLISHING THE SOCIETY

The prospectus sets out very clearly the aims that were to drive the Society for the next forty years. In the first place it was emphasised that the Society's primary aim was to open more occupations to women. Since two million

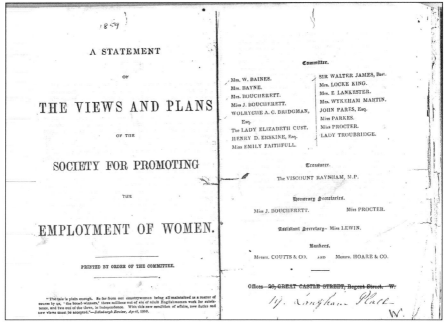

SPEW Prospectus 1859
(Girton College Collection)

unmarried women needed to work for a living, the pamphlet argued, the "great want of employment for women" led to distress and suffering. "The three great professions open to receive them - Teaching, Domestic Service, and Needlework - are over-crowded to such a degree as to render competition excessive and to beat down wages to a point at which it is difficult to live." Thus workhouses were full of able-bodied women who were then "driven out to live as best they may . . . and all this misery is inflicted on them for no fault, but that of having come into a world where there is no employment for them." Was this, the prospectus asked, natural, what God intended? "Or is it that there is something wrong in our social arrangements, whereby they are unfairly deprived of occupations that were intended for their particular benefit?" Male wages, on the other hand, were so high that bounties for soldiers and sailors had had to be raised, and in some areas men could earn enough in three days to spend the rest of the week in drunkenness. "Surely," it went on, "there is something wrong with this disproportion, something unnatural, and that was never intended. Let us then look round, and see whether men are never to be found occupying easy, remunerative places that could as well or better be filled by women; places that originally belonged to them, and that they would have remained in possession of to this day, had not artificial means been used to displace them."

The second aim of the Society was then outlined. One of the great handicaps preventing women moving into the "places that originally belonged to them" was their inadequate training, for example, the neglect of arithmetic in their education. The Society therefore proposed to set up a school to remedy this. "Girls educated in this school would be capable of becoming clerks, cashiers, and ticket-sellers at railway stations." Plans to establish training classes for hair-dressing, printing and watch-making were also mentioned in the prospectus. Once these girls were trained, it was argued, they would themselves take on female apprentices, and the occupations would gradually become feminised.

A very busy time for Jessie Boucherett followed:

> From the end of August 59, when the Prospectus was first distributed, to the beginning of November, every letter was forwarded to me from the office to be answered, the Secretary proving incompetent. The letters of enquiry were numerous and I was often writing all day, but the result was that when the Committee met in November they found £170 in the bank. (GCIP SPTW 4/1)

The Committee also found that great progress had been made in creating a public awareness of the Society and its aims. In October the National Association for the Promotion of Social Science, an organisation concerned with public policy and public welfare, and headed by leading reformist politicians and philanthropists like Lord John Russell, Lord Brougham and the Earl of Shaftesbury, held its Annual Congress in Bradford. Both Bessie Parkes and Jessie Boucherett presented papers on women's work that created a great deal of public interest. Bessie Parkes wrote ecstatically to Barbara Bodichon:

> There is <u>another</u> leader in today about our question . . . the whole kingdom is ringing with our Bradford Paper & subscriptions pouring in at the EWJ Office . . . . - all the weekly papers are full of it too. (GCPP V 94 BRP to BB, 17-11-1859)

It seems that, after the Congress, the Society and its aims were accepted as part of the progressive agenda of the mid-century. The Council of the National Association for the Promotion of Social Science appointed a committee of six men and six women "to consider and report on the subject of Female Employment", four of the women being Jessie Boucherett, Bessie Rayner Parkes, Adelaide Procter and Emily Faithfull, all members of the SPEW Committee. In consequence Jessie Boucherett and Adelaide Procter approached G.W. Hastings, the Secretary of the NAPSS, to propose that the SPEW become formally attached to the Association. This was agreed to on December 8, 1859, the NAPSS providing a number of distinguished men to serve as Officers and on its Committee. The Title Page of the Annual Report reproduced here lists the names of men well-known for their interest in social reform, many of them members of Parliament. Lord Shaftesbury remained President until his death in 1885, presiding at most of the Annual Meetings, and the Minutes of the early meetings of the SPEW indicate that most of those on the Committee attended regularly in the early years.[2]

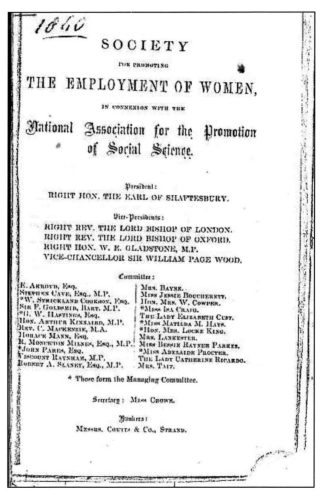

SPEW Officers and Committee Members (AR 1864)
(*Girton College Collection*)

Other organisational changes occurred during the Society's first year. In December 1859 a seven year lease of a house at 19 Langham Place was taken by Lady Monson, an older friend of Matilda Hays (1820-1897), the co-editor with Bessie Parkes of the *English Woman's Journal*, and the SPEW, the *English Woman's Journal*, and Bessie Parkes's Reading Room were all accommodated there. The Committee of the SPEW however met in a room at 3 Waterloo Place, the headquarters of the NAPSS. In January 1860 Sarah Lewin (1812-1898), who already worked for the *English Woman's Journal*, was confirmed as Assistant Secretary of the SPEW at 5s. a week, and in March 1860 the first Secretary, Emily Faithfull, who seems to have been paid about £50 a year, resigned, her place being taken by Jane Crowe, a long time friend of two women who were later to play major roles in the Women's Movement, Elizabeth Garrett Anderson and Emily Davies. The 1861 census records both Jane Crowe and Matilda Hays as living in the upper floors of the Langham Place building.

The regulation of the Society's affairs soon took a form it was to preserve for many years. The Committee met fortnightly with the Chair being taken at each meeting by one of the Committee members present. From January 1860 on, detailed notes of the discussions and decisions were made by the Secretary and copied into a large bound Minute book, being read and signed by the Chair at the next meeting. (These books have been preserved and form the basis for most of the account that follows.) From the early days there was also a smaller Managing Committee which dealt with day to day affairs and reported to the main Committee. Records of its earlier meetings do not survive, but in January 1870 the Secretary initiated a second series of Minute Books which were continued until the two Committees were merged in June 1902.

The affiliation with the NAPSS caused some problems in the early years. It seems that Viscount Raynham, whose support had been so welcomed by the founders, did not approve of the change. The Minutes for February 7, 1860, recorded:

> Mr Hastings then stated that Lord Raynham refused to acknowledge the affiliation of the Society to the National Association, and had given orders to Messrs Coutts & Co to refuse any more money paid to the account of the Society for Promoting the Employment of Women, and to decline cashing cheques drawn by the order of the Managing Committee.

The difficulty was overcome by holding a meeting of subscribers on February 17 (a copy of the printed handout prepared for the meeting still exists) at which the changes were approved, though Lord Raynham played no further part in the Society's affairs.

Another dispute relating to the NAPSS led to the resignation of three of the Society's earliest members, Bessie Rayner Parkes, Adelaide Procter and Matilda Hays. On April 29, 1862 the *Times* published a rather intemperate letter from Matilda Hays accusing men of seeing women simply as "breeding animals". A member of the NAPSS Council, the barrister Andrew Edgar, took exception to this and wrote to the SPEW demanding that she resign. At its next meeting the Committee unanimously passed the resolution "That the Committee having heard Mr Edgar's letter read, decline to enter on the subject contained in it", but enough must have been said informally to upset Matilda Hays and her two close friends, and by June 1862 all three had left the Society. This did not, however, cause a real rift. The *English Woman's Journal* continued to report positively on the Society's affairs (on February 12, 1864, it was referred to in the Minutes as "the regular organ of the Society"), and shared Langham Place amicably with the Society's office. Indeed, in February 1864, the *Journal's* financial situation having declined while the Society's stabilised, the Society moved into the more accessible, though more expensive, ground floor rooms, allowing the editorial work of the *Journal* to be done there without charge.

Furthermore, the resignation of the early enthusiasts does not seem to have hampered the Society's progress. Although the male attendance at Committee meetings gradually slackened, new deeply committed women were recruited (see the account below), and in 1865 the final feature of the Society which determined its functioning in the nineteenth century was put in place. When Jane Crowe resigned as Secretary on health grounds it was decided that a permanent full time appointment should be made and Jessie Boucherett promised to guarantee the first year's salary. According to the Minutes it was resolved:

> That the following advertisement, "Society for Promoting the Employment of Women. Wanted, a lady of active habits, and with some knowledge of business to act as Secretary to the above Society. Salary £100 a year. Apply by letter, before 26th August, to the Hon. Sec. Pro.tem. Miss Crowe, 19 Langham Place, London W.," be inserted on or about the 1st August in the Spectator (twice) Morning Star, Pall Mall Gazette--- and, that the Managing Committee be empowered to receive applications and to select from among the candidates those whom they consider the most eligible. (GCM 27-6-65)

The Committee interviewed seven of the applicants and chose Gertrude King. In her letter of appointment she was told:

> The Minute under which you are appointed is as follows: "That a Lady be appointed at a salary of £100 a year, who in addition to the usual duties of Secretary, should negotiate with Employers for the apprenticeship of girls to businesses, and for the increased employment of women in those which are already open---and that she be expected to give the chief part of her time to the work of the Society, but that the distribution of it be left to her own discretion." The management of the accounts will for the present, be in the hands of the Assistant Secretary.__

The appointment will date from September 5th and will be terminable at a month's notice on either side.

As it turned out Gertrude King held the post for the next fifty years, organising and supervising the moving of the office to 23 Gt Marlborough St in 1867, and then to 22 Berners Street in 1872.

MISS KING.

Gertrude King
1832-1928
(From The Quiver, *1889, p.114)*

SOME LEADING FIGURES

Jessie Boucherett was not only the founder of the Society, she was a dominating presence throughout its first fifty years. As the next two chapters will show she had very strong ideas about the direction it should take, and was prepared to use her own money to have them implemented. She was the youngest of four children, none of whom married, in a wealthy landed family settled in North Willingham in Lincolnshire, and this assured her of an independent and very substantial income for life. When her father died in 1857 she received a capital sum of £10,000, her mother's death in 1873 put her in possession of a further £16,000, and when her remaining brother died in 1877 he left her £1,000 a year for life. She inherited the estate herself when her elder sister died in 1895. (Jordan and Bridger 2006)

Her work for the Women's Movement, which began when she visited the *English Woman's Journal* office in 1859, formed the core of her life. When the successor to the *Journal*, the *Alexandra Magazine*, ceased publication in December 1865, she put up the money for a replacement, the *Englishwoman's Review*, which ran from January 1866 to July 1910, and operated as a sort of newsletter recording the progress of the various Women's Movement campaigns. One of these, the women's suffrage campaign, was the second great enthusiasm of Jessie Boucherett's life, and actually began in the SPEW office in May 1866 with Jessie Boucherett putting down £25 to finance it (Hirsch 1998: 217). She also used the Society as the base for her opposition to protective legislation targeted solely at women, which she first raised at a Committee meeting in 1873 (GCM 19-5-73) and which was a compelling interest from then until her death. She managed to convert most of the Society's active Committee members (though not its President) to her views. In her will she left £2,000 each to the Society and to the Freedom of Labour Defence Fund she had established in 1899, and, among a number of lesser legacies, £700 to Gertrude King.

The Committee member who took over the leadership role on Jessie Boucherett's death in 1905 was the Hon. Victoria Grosvenor (1833-1913), an unmarried daughter of Lord Ebury, who lived with her family in Hanover Square. An In Memoriam notice in the 1913 Annual Report read:

> By the death of the Honble. Victoria Grosvenor the Society has sustained an irreparable loss. From the time she became a member of the Committee in July 1865 [In fact she attended her first meeting on February 10, 1864] till the day of her death February 13, 1913, she was its true and constant friend. She became Hon. Treasurer in 1888, and has for many years taken the chair at the bi-monthly meetings of the Committee. She was perfect in this capacity, courteous to every one, always keeping to the point in question till a decision was reached. Though herself a staunch Churchwoman, and devoting much of her time to Church matters and Church associations, she was thoroughly broad-minded and never begrudged time or thought bestowed on the work of the Society, which is entirely free from religious or political bias. Her practical commonsense and sound judgment were invaluable, while her genial kindness and bright disposition won for her the love and respect of all who worked with her. She never gave up till absolutely obliged to do so, her last signature to the minutes being dated January 10, 1913.

Almost as long-serving was Jane Crowe (b. 1830), who joined the Committee on her resignation as the Society's Secretary in 1864, attended her last meeting on October 13, 1905, and was one of the most assiduous in making inquiries on behalf of the Society. She was artistic, on one occasion winning a prize for a printed blind, and the Committee tended to look to her for advice when placing women in art-related occupations.[3] After leaving Langham Place she shared a house for a time with the medical pioneer, Elizabeth Garrett, and then at some time in the 1870s moved to Tunbridge Wells. She and her friend Miss Harker-Smith[4] made substantial contributions to the Society when it seemed likely to have to draw on its investment funds (GCM 27-11-1908, 10-12-1909)

Two women who played a significant part in the wider Women's Movement were members of the Committee for varying lengths of time. Emily Davies, the pioneer of women's university education, served from 1865 to 1873, and Charlotte (Mrs William) Burbury, (1832-1895), sister of Professor Kennedy of Cambridge, who was also active in the suffrage, medical and educational campaigns, serving on a number of committees and boards, and who became a practised public speaker on women's issues, served from 1869 to 1889 (Crawford 1999: 87, 157-9).

One member who joined the Committee in 1865, Mary Ponsonby, wife of a former equerry to Prince Albert who in 1870 became the Queen's Private Secretary, may have played some part in gaining the Queen's patronage for the Society. When in 1864 the Committee heard that the Dublin Society for the Employment of Women had received royal patronage, they put out feelers for similar support, but were told that the Queen did not grant this to societies as small as the SPEW, "although she considered the object of increasing female employment a commendable one" (GCM 12-1-64, 12-2-64). During the next few years one particular member, Mrs Locke King,[5] brought up the issue a number of times but the Committee remained wary of another refusal. Finally, however, on January 26, 1869, Mrs Ponsonby told the Committee that the Queen had consented to being listed as a patroness.

At a Committee meeting early in 1864 the possibility was discussed of "inviting lady members of rank to become vice-Presidents:--Vice-presidents having a right to attend Committees and vote like ordinary members---by which means one or two vacancies would be created to be filled up with ladies who would undertake to help in the office such assistance being much required" (GCM 12-2-64). This seems to have resulted in the appointment of a Miss James and a Miss Lawrance in May 1864 (GCM 10-5-64). Sara Lawrance, who remained a member until 1888, had already acted as Secretary in Jane Crowe's absence, taking the Minutes at Committee meetings, but we have been able to find out nothing about her apart from the fact that she was an early member of the feminist discussion group, the Kensington Society, and seems to have had something of a crush on Bessie Parkes. We know even less about Miss James, who over the years made donations amounting to £41.18.6 to the Society, and remained on the Committee until 1892. Yet, as will appear in the next chapter, both women put a good deal of effort into sorting out one of the Society's difficulties, and it can perhaps be assumed that they provided the Secretary with support on less crucial occasions.

Sarah Lewin (1812-1898), the Assistant Secretary, was rather older than most of the other workers for the Society, and came from a much more modest background. (She was not, as is sometimes erroneously stated, related to the Jane Lewin who supported Maria Rye's emigration efforts.) She began working as bookkeeper for her butcher uncle when she was nineteen, but on encountering a copy of the *English Woman's Journal* became committed to the Women's Movement for the rest of her life. In January 1860 she was appointed Assistant Secretary to the SPEW "at a salary of five shillings a week", and except for a brief interlude when she worked primarily for the *English Woman's Journal*, continued in this position until failing eyesight caused her to retire in 1889. By that time she had been renting an upper apartment in the Society's premises in Berners Street for many years and her salary had risen to £50 a year. She was presented with an illuminated address and a testimonial present of £150 in a special purse and invited to join the Committee, which she attended regularly thereafter. She made a present of £100 from her savings to the Society and also donated "her large Chippendale case which has always occupied the right hand corner [of the office] by the fireplace". (EWR 1898; GCM 11-1-1860, 6-07-1889, 18-10-89)

At a Meeting of the General Committee held on Friday, January 11th 1895
Present:
F.D. Mocatta Esq. in the Chair
Miss Jessie Boucherett.
Mr. Bullock.
Mr. Fitch,
Mr. Gerard Ford.
Hon. Victoria Grosvenor
Miss Lewin.
                    Gertrude J. King Sec'y

The Minutes of the previous Meeting were read and confirmed.
A Report of the work of the Society during the quarter ending December 31st 1894 was read and approved.
A statement of the accounts for the same quarter was submitted and passed. Donations amounting to £47.7 have been received during the quarter. £10 from Miss Jessie Boucherett for the General Fund, and £3.4 for the Book-keeping Class; £25 from Miss Meynell Ingram; £5 from the Skinners Company; £3 from Hon. Dudley Fortescue; 10/6 from Miss Giuseppi, an old pupil of the Book-keeping Class; 12/6 from two ladies who have been helped by the Society.
        As the funds of the Society available for general purposes were very low, letters had been sent to 19 of the City Companies asking for help. The Sadlers Company have responded by sending a donation of £5; the Mercers say that they cannot contribute at present, but replies have not as yet been received from the other companies.
        As the Book-keeping Class has not been altogether satisfactory, lately the Managing Committee decided to seek a new teacher. Miss Toplis recommended a lady - a B.A. of London - who is on her staff as a teacher of arithmetic and Mathematics, - but she has had no experience at all in Book-keeping or in business, and it was decided that a thorough knowledge of Book-keeping and some experience in business are essential. One of the candidates for the post, Miss Annie Simpson, attended the class some years ago, and gained a good certificate, & she had since taken a First Class Certificate at the Society of Arts. Miss Simpson has held a situation for 6 years in Miss Amy Bell's office, & Miss Bell speaks very highly of her knowledge of book-keeping and accounts. The other candidate, Miss Whitewright was also a pupil in the Class, and gained a certificate in 1890. She has since had experience in Book-keeping, but not as

Page of Minutes written by Gertude King
(Girton College Collection)

The lynch-pin of the Society, however, was, as will be seen from the accounts that follow, the Secretary Gertrude King (1832[6]-1928). Her father, a man of considerable scholarship, ran a private school for boys in Marylebone. She does not seem to have followed a career before taking the position with the Society, though she may have taught in her father's school. The censuses show that after her parents' deaths she continued to live in the Marylebone district with her brother-in-law, James Menzies, a tutor for university entrance, and his family and scholars until his death in 1900, when she set up house with her niece, Gertrude Menzies (b. 1864) (LSE HARRISON 1/95.21). She devoted her life to the Society. She ran the office (maintaining the fabric as well as supervising the activities), controlled the finances, kept the Minutes (her clear, unfaltering handwriting is an incalculable boon to the researcher), interviewed applicants, visited employers, supervised the classes held and the casual clerical work undertaken in the office, attended conferences, and undertook any other tasks requested of her. She retired in 1915 after fifty years' service, and was given a small pension. On her death her protégée Constance Hoster wrote: "Only those who knew her as it was my privilege to know her could realise her wonderful influence, her brilliant brain-power, her insight into character and the absolute sweetness and unselfishness of her disposition. ...The past, present and future generations alike owe Gertrude King a deep debt of gratitude. In her quiet way she was a pioneer in her generation." (*AR* 1929)

---

1   She explained her decision to Barbara Leigh Smith (now Barbara Bodichon): "As to my allowing my name to be on Miss Boucheretts Committee; I mean to join every Committee in aid of women, however absurd. You see, dear Barbara, there is little or no sound thought in the kingdom on this subject; but a deal of strong feeling gradually rising - Therefore we must sail with the tide, & persuade people into one's own views gradually, or nothing will be done." (GCPP V 90. BRP to BB, 13-9-1859).

2   By 1866 the attendance of the male members had slackened considerably, perhaps partly because since 1864 meetings were no longer held at 3 Waterloo Place, in the heart of male clubland, but at 1 Adam Street, Adelphi, a much more taxing walk from Pall Mall.

3   See GCM 18-12-66, 30-06-68, 03-11-69, MCM 2-11-70, 31-5-71, 1-5-72, 12-6-74, 3-11-74, 31-1-79.

4   Miss Harker Smith left £3,000 to the Society in 1914.

5   Mrs Locke King later pressed, this time unsuccessfully in spite of a threat to resign, to have Mrs Gladstone's name dropped from the list of patronesses (GCM 24-4-74, 12-4-78).

6   This date is based on the age given to the census-takers in 1841. In later censuses 1834 and 1836 are implied, while her obituaries give her age at death in 1928 as 98.

7   In 1905 the Committee voted to increase her salary by £10 per annum "as a mark of [its] sincere appreciation of her devoted services." (GCM 12-1-1906).

CHAPTER 2

Breaching the "Chinese wall of prejudices": 1860-1880

It will be the true, the lasting glory of Florence Nightingale and her band of devoted assistants, that they have broken through what Goethe calls a 'Chinese wall of prejudices:' prejudices religious, social, professional; and established a precedent which will indeed multiply the good to all time.
(Jameson 1855: 113)

The SPEW office at Langham Place[1] must have been a busy place. The Secretary, the Assistant Secretary and their voluntary helpers seem to have kept it open to visitors for most of the day, while the members of the Ladies' Reading Room (who had access to "a luncheon room, and a room for the reception of parcels" on one of the upper floors (EWJ 4:21, p. 288)) must frequently have passed through. There were also callers who, having heard of the Society's aims, were hoping the Society could find them suitable employment.

The Society seems to have accepted that finding work for these women, and for those who wrote asking advice, was a major responsibility, and well into the twentieth century the office combined the functions of an employment agency and a careers advisory service. Unfortunately a great many of the Society's earlier clients were women well into middle age: widows, those with husbands who from illness or business failure were no longer able to support them, those left without support when the parents or relatives with whom they had lived died. The 1875 Annual Report commented on the problems these women created:

> The timidity which makes women ashamed to be known to work, is most difficult to deal with: it is not at all an uncommon thing for a lady to apply to the Society for employment, but to refuse to give her name; the mention of references strikes her with dismay. There are ladies who are so afraid of being known to do anything towards their own maintenance that they beg to be allowed to work under an assumed name; these poor ladies will submit to any privation, undergo any hardship, to keep up appearances. (*AR* 1875)

These were of course exactly the kind of women whose situation the Society had been founded to address, but the social and economic changes that its founders envisaged, that more occupations should be opened to women and that all women should be trained for an occupation, had still to be implemented and these were not women capable of implementing them. Fortunately the Society also attracted younger women from rather less genteel families living in the surrounding districts, who were less inhibited, and these young local women became the subjects for the Society's experiments.

Rather more than a quarter of the Society's income from donations and subscriptions went on supporting the office. In 1863-4, for example, the income of the Society was £432.13.5, and the money spent on rent, salaries, and general expenses was £152.3.1.[2] Nevertheless this left a modest but significant sum for devoting to the Society's broader aims. At first it was intended that the Society should use these funds to set up classes to teach girls skills such as printing, hairdressing and book-keeping which would lead to their employment in these trades in the wider community. By 1865, however, the Committee had come to realise that most skilled occupations were entered by apprenticeship, and that women would have little chance of breaking into them unless they followed the male pattern of training. It was in the process of organising apprenticeships that the scheme which has since become the Society's main function, the granting of interest-free loans for training, evolved. The *Annual Report* for 1867 described how this came about:

During the past year the principal efforts of the Society have been directed to the apprenticing of girls to special branches of industry, the Committee regarding this as the best means open to them at present of improving the social position of women. In all businesses which are at all remunerative premiums are required with apprentices, and, as it is a new idea to parents to start their daughters in life otherwise than by marriage, the difficulty of obtaining a premium is a constant hindrance to the efforts of the Society. The Committee are happy to state that the liberality of friends has partially obviated this difficulty, and they have been assisted to establish a Fund to aid, by loan or otherwise, such girls as are willing to sign indentures, but whose friends are unable to provide the necessary premium. The contributions to this fund amount to £85.14s.; of this sum £64 has already been employed in apprenticing two girls to glass engraving. The balance in the hands of the Committee is not sufficient for the premium of a third.

The apprentice as a rule, is to repay the sum advanced for her premium out of her earnings, but as this can only be done by small instalments, it will be some time before the Society can be repaid; it is hoped that after a few years timely assistance may often be rendered to promising girls at a very moderate cost to the fund, and such assistance, it is believed, will on every account be preferable to the ordinary mode of giving money to necessitous women for the temporary relief of distress. Before any girl is apprenticed, the utmost care is taken to ascertain that the tradesman with whom she is to be placed is, in all respects, worthy of the trust, and that the work to which he undertakes to train her is such as may be properly done by women.

Before signing her indentures, a girl is required to serve a certain time in the business on trial, that it may be seen whether she has a fair chance of attaining proficiency, and that she is sufficiently sensible and orderly to conform to rules and hours.

Though the provision of loans for training has, one hundred and fifty years later, become the main purpose of the Society, during the first twenty years this was seen as merely a means to the Society's primary aim of opening new occupations. The extent to which this end was achieved can be best estimated by looking separately at its endeavours in the various fields singled out as promising.

CLERICAL WORK AND THE CIVIL SERVICE

The need to find new occupations had dominated discussions in the earliest days of the Society's history, and looking at the decisions made, it seems that the Committee saw clerical work of various kinds as the most promising avenue to pursue. It had been argued by Anna Jameson as far back as 1846 that this was suitable work for women:

> She can write a good hand, and is a quick and ready accountant. She might be a clerk, - or a cashier, - or an assistant in a mercantile house. Such a thing is common in France, but here in England, who would employ her? Who would countenance such an innovation on all our English ideas of feminine propriety? I have heard of women employed in writing and engrossing for attorneys, but this is scarcely an acknowledged means of assistance; they are employed secretly, and merely because they are paid much less than men. (Jameson 1846: 236)

Although it was not unknown for women to undertake clerical work at this period, such work was usually done within a small family business by wives, daughters and sisters of the male heads of the families. The census of 1861 listed only 34 female accountants and 274 female commercial clerks, which suggests that very few women did this sort of work for wages outside the home.

The Committee members seem to have felt that office work had two separate branches, the copying of letters and documents and book-keeping. By the end of January 1860 classes had been organized to teach these two skills, and a room hired in Queen's Square, Bloomsbury, where they could be conducted. For five hours daily the room was used for law-copying classes[3]

Alexandra Magazine Advertiser.

Institution for Needlewomen, 2, Hinde Street, Man-chester Square. Under the immediate patronage of H.R.H. the Duchess of Cambridge; H.R.H. the Grand Duchess of Mecklenburg-Strelitz, H.R.H. Princess Mary of Cambridge. Patrons: The Lord Bishop of London, the Lord Bishop of Oxford. President: Earl of Shaftesbury. Ladies are invited to visit the above Institution, where orders for Needlework of all kinds are received and skilfully executed. During the last year above 10,000 garments were cut out and made up by the Society's Needlewomen.

Association for the Sale of Work, by Ladies of Limited Means, 66A, Berners Street, Oxford Street, London, W. Founded in 1858.

Patronesses.

The Duchess of Beaufort.	The Viscountess Middleton.
The Countess of Shaftesbury.	The Hon. Mrs. R. Adams.

and others.

Treasurer.—H. Gerard Hoare, Esq., 37, Fleet Street.
Hon. Secs.—Mrs. C. R. Hoare, 2, Orsett Terrace, Hyde Park.
Mrs. Lockey, Bath. | Mrs. Lanfeur, Reading.

Cork Protestant Orphan Female Home, Opened March, 1856, for the reception of twelve girls, to be trained as servants. Since the beginning, fifty-nine girls have been received into "The Home"; forty-four of these are now comfortably placed in situations.

The Home is entirely dependent on voluntary contributions. The Honorary Superintendent, Mrs. Tooker, the Mardyke, Cork, will be grateful for any aid towards this undertaking.

Nurses' Training School, Dover Street, Liverpool.— The Liverpool School and Home for Nurses is intended to meet and supply a want universally felt by medical men, and others, namely, to provide trained nurses for the poor, hospital, and private sick nursing.

Young women wishing to qualify in this School, should be between the ages of twenty-five and thirty-five years; of unexceptionable character and good health. They should be able to remain one year as Probationer, receiving £14 4s., and two years after, as Nurse, at wages, varying according to ability, between £16 and £20.

Further particulars may be had on application to the Lady Superintendent at the above address.

Miss Rye's Law Copying Office. 12, Portugal Street, Lincoln's Inn. Law Papers of all kinds, Specifications, Bills of Quantities, Parish Returns, Ships' Books, Sermons, and Petitions, carefully copied and punctually returned. Deeds engrossed. Envelopes addressed. Miscellaneous MSS. copied in running hand. References and Specimens of work done may be had on application to the Manager, Miss N. E. Francies.

N.B.—Only Female Clerks are employed in this Office.

Photographic Printing and Colouring.—MRS. BURKE begs to announce that she continues to execute every variety of Photographic Printing, both for Amateurs and the Profession, on reasonable terms. Having always been employed by the best houses, Mrs. Burke feels justified in promising First-class work, both as regards beauty and durability. Price Lists and Estimates sent on application. Cartes de visite and pictures of larger size either slightly tinted or highly-finished in miniature style. Lessons given. Address, 11, Eton Street, Gloucester Street, Regents Park, N.W.

Cork Protestant Hall.—President, The EARL OF BANDON. This Hall was built for the purpose of providing accommodation for Lectures, Sermons, Religious Meetings, &c.; and is specially devoted to the maintenance of Scriptural truth and loyalty. Application for the use of the Hall to be made to

RICHARD BEARE TOOKER, (*Hon. Sec.*)
The Mardyke, Cork.

A page of advertisements from the Alexandra Magazine, May 1864
(Girton College Collection)

organised by Maria Rye (1829-1903), an early supporter of the married women's property campaign and a founder member of the Society, while on two evenings a week a book-keeping class was held.

Law-copying

Both ventures proved not only helpful to the individuals who attended the classes but also successful in spreading the idea that office work was appropriate to women and that employers could benefit by hiring them. The law-copying classes soon became a business for copying documents of all kinds. In April they were moved to premises costing £65 a year at 12 Portugal Street, Lincoln's Inn Fields, and the Society distributed a circular addressed to solicitors inviting them to furnish work to the Law Copying class (GCM 3-4-60). In August Maria Rye reported that there were "8 'rapid writers' and 2 learners" in the office (EWJ 5:391), and in September Barbara Bodichon arranged to lend her £200 so that she could run the office as her own private business (Diamond 1996: 48-55). She seems to have managed creditably for the next three years, relying on the Society to promote the office and lease the building in Portugal Street. (Boucherett 1884:98; Diamond 1999: 47-53; E. 1864; PP1875) In January 1862 she wrote to Barbara Bodichon, "My business is progressing slowly—very slowly—but still progressing,—we made in the year—the first year I had it £300!! nearly £200 however went for wages—& the greater part of the rest for house expences—still it was not bad when you think of all our ignorance & inaptitude", and by March 1862 she was able to pay £5 interest on her loan (Diamond 1996: 51).

Soon, however, her energies began to be absorbed by the Female Middle Class Emigration Society (FMCES), an organisation she established in May 1862 with Jane Lewin (1828-1914), a member of a wealthy radical family, to promote the emigration of governesses to the colonies. In November 1862 she set out on a voyage to New Zealand and Australia on behalf of the FMCES and spent most of the next two years out of the country. Meanwhile Jane Lewin seems to have kept an eye on the law-copying office in her absence (the FMCES office was in the same building), and by 1865 had taken over the proprietorship from Maria Rye and the lease of the building from the SPEW and was running it with a salaried manager (GCM, 17-01-65). Its progress continued to be reported in the Society's Annual Reports until, in 1876, the Committee became dissatisfied with inaccurate claims for its success made by the current manager, a Mrs Sunter, and severed the connection (GCM 28-4-76).

The venture did, nevertheless, play a part in opening clerical work to women by establishing the viability and respectability of document copying offices run by women and employing women. Thus, as will be described in more detail in Chapter 3, when the typewriter appeared in the 1880s, the Society had the confidence to set up a successful typewriting agency on the Portugal Street pattern.

Book-keeping and the Commercial School

The second venture initiated in January 1860, the teaching of book-keeping, seems to have been even more influential in opening clerical work to women. Jessie Boucherett was particularly interested in training women for this work, and in May 1860 proposed a scheme of her own to replace the Committee's earlier efforts. On her prompting, the Society set up a school which offered a general education for girls up to fourteen where the emphasis was on writing and arithmetic, and classes for older girls where they were taught book-keeping and generally prepared for clerical work. To avoid controversies over religious education Jessie Boucherett became the proprietor of the school and took responsibility for the expenses, while the book-keeping classes for older girls were organised and subsidised by the Society, but held initially at the school's premises in Charlotte Street. The school flourished, with numbers reaching 80 by 1865, when it moved to new premises at 45 Great Ormond St, but the 'adult' classes were not so immediately successful, the numbers falling on occasion to as low as four. The Annual Report for 1864 gave some of the reasons:

> Several young persons are quite ready to take situations as clerks or book-keepers; and subscribers and friends of the cause would greatly oblige the managers of the classes by mentioning this fact to their tradesmen, whether in town or country. The young persons who attend the classes are usually either girls without parents or else whose parents are unable to obtain situations for them, so that they depend entirely on the Society's Register for employment, and are often obliged to wait a long time before they can be provided with it. The girls in the school [chiefly tradesmen's daughters] are more fortunate in this respect, as their parents are generally able to find situations for them by private interest.

With the appointment of Gertrude King as Secretary in September 1865 the situation for the adult classes improved. After the move to 23 Great Marlborough Street the classes were held at the office and she took responsibility for finding situations for those who were given certificates. Many years later she told the Committee that "she learnt to know to some extent the characters and capabilities of students while they were attending the class, and could generally select those who were suitable for various posts" (GCM 8-1-97). One of the earliest students at these classes, Mary Harris Smith (1844-1934)[4], whose first position was found for her by the Society, moved on to increasingly responsible positions and became in 1920 "the first and only woman Chartered Accountant in the world" (*AR* 1920). Between 1891 and 1926 she carried out the annual audit of the Society's accounts.

A good deal of casual copying work was offered to the Society by supporters and their contacts, and Gertrude King insisted that much of it should be done under her eye at the office. This put her in a good position to give advice and training to inexperienced women hoping to make a career of the work, and also to make reliable recommendations to employers. In 1869 (the first year when figures were published in the Annual Report), it was recorded that 17 such commissions were given to the Society. By 1885 the number had risen to 252. The author of an article in *The Quiver* described herself as flicking through the Employment Register and reported:

> And here is a page of what is called "odd office work," for which over £170 has been paid during the year:- "Addressing envelopes, directory, copying specifications, petitions, appeals, streeting boroughs, alphabetical list of voters;" we look up from the page and inquire. Neither sectarianism nor political bias accepted here! We learn that lists of voters were prepared, boroughs streeted, and cards and addresses sent out at the last election for the Conservative, Liberal, and Radical candidates! Ten thousand addresses left the office, for which five shillings per thousand was received. (Beale, 1889: 113).

In November 1874 Gertrude King gave an account of the Society's work in the clerical area to the Civil Service Inquiry Commission. She told the Commissioners that they had little trouble finding work in shops and warehouses for the tradesmen's daughters who attended the school and the book-keeping classes. The "ladies", who had trained when rather older, tended to reject this sort of employment, but a number had been found work in the offices of large charities like the Society for the Propagation of the Gospel. When asked if their candidates were "often returned upon your hands as inefficient", she replied:

> When they once make a start we very seldom have them back again. Before we send them out we have them examined. We have a class, and the girls attend this class until we think that they are competent, and then Mr. Proctor, of King's College, holds an examination for us; and no girl is sent out with the Society's recommendation unless she has passed a satisfactory examination. Mr. Proctor's highest marks are usually about 100, and if the candidate does not get 75 the certificate is withheld.
>
> She said also that employers were asked to report any problems, and that when girls left situations "they almost always came to the office" since she had got to know them while they were attending classes. (PP 1875, VOL XXIII: 218-9).

Shorthand

A year earlier, in September 1873, the Society had pioneered the teaching of yet another of the clerical skills, shorthand. It was reported in the periodical *Labour News* that a Mrs Rose Crawshay (never a member of the Society but with a later history of concern with women's work), was offering to contribute £5 towards shorthand classes for women. Gertrude King reported this to the Committee and suggested that the Society could offer its office for the purpose. Mrs Crawshay was approached and she agreed, if a class were formed, to pay the fees for two or three girls. Gertrude King went ahead with the plan and the Minutes recorded:

> The Secretary stated that in compliance with the order of the Committee she had spoken to Mr Grant, son of Mr Peter Taylor's private secretary [Mrs Peter Taylor was a major figure in the wider Women's Movement] who had been strongly recommended to her & who is at present engaged on a newspaper and that he offered to teach short-hand writing to two or three intelligent girls for 10/6 a term, giving them one lesson of 1½ hours once a week; He thought one year's teaching would be sufficient if they practised well
>
> Resolved that the class be started as soon as two or three intelligent girls could be found but that no expense be incurred by the Society in the matter. (GCM 25-6-73)

Three months later it was reported "that the shorthand class had been commenced under Mr Grant on Sept 16th that he had five pupils one paying her own fees three paid for by Mrs Crawshay and the fifth being Mr Grant's sister" (GCM 17-9-73).

Again the progress was slow and rocky. Only two of the first pupils acquired real competence, but one of them, Miss Pritchard, 83, Edgware Road, managed to build a successful career. The Annual Report of 1877 noted that she "reports at Meetings, takes down and writes out business letters, writes out shorthand Reports, and gives lessons" and that of 1878, that she was "now fully employed". For several years the scheme lapsed, but in 1879, a "demand having arisen for Clerks and Book-keepers who understand shorthand", a further attempt was made. These classes lasted until 1883, when it was felt that this need was now being filled by Isaac Pitman's recently founded Metropolitan School of Stenography in Chancery Lane (GCM 12-10-1883), and the Society's clients were directed there.

In 1884 Jessie Boucherett wrote of clerical work for women:

> To-day there is almost an unlimited field of employment for women in this direction. A girl who is a good arithmetician, writes a good hand, and obtains a certificate for double entry, is sure of a situation, and if in addition she learns to write short-hand, she may aspire to a superior position. Ordinary book-keepers (not short-hand writers) receive at first about fifteen shillings a week without board and lodging; at the end of each year their wages are generally raised two or three shillings a week until they reach twenty-five shillings, while some experienced accountants receive thirty or thirty-five shillings a week. The number of women commercial clerks increased between the years 1861 and 1871 from 404 to 1,755, and it is now probably much larger. [In the census of 1881 it was recorded as 5,989.]

The Society took a good deal of credit for this change. In 1879, on the twentieth anniversary of the founding of the Society, the Annual Report claimed:

> There is every reason to believe that the advance has been steady, and that the census of 1881 will show a proportionate increase in numbers. That the Society has been one of the main agents in bringing about this result, in opening new fields of occupation for women, and thereby increasing their usefulness and--as a natural consequence--their happiness is, the Committee believe, indisputable.

The authors of this book are inclined to agree with the Society's claim at least as far as clerical work is concerned. As one of us has written, using as evidence the numbers of clerks returned in the censuses:

> A small number of merchants had apparently seen these advantages [of hiring young women as clerks] by 1841, but . . . they were widely scattered throughout the country, and their example seems not to have been copied by their neighbours. Lancashire, with 19 female commercial clerks, had the largest number outside London while many counties returned only one. Nor was their lead followed during the ensuing twenty years, for during this period the number of female commercial clerks rose only from 162 to 274. During the 1860s, however, many more employers seem to have come to the same realisation, though taking on girl clerks still seems to have been a matter of individual initiative rather than spreading local practice, since even in 1871, out of a total of 1,466 female commercial clerks, only London with 577 and Lancashire with 161 had more than 100.
>
> Such a widely scattered, apparently idiosyncratic pattern of change suggests a series of individual responses to some nationwide prompting, and, since economic conditions do not seem to have changed radically in this decade, the prompting which suggests itself is the Society for Promoting the Employment of Women's propaganda campaign. It was members of this society who during this decade were arguing that employers need not be bound by the customary and the usual, that just because women had not so far been seen in certain occupations they should not forever be excluded from them. Moreover they suggested motives for making changes which went beyond simple self-interest. They appealed to public spirit as well. The Women's Movement continually stressed the plight of the "surplus women", and appealed to employers to do something about it. Surely the most likely explanation for the big increase in the number of female commercial clerks during the 1860s is that certain men all over the country made the double discovery that if they abandoned their customary "knowledge" of the proper sort of clerk, they could both save themselves money and regard themselves as progressive, public-spirited businessmen. (Jordan1999b: 192-3)

The Post Office

We also believe that the Society played a part in the creation within the Civil Service establishment of secure pensioned positions for women. There was, it seems, a fairly widespread awareness of the SPEW and its aims within the most go-ahead section of the Civil Service, the Post Office. From its earliest years the SPEW had been sending girls to work for the International and Electric Telegraph Company which had been employing women in its Central Office since 1853, and when in 1870 the Post Office took over the Telegraph Service, Frank Scudamore, the officer in charge of the transfer, became aware of the cheapness and efficiency of female labour and in his report on the transfer noted that women with the appropriate education would work for lower wages than men, that young women could tolerate sedentary and repetitive work better than young men, and that these women did not clog up the promotion system because most of them left to be married after five to ten years (Scudamore 1871: 78-9). Within a few years women were employed, not just to operate the telegraph machines, but for simple clerical work in the Telegraph Clearing House and the Returned Letter Office. These women were described as being from "the class from which assistants behind the counters of shops are recruited" (Jordan 1999b: 181) and did the work of very low level clerks. Then when, in December 1873, the Controller of the Savings Bank asked for some of the "boy clerks"

The Central Telegraph Office in 1874
(From The Illustrated London News, 1874)

and "writers" who currently made up his staff to be replaced with more responsible, but more expensive, "Third Class Clerks", the Secretary to the Post Office, Sir John Tilly, responded by suggesting that he consider using "educated women" (POST 30/275 D [E 3613/1875] File No. I). For several months the Controller resisted, but Tilly was firm, and by July 1874 it had been decided that the establishment was to consist of a Lady Superintendent with a salary rising from £165 to £300 and 62 clerks in three grades with salaries ranging from £40 to £150. Tilly then wrote to the Treasury:

> Assuming that your Lordships adopt my propositions the question will arise as the best mode of proceeding in order to obtain candidates.
>
> They must be persons who have been somewhat carefully educated and to my mind it is very undesirable to collect a crowd of young ladies by public advertisement and subject the good majority of them to trouble and expense only to end in disappointment. . . . I think therefore the competition should be limited and that the candidates who must in that case be nominated should be in the proportion of three to each vacancy to be filled.
>
> I should propose, as the most convenient arrangement, to place myself in communication with persons who take a prominent part in obtaining employment for educated women and by this means I have little doubt that a sufficiently large number of suitable candidates can be readily collected. (POST 30/275 D [E 3613/1875] File No. IV)

An appropriate examination with papers in Handwriting and Orthography, English Grammar and Composition, Arithmetic (including vulgar and decimal fractions), and Geography was devised and the first female clerks began work on July 16, 1875. (Jordan 1999b:180-184)

The Society had a good deal of contact with Civil Service officials during this period and it seems highly likely that Gertrude King was one of the "persons who take a prominent part in obtaining employment for educated women" approached by the Post Office. Certainly her name was not unknown in these circles. In 1870 on the instructions of the Committee she had written to Frank Scudamore on behalf of the women in the Telegraph Office, and in 1874, after Committee members had lobbied members of the Civil Service Inquiry Commission, she was called to give evidence on women clerks. One outcome of this was that Mr Walrond, one of the Commissioners, asked her to find women to mark Civil Service examination papers, and she recommended teachers from the North London Collegiate School, then on holiday. On January 1, 1875 the Minutes recorded:

> The Secretary reported that the Civil Service Commissioners had resolved to try the experiment of employing ladies to examine the papers of candidates for clerkships in the Custom House offering them 6/- a day; that on Dec 31st two ladies had attended at the office of the Civil Service Commission to receive instructions as to the method of correcting the

papers, that on the 2nd, 4th, & 5th twelve ladies had been employed in correcting the dictation and spelling, that three of these who had passed the Cambridge Senior Examination had been kept longer to examine the Arithmetic. The ladies corrected on an average 25 papers a day each, but no report has as yet been received from the Commissioners.[5]

On April 9, 1875 Gertrude King informed the Committee that the Post Office was looking for candidates for its positions, and on April 28 the Minutes recorded:

> The Civil Service Commissioners having sent for two ladies to superintend the Examinations for the clerkships in the Post Office Savings Bank, the Secretary stated that Miss Nicol and Miss Andrews had superintended them for two days, & had afterwards been engaged for three days in looking over the dictation and arithmetic papers.
>
> The papers given to the candidates were inspected.

Although there is no record of women on the Society's books being put forward for the examinations, five of the successful candidates were ex-pupils of the North London Collegiate School, whose founder and headmistress, Frances Buss, was a member of the Society's Committee from 1875 to 1888, suggesting again the involvement of the Society.

After 1876 the Society played little part in the recruitment of women for the Post Office or the extension of their employment into other areas of the Civil Service. Although its role was significant in breaking down the "Chinese wall of prejudices" and ushering through the pioneers, as had happened with clerical work country-wide, the movement of women into these areas gained its own momentum and proceeded without the Society's help.

THE SKILLED TRADES

From the beginning the Society had been interested in introducing women into the lighter male trades, but the situation here, though they did not know it, was not nearly so promising. In clerical work employers desperately needed what two sociologists have called an "unpromotable category" of workers which made attractive male career ladders possible for the few. Large numbers of similarly educated and trained employees were necessary but there were few positions of managerial responsibility to which workers could be promoted. Young women with the characteristics Frank Scudamore's report had identified provided a solution to these problems, as had already been recognised by employers in such occupations as elementary school teaching and retail work (Cockburn, 1991: 63; Cohn, 1985: 93-7; Crompton, 1984: 243; Scudamore, 1871: 78-9)

This need was nothing like as pressing in the skilled trades. The skills workers developed during a trade apprenticeship were far more specialized than those needed for clerical work. In most trades the repetitive low-grade work was done by a shifting group of apprentices who then went on to extend their expertise by working as journeymen for much higher wages, or set up in business for themselves. Though the Society managed to carve out a niche for women in a number of the male trades, in none of them did this lead to the mass feminization that followed their initiatives in clerical work, though in two at least, hairdressing and hospital dispensing, it could be argued that the Society prepared the ground so that when economic conditions changed and an "unpromotable" workforce of women became just what employers needed, there was no longer a "Chinese wall of prejudices" to prevent their seeing it.

Printing
In the early years, the Women's Movement's most widely publicised initiative in the skilled trades area was the attempt to introduce women into printing. In March 1860 Emily Faithfull in partnership with George Hastings,

The Victoria Press in 1861
(From The Illustrated London News, *1861*)

the Secretary of the NAPSS, established the Victoria Press as a private commercial venture and undertook to have girls trained as compositors.[6] The relationship between the Society and the Victoria Press was spelled out in the 1864 *Annual Report*:

> Letters from employers and applicants being not infrequently sent to the Victoria Press, under the impression that Miss Faithfull belongs to the Society, and is the right person to apply to for situations and assistants, by which considerable inconvenience is occasioned to all parties, it is thought advisable to explain the real state of the case.
>
> The idea of teaching women to print originated in the Society, and it was at one time contemplated to establish a woman's printing press in connexion with it; a small sum of money (£50) was collected for this object, when the Committee came to the conclusion that the undertaking would be more likely to succeed if it were left to private enterprise.
>
> Miss Faithfull took up the project, and the £50 was spent in apprenticing girls to her. Beyond this, the Society has had no share in the undertaking, the credit of which belongs to Miss Faithfull alone; neither has Miss Faithfull had any share in the management of the Society since the establishment of the Victoria Press, more than four years ago.

The Minutes of February 14, 1865 suggest, however, that a rift soon afterwards opened between the Society and the Victoria Press, the Chairman at that meeting, Sir Francis Goldsmid, reporting that "he had been authorised by Miss Faithfull to say, that she did not desire to be employed in future as the printer of the Society."[7]

The Society then transferred its patronage to John Bale and Sons of 78 Great Titchfield St, St Marylebone. He undertook their printing and applied to the Secretary when he needed new apprentices, and this happy relationship continued into the next century. Indeed when new technology overtook the printing trade in the early 1900s, the Society raised a fund so that the Bales could hire first a linotype and then a monotype machine for the girls to learn on.[8] Other printing firms, too, approached the Society for apprentices. The Women's Union Printing Office, established by Emma Patterson (1848-1886, later a pioneer advocate of women's trade unions) at 38 Castle Street, Holborn in 1876 took a number of their girls (GCM 28-4-76, 13-10-76, Annual Report 1878; Drake 1984: 10-12; Crawford 1999:530)[9] and in 1877 Mr Hurd, of Bedford Street, Commercial Road "resolved to try the experiment at the suggestion of Mr Bale" (MCM 7-12-77). He persevered with the experiment, approached the Society again for apprentices in 1884 (GCM 10-10-84) and in 1888 informed the Secretary "that he now employs women only as compositors"(MCM 23-11-88). Emily Faithfull's efforts were also sufficiently publicised for other women's printing offices to be established in Dublin and Edinburgh (MCM13-10-76), where they too appear to have inspired several local firms to take on women.[10]

The numbers, nevertheless, remained small. The census figures show a rise in the number of women employed in the printing industry generally from 419 (1.4% of the total) in 1861 to 9693 (9.1, %) in 1901. The figures for 1911 make it clear, however, that the percentage was not as high in the area, typesetting, with which the Society had concerned itself. In that year 602 women (1.6% of the total) were recorded as "hand compositors" and 92 (2.4%) as "machine compositors".

Hairdressing

The 1859 "Statement" issued by the Society had singled out hairdressing as a likely field into which to introduce women. Women had apparently run independent businesses as hairdressers until the mid-eighteenth century, when a fashion for French hairdressers had driven them out of the occupation (Pinchbeck 1930: 291-2), and by the mid-nineteenth century women with this skill seem to have been employed primarily as ladies' maids, though there were a number who, as widows, had taken over from their husbands.[11] Emily Davies, even before she became a member of the Committee in 1865, pressed strongly for the Society to move in this direction[12], suggesting from time to time that the Society should set up a hairdressing class and then its own hairdressing shop (MCM 8-1-61, 14-10-62, 10-5-64, 21-7-1864). This proposal was never acted on, but from 1861 onwards the Committee began placing girls as apprentices with individual hairdressers, on occasion providing loans to pay for the premium. The only employer named in the Minutes in the 1860s was Mr Atwell of Church Place St James', but there must have been others since, according to the 1866 Annual Report, seven girls were being trained. The 1869 Report claimed that the experiment had now entered a new phase of stability:

> It is some years now since the Committee first endeavoured to introduce women into this trade, so well suited to them. They have met with much opposition, as few masters care to incur the inconvenience and risk of making innovations in their establishments, or of training women to proficiency in their art. Now, however, we have much pleasure in calling attention to the establishment of Mr Douglas, 21 and 23 Bond Street,[13] where a large and efficient staff of female attendants is always waiting. He had some difficulty in finding young women who had received thorough training in the art, but some of those he engaged were the daughters of hair-dressers who had been trained by their fathers, while one was a young woman, who, by the assistance of the Society, had served a regular apprenticeship to a hairdresser, and who in former Reports has been recommended as competent for her work.
>
> Mr Douglas has spared no pains in making these young women thoroughly proficient, and in instructing others whom he has taken into his service. He states that his experiment has proved very satisfactory;

indeed he has found female assistants so popular that he has been obliged considerably to add to their number.

Another Bond Street hairdresser with shops in both London and Brighton, Mr Truefitt, soon followed his example, and the Report noted: "The girls formerly apprenticed by the Society naturally find employment in these shops."

A number of glimpses of the careers of women introduced by the Society appear in the Minutes. In November 1869 Committee members were told that "Emily Truelove, who now thoroughly understood her business would have been engaged by Mr Truefitt if she had been taller,[14] but that in consequence of being short, she found it very difficult to obtain a situation, & would be much obliged to any ladies who would give her employment". Help must have been forthcoming because in May 1872 it was reported that she now had "a situation at a hairdressers at 7 East Street Brighton where she is getting on nicely" and in April 1875 her further successful progress was recorded:

> Emily Truelove, who had learnt hairdressing through the agency of the Society and had held good situations since the expiration of her apprenticeship, being anxious to purchase a business asked whether the Society could help her to do so by a loan. She has £60 of her own & the price of the good will, fixtures, &c, is £100. She hoped to be able to repay the loan in a very short time. She is engaged to be married to a hairdresser and thought if they could get this shop, they would be able to get on very well in it.
>
> It was not considered that a loan for such a purpose came within the scope of the Society, but it was thought that there were other Societies from which such a loan could be procured.

The progress of Clara Roy, "the daughter of a coast guard officer, now dead" was less satisfactory. In April 1871 she was apprenticed to Mr. Atwell but did little to promote the Society's aims. The Minutes of July 18, 1873 reported:

> The Secretary stated that she had seen Mr Atwell about taking another apprentice, but that though he had a vacancy for one, he refused to take another on the same terms as he had taken them before because he had had so much trouble with Clara Roy, who had been recommended by Mrs Stopford Brook. He complained that she was unpunctual, idle, and that she caused mischief in his house. That by her indentures he was obliged to pay her 10/- a week & she did not earn as much as that. He promised to reconsider his terms, reserving to himself the power of inflicting fines &c. and to send them in writing to the Committee.

Although the Society continued to apprentice one or two girls to the same small group of hairdressers throughout the 1870s, there was little indication that the practice was being widely copied. The Annual Report for 1876 noted "Hair-dressers are still reluctant to take girls, and no fresh opening in this trade has been found during the year". The census returns suggest that the feminisation of the occupation was not rapid, and that, as with printing, throughout the nineteenth century the Society did little more than contribute to carving out a niche for women in a predominantly male occupation. Although the censuses show that the numbers of women recorded rose from 419 in 1861 to 1,745 in 1901, they increased from only 3 to 5 percent of the total numbers in the occupation. Things may, however, have begun to change in the early years of the twentieth century. By 1911 the proportion had risen to 10 percent, while the number of female hairdressing businesses employing others had risen to 401, 92 of them conducted by single women, and the rest by married women and widows.

Hospital dispensing

An occupation where it seems more certain that the Society's initiatives led ultimately to feminization was hospital dispensing, its major contribution being to ensure that, when changed conditions made young women an appealing labour source for employers, there was no Chinese wall of prejudice to prevent their seeing it. The Society's interest in the occupation arose because a number of the leading Society members were part of the wider group concerned with other Women's Movement issues. In 1866 the medical pioneer Elizabeth Garrett (later Garrett Anderson) opened St Mary's Dispensary for Women, a charitable institution offering medical advice to the poor women of Lisson Grove. Its Committee's membership overlapped considerably with that of the SPEW. Lord Shaftesbury was President, the Hon. Maude Stanley was a member of both Committees, and Barbara Bodichon, Jessie Boucherett and Lady Goldsmid (who on her husband Sir Francis's death took his place on the SPEW Committee) were substantial subscribers. Perhaps most significant of all, Jane Crowe, the first Secretary of the SPEW, and still an active Committee member, shared a house with Elizabeth Garrett (Manton 1965:167-70).

Although the Dispensary initially employed a man to make up the doctor's prescriptions, it was almost immediately arranged that one of the Society's protégées, should be apprenticed to him to learn the trade. In 1868 she was appointed dispenser in his place and began training other young women. It is possible to disentangle from records of the Society, the Dispensary (soon to become the New Hospital for Women) and the pharmaceutical press some details of the young women who were thus introduced into the occupation. It seems likely that the first of these was Jane Minshull, aged 24 in 1866, the eldest daughter of an East End brush and bristle merchant, who held the position of dispenser at the hospital until 1874, while the Minutes of 1870 mention "Miss Macaulay, the daughter of a Surgeon who had died in the Crimea", being apprenticed at the hospital.[15] Isabella Clarke, (born 1843, the daughter of a solicitor), who went on to a distinguished career as the pioneer woman pharmacist, also gained some of her training at the hospital, though not through the direct introduction of the Society. Jane Minshull probably also trained her younger sister, Rose Minshull, and the even younger Louisa Stammwitz (born 1850), one of four children of "a tailor employing 12 men", both protégées of the Society. The Society's Annual Report for 1870 mentions also that apprenticeships had been found for clients at a dispensary for women and children in Bethnal Green, and at the Dispensary for Skin Diseases, Poland Street, in the Oxford Street area, and that these women now held the post of dispenser at the institutions where they trained. In 1875 Louisa Stammwitz took over from Jane Minshull at the New Hospital for Women, and in 1876 Isabella Clarke's younger sister, Alice Clarke became her assistant, becoming chief dispenser herself in 1879. The census of 1881 reveals that the third of the Minshull sisters (Flora) had also entered the occupation.

In 1873 Rose Minshull and Louisa Stammwitz were drawn into a campaign, initiated by two women whose ultimate aim was to study medicine, to have women trained as pharmacists and accepted into its professional body, a campaign vigorously promoted by a radical member of the Council of the Royal Pharmaceutical Society, Robert Hampson. Both the Society's protégées sat for the Preliminary examination which entitled them to attend professional lectures, and passed it with ease, Rose Minshull coming first out of 166 candidates. They then proceeded to study for the Pharmaceutical Society's Minor examination which gave them the right to conduct their own chemist shops, and the Major examination which allowed them to call themselves pharmaceutical chemists. In 1874 Isabella Clarke joined the campaign and, no doubt because she had the time and money to devote all her energies to the project, had passed both examinations by 1875. The other two passed the Minor in 1877 and the Major in 1879. A few months later Robert Hampson finally won his long battle with the Pharmaceutical Society to have women accorded the same rights as men. Though the members had not been willing to accept the abstract principle of women's right to membership, the fact that women had had, as one of the Council put it, "the necessary moral courage to undergo the ordeal of *two* or *three* examinations, where fifty per cent. are plucked [i.e. fail]" made them change their minds. The names of all three were added to the list of members (Jordan 1998).[16]

The Pharmaceutical Society thus became the first of the legally constituted professional associations to admit women to membership, and the SPEW must be seen as playing a significant role in this achievement. Yet, during the next decade, only ten more women took advantage of the new opportunities, none of them SPEW protégées (Jordan 2001). During the 1880s a number of young women applied to the Society for loans and for help in finding apprenticeships, but none succeeded in gaining the qualification, perhaps because none of them had the academic ability and determination of the pioneers. In 1883 a Miss Bridges had been offered a loan of £50, but had been "frightened at the Latin in the preliminary Examination". The offer was then passed to Mary Kimber, 17 Bonchurch Road, North Kensington, who accepted it and began work under Isabella Clarke. The 1886 Minutes, however, recorded that she had had to give up pharmacy because "she is unable to grasp the Chemistry" though she could understand Botany and Dispensing. The Committee expressed regret and hoped that "she will get work as a dispenser" (MCM 15-6-83; GCM 12-10-83, 2-7-86).

This more lowly calling of hospital dispenser became one of the Society's successes, becoming rapidly feminised from the mid-1890s onwards. From the 1870s there was a growing trickle of women into these positions, particularly in Birmingham where the Birmingham and Midland Hospital for Women founded in 1871, appointed a female dispenser in 1872, and where the practice spread to other hospitals. In 1887 the Society of Apothecaries opened its examinations to women, including the examination for the Apothecaries' Assistant's Certificate, a qualification that had been offered by the Society of Apothecaries since the beginning of the century though not much patronised. This examination was much less demanding than the Pharmaceutical Society's, and the fees were lower, and in 1889 five female dispensers from Birmingham applied to sit for it. Other women followed their lead, and by the end of 1894 29 women had gained the Assistant's Certificate, in five years overtaking in numbers the 26 who had passed Pharmaceutical Society examinations in the last twenty.

And then in 1895 a change in industrial conditions occurred which made the hiring of women much more appealing to employers. In that year the Local Government Board, which had power to regulate all local government activities, ruled that those dispensing medicines in workhouse infirmaries and prisons must have some form of qualification, listing the Apothecaries' Assistant's Certificate as acceptable. Up to this time it had been customary to have much of the routine dispensary work done by untrained, low-paid hospital porters and "dispensary boys", but now a situation was created, like that in clerical work and teaching, where an educated, but cheap and "unpromotable", category of worker was needed. The transition and its speed can be seen in the increase in the numbers of women (and decrease in the numbers of men) taking the examination during the next five years. In 1894 65 men and 14 women (18% of total) gained the certificate whereas in 1900 there were only 36 men compared with 100 women (74% of total). The Assistant's Certificate continued to be the qualification of choice for hospital dispensers into the twentieth century, its most notable holder being the novelist Agatha Christie, who gained it in 1917 and whose first detective story, *The Mysterious Affair at Styles*, was built on a poisoning case she had come across in her studies (Jordan, 2002).

Plan-tracing

Another predominantly male area where the Society helped to carve out a small niche for women was the tracing of engineering and architectural plans. The first steps seem to have been taken without reference to the Society (though probably as an outcome of their propaganda), by an engineering firm, Messrs Easton and Anderson of Southward Street. It seems likely that when in the early 1870s the firm set up a room in their offices where their own tracing could be done and employed a young woman, Elizabeth Crosby, to train and supervise a female staff, the moving spirits, Mr Easton and Miss Crosby, were prompted by the Society's publicity to discover whether plan-tracing was a suitable new occupation for women. By 1875 six young women were working there, earning about £1 or 25/- weekly, and the next development makes it fairly clear that Mr Easton saw this as a public-spirited enterprise, rather than one dictated by the firm's commercial needs. He suggested to Elizabeth Crosby that she should approach the SPEW to sponsor an independent venture to extend this work to other women and other firms. The Minutes reported the plans she outlined to the Committee:

> Mr Easton has suggested to her that more women might be employed in this way if work could be procured from other engineers. This of course could not be done unless the ladies could have an independent office. There would be considerable difficulty in getting work from engineers as they do not like their plans to go off the premises. These difficulties may be overcome as there are one or two offices at which tracings are made, and if an office were established under the auspices of a society such as this, Mr Easton thought that the scheme would not be viewed with the same amount of jealousy as it would be if started under his immediate patronage. He was quite willing to do everything in his power to promote the scheme: he would allow reference to be made to him as to the capability of the ladies he now employs, the accuracy and neatness of their work. (MCM 12-3-75)

In response to the Committee's questions Miss Crosby said that she was ready to manage the scheme herself, that Easton and Anderson would send work to her office, and that all she wanted from the Society was a guarantee of the rent for the premises during the first year. A week later she wrote to the Committee assuring them that Mr Easton would take back his present employees if the plan failed after a year.

In May Miss Crosby wrote postponing the opening because "we hear that work is slack in all offices", but discussions continued about the level of the Society's help. In June Jessie Boucherett endorsed the scheme by making a donation of £25 as an initial fund to pay salaries, and by December the Society had received promises of £72 towards the rent, while Mr Easton offered the top floor of a property he owned at Queen Anne's Gate for £60 a year, and "promised to transfer to it the desks, stools, &c now used by the ladies". The office finally opened on January 31, 1876, its business cards reading "Ladies' Tracing Office for Engineers' and Architects' plans. Miss E.R. Crosby. 42 Queen Anne's Gate, Westminster."

The office prospered. Gertrude King paid a number of visits to it and commented favourably, while the Minutes reported:

> Read a letter from Miss Crosby giving a sketch of the progress of the Ladies plan tracing office from its opening on January 31st to July. From this it appeared that independently of the work done for Messrs Easton and Anderson which is pretty constant, 32 orders from 16 different sources have been executed. Notes were enclosed in which the work done by the ladies was commended. Miss Crosby stated that as a rule she takes home the work herself and that the comments were generally spoken not written. She had at work with her three ladies who are thoroughly efficient, one who has been with them 5 months, and a fifth who has been only three weeks. This last is the daughter of an architect and has had a little practice in the work.
>
> During their five months work the best worker has earned on an average £1..1..8 per week, the second 19/- and the third nearly 17/-.
>
> Miss Crosby herself has worked only when they have been much pressed, and is not a paid worker. She writes - "If we were prosperous enough, after securing our Rent and other expenses to have a margin, I should then consider myself justified in receiving remuneration, but not till then." (MCM 7-7-76)

Things seemed just as good at the end of the year, the Minutes reporting:

> Read a letter from Miss Crosby stating that the plan tracing circular had been delayed owing to the great pressure of work during the last fortnight. All the ladies working at the office had been fully occupied and had had almost more than they could get through. She also stated that she had been going through the accounts and she thought they would have between £20 & £30 in hand towards next year's rent. As during the first year there have been many expenses which will not occur again and as a connection had to be formed, this report was considered very satisfactory. (MCM 8-12-76)

Similarly satisfactory reports were received for a further year[17] until Miss Crosby announced that she was to be married[18], and that she wished to pass the management of the office to her most experienced worker there, a Miss Long. She also offered to repay out of her profits the £65 still owing from the Society's initial grant. The Society, prompted by Gertrude King, approved this change, and re-lent the £65 to the business as conducted by Miss Long (MCM 10-5-78).

The office continued to receive regular visits from Gertrude King and to have its progress recorded in the Society's Annual Reports. At the end of

1882 Gertrude King reported not only substantial expansion of the original office but a situation that suggests that the project was moving beyond the experimental stage:

> The Secretary stated that in addition to her own two offices Miss Long had been asked to start an office for a large firm of engineers in Lambeth where four ladies would be constantly employed, & another for the Meteorological Society. The ladies about to work in these offices will have been trained by Miss Long, & she has at present 20 in her office. (MCM 8-12-82)

The office maintained its strong ties with the Society, the 1883 Annual Report recording that "six ladies have been introduced into her office during the year through the agency of the Society", and in 1889 Miss Long applied to the Society for a loan to buy equipment for the "sun-printing of plans". Gertrude King went to considerable trouble to master the details of the process and explain them to the Committee, and a loan of £25 was arranged, the Society in this demonstrating an awareness that changes in technology could dislodge the fragile hold women had on these new occupations, an awareness that was to surface again with printing in 1900. In fact the new equipment proved so profitable that Miss Long was able to repay the loan within a year. [19]

In November 1902 Miss Long sold the business for £300 to the father of two former pupils who intended to carry it on together, and out of the proceeds finally repaid the money lent by the Society in 1876 (GCM 28-11-1902). The Society's Minutes indicate that other plan-tracing offices employing women had been springing up, and the practice of employing women seems to have spread beyond the capital. Joan Bakewell, in her autobiography (2003:17) records that her mother, who began working in a Manchester engineering office in 1915 at the age of thirteen, took evening classes in experimental mathematics, practical drawing, mechanics and physics and became a plan-tracer.

ARTISTIC TRADES

All the efforts described so far resulted either in a previously male occupation becoming feminised, or in a niche being created in one for women. But there were also ventures undertaken by the Society where the results could almost be described as disastrous, where the Society made injudicious decisions about policy, gave bad advice, and lost money. This was particularly the case with the Society's early attempts to introduce women into trades with an artistic aspect, specifically photography, glass-engraving, and gilding. From the beginning the Society had felt that, since drawing, painting and embroidery were "accomplishments" that formed part of the standard curriculum in girls' schools from the most aristocratic to the cheapest, the various artistic trades were particularly suitable for women. In the 1860s, as has already been shown, the Committee believed that the most appropriate way to open new occupations for women was to set up classes where they could be trained and then either to turn the classes into a commercial business where the trainees could be employed, as had happened in the cases of printing, law-copying and plan-tracing, or else try to find work for them in the broader labour market as happened with book-keeping and hairdressing. In their ventures into the artistic fields, however, the Committee members seem to have made a number of misjudgements, both of character and of the industrial situation, which did little to advance the Society's aims.

Photography

In the case of photography, the Society made efforts to find women who could do for this occupation what Emily Faithfull and Maria Rye had done for printing and law-copying but were met with disappointment. Without any prompting commercial photographers had began employing girls with some art training to help in the developing, printing and colouring of photographs, and from the Society's beginning it was found possible to place girls who asked for help in such positions (*AR* 1861). In 1863 the Committee approved a loan of £25 to allow a Mrs Burke, who had been working for a leading firm, to set up for herself as a photographic printer. Jessie Boucherett threw herself enthusiastically into the scheme, Emily Davies writing of her to Barbara Bodichon: "She intends to stay [in London] two or three weeks, or perhaps longer, according as things turn out. Her immediate business is to set up Mrs. Burke." (Davies 2004: 85)

Members of the Committee noted, however, that there were almost no women employed to take the actual photographs, and the Annual Report of 1864 recorded their intention to address the problem:

> As several lady amateurs are very good photographers, it seems certain that a want of the means of good instruction is the cause of this inferiority among professional female artists. The Committee desires therefore to set up an establishment---or rather to assist some lady to set up an establishment of her own---where respectable young persons of the middle ranks may be taught the superior as well as inferior branches of the trade.

Their attempt to fulfil this need embroiled them with two women who seem to have done little more than waste the Secretary's time and the Society's money. The first was a Miss Horsburgh of Southwood Lane, Highgate, who approached them on February 12, 1864, and the second a Mrs Kemp of Douglas Street, Deptford, who with her husband, asked in 1865 for "assistance in establishing a Photographic business on terms suggested by the Society's Annual Report 1863-64". Miss Horsburgh appears to have wanted no more than financial backing to set up a studio or school, but the Kemps talked the Committee into an agreement that:

> . . . the Commee will pay for the thorough instruction in photography for any approved candidate, if the cost do not exceed £20, provided, should she attain proficiency, she will undertake to establish and conduct at her own risk, a photographic business in which female apprentices shall be taught, the Society advancing £150 to be repaid by instalments of £30 per annum if Mr Bosanquet continues willing to lend £100. (GCM 4-9-65)

By November 14 the Managing Committee had decided that both applicants were capable of establishing photographic businesses on the Society's terms and had agreed to pay for Mrs Kemp to be trained "as advised by Mr Dawson, Prof of photography at Kings'College".

Thereafter nothing went right. Mrs Kemp, after borrowing £5 for photographic equipment, found that her sight was not up to the photographic course and was replaced on it by her sixteen-year-old daughter. The Society's efforts to persuade the two women to go into partnership came to nothing, and each set up a separate establishment, Miss Horsburgh in partnership with a Mrs Yates who had studied photography at King's College. The Kemps got themselves into deep financial trouble and when asked to begin repaying their loan at the end of 1866, revealed that they had been forced to sell their furniture to pay their rent. In October 1867 Miss Horsburgh decided that she must go abroad for the sake of her health and began looking for someone to take over her school. By the end of 1868 she too was badly behind with the repayments of her loan.

In the event the occupation was opened to women without any particular intervention by the Society. Quite a number of women entered it as a result of their own artistic ambitions, and there appears to have been no "Chinese wall" preventing them from getting clients. For the rest of the century the Society's contribution was primarily supporting individuals, making loans for their training or to help them set up in business, and using its connections to find openings for them when trained. In 1865, for example, "It was agreed that £10 be lent to Miss Cantelo [a protégée of Bessie Parkes's] of Newport, Isle of Wight for the purchase of apparatus for her photographic business to be repaid at her own conscience" (GCM 4-7-65). In 1874 the Hon. Victoria Grosvenor recommended the Misses Dawson "who have a studio at the polytechnic, & who appeared to be willing to give instruction in photography". The Secretary called on them and found that "Miss Dawson will be happy to give private lessons or to take a young lady as an apprentice" (MCM 12-6-74). In 1900 "Miss Blanche Elmes, Glencairn, Grove Park, Chiswick applied for a loan of £10 to enable her to learn Photography under Mrs Fielding, 108 Hammersmith Road" and a loan of £20 (the full cost of the premium) was granted to her (GCM 14-12-1900).

Glass-engraving

In the case of photography it would seem that the Society's plan was a viable one, but that the women chosen to carry it out proved inadequate. The Society's attempts to open two other occupations, glass-engraving and gilding, to women appear, however, to have been in themselves ill-judged, and to have resulted in the training of two quite talented young women for occupations where there was no place for them.

In the 1860s the Society believed it had found a skilled craftsman who could teach young women the art of glass-engraving and arranged for four girls to be apprenticed to him. From this distance in time it appears that Mr Fallon may have hoped his offer to take female apprentices would save a business in financial difficulties. Though on two occasions he claimed that his troubles arose from "the refusal of his men to work, when they found he was introducing female labour into the trade", the complications suggest that the trouble really sprang from his own financial incompetence. In early 1868 he told the Society he was about to be evicted from his workshop, and when Miss James and Miss Lawrance (see Chapter 1) visited him, they found that he had rented large premises with the idea of subletting but had failed to find a tenant. They then canvassed the Society's supporters and raised enough for a loan to cover his difficulties. Fallon then managed to get another loan from the Society for equipment. Telling the Committee "that he felt confident of the ultimate success of the girls, that hitherto they had quite answered his expectations, and were already able to execute inferior work, if he could secure a sufficient number of lathes for them", he persuaded the Committee to disgorge from the loan fund "£45 to the absolute purchase of three lathes with spindles and copper wheels attached" and "£3 to be paid in wages to the girls apprenticed to Mr Fallon" (GCM 14-1-68) .

But the collapse of his business was only postponed. On October 3, 1868, he was arrested for debt, "having become security for a friend who had failed", and the Secretary had to move quickly to remove the lathes the Society had paid for to the Society's office at 23 Great Marlborough Street. On November 11, it was agreed to allow him to borrow the lathes "on his procuring a letter from his assignees acknowledging them to be the property of the Society", but it then emerged he had not paid the girls wages for some time, and one, Miss Brain[20], wanted to give up. The difficulty was temporarily solved by Jessie Boucherett who commissioned the Secretary "to allow Mr Fallon 15/- a week for three months in order to pay three of the girls 5/- a week each for that time" (GCM 3-11-68). Predictably, however, Fallon's business failed finally in the middle of 1869, and the Committee was left with apprentices who had paid their fees but not received the instruction to which they were entitled.

Two members of the Committee came to the rescue, one (not identified) arranging to pay for two of these apprentices, Elizabeth Walter and Ada Stone, to receive lessons from a skilled German engraver, Mr Eisert[21], and the other, Miss James, hiring a room in which they could work with the lathes the Society had bought. Things did not go entirely smoothly, the minutes noting:

> Mr Eisert having repeatedly complained of the idleness and inattention of Ada Stone the Honble Maude Stanley undertook to speak to her on the subject, and to tell her that the Committee had decided to allow her to continue under Mr Eisert's instruction for six months more, but if during that time she did not work industriously they would not permit her to remain longer. (MCM 18-5-70)

Elizabeth Walker, on the other hand, appeared to be everything the Society could desire. Later in 1870 her work was entered in a Workmen's International Exhibition, where she won a prize and where Queen Victoria bought the water-jugs and goblets she had engraved (GMC 16-11-1870). The Society then tried to use her to expand the women's presence in the trade, at first having her teach a new apprentice under Eisert's guidance and then, when the pupil withdrew, paying rent for a room where she could work, and, the Annual Reports suggest, keeping samples of her work at the office and arranging commissions for her from the Society's patrons. Unfortunately she seems to have been unable to get enough work to survive, and the last mention of her in the minutes is a record on July 24, 1872 of her announcement that she meant to give up the work on October 1.

Gilding

The Committee members were not discouraged by the glass-engraving fiasco. On October 16, 1872, only a few weeks after Elizabeth Walker's withdrawal, the Managiing Committee Minutes recorded:

> The Secretary stated that she had been making inquiries about carving and gilding for women, that Mr Heggie of 18 Great Portland Street and Mr Chance of London Street Fitzroy Square, agreed that it was an excellent business for women, that it could be readily learnt, and that the earnings from it were good, a really good workman being able to earn two guineas a week. Both had known women who assisted their husbands or relatives in the business. Mr Heggie stated that he had a son who had been trained for a picture dealer who would teach one girl for a month, or should this fail he could find a gilder who would give all the necessary instruction for £10. The tools required would cost 5/- for each person. He thought a fair business might be started for £20 or £30 if the Society had a room in which the girls could work. He said that frames could be bought wholesale much more cheaply than they could be made by women as they were made by machinery. The Secretary stated that Miss Boucherett had heard these particulars and wished that the attempt should be made and offered a room for the purpose at the School at 41 Regent Square.

A teacher was quickly found, the secretary reporting:

> Mr Lawson could not spare the time from his regular business, but said that his wife who was a very good gilder, and could teach quite as well as he could himself would teach a class for four hours a day, two in the morning and two in the afternoon for three months for £1 a week and two hours a day during the next three months for 10/- a week that he would himself see that everything went on well and do his best to get them common work to practice upon. (MCM 16-10-72)

In November the Committee inspected a specimen of gilding done by Mrs Lawson which the secretary had shown to Mr Chance of Loudon Street, who had pronounced it very good, and it was decided that Mrs Lawson should be employed to teach a class of up to four girls (GCM 30-10-72, MCM 27-11-72). By December arrangements for the class had been finalised, the minutes reporting that:

> ... the benches which had been used for glass engraving had been applied & refixed for the gilding and that materials necessary to commence work, including a dozen small frames had been purchased, the sum expended for these purposes amounting to £1..15..9.
>
> As the girls could not as yet do much by themselves it was arranged that they should work till 5 o'clock only, Mrs Lawson being with them from 9 till 11 in the morning, and from 2.30 till 4.30 in the afternoon.
>
> As there was a woman living in the house, who took charge of the rooms used for the school, it was resolved to make an arrangement with her to light the fire & clean the room for the gilders. (MCM 18-12-72)

Two girls, Emily Garwood and Emma Darwin began work on December 16, and another, Mary Johnson, joined them later. Things seem to have gone swimmingly throughout the first half of 1873, the girls learning rapidly and gilding a number of frames bought for them by the Society, and sold through the office (MCM 15-1-73, 30-5-73, 11-6-73, GCM 30-1-73). At one point Mrs Lawson became ill and Mr Lawson took the class, reporting that the girls "had made most satisfactory progress and already knew as much of the business as his apprentice who had been with him nearly a year." (MCM 19-2-73)

When, however, the lessons came to an end and the girls set out to get work for themselves things were not so promising. In July it was reported that the girls "having spent two or three days in seeking work at various shops found considerable difficulty in procuring it", though they had received some commissions from Mr Chance of Loudon St (MCM 18-7-73). In October things were not much better:

> The Secretary stated that Mary Johnson the youngest of the gilders had been working for a short time as improver at a shop in Church St

Edgware Road, that she had got on fairly there & had a promise of further employment at the same place as soon as they were busy. The other two girls had been working some weeks for Lawson having at first worked at his shop but that this had caused so much unpleasantness among his men that he had been obliged to let them have the work at their work room in Regent Sqr. (MCM 17-10-73)

They seem to have struggled on in the premises provided by Jessie Boucherett into the next year, but in January Emily Garwood gave up because "she seldom earned more than 6s and some weeks nothing", and the Secretary explained to the Committee that it took time "to form a connection", and that "she thought if the girls would only wait they would in time get plenty of work. Emily Garwood will be glad to resume the gilding if Emma Darwin should be fortunate enough to get more work than she can do single-handed" (GCM 23-1-74). Committee members offered work when they could. In March the Hon. Maude Stanley provided Emma Darwin with ten days of work, and in May she began working for Mrs Hankey "& is likely to be engaged there for some time" (MCM 13-3-74, 22-5-74). By April 1875 Emma Darwin was forced to look for alternative work, though the Annual Report of that year implied that she was ready to take on gilding if any were offered to her (GCM 9-4-75). The Annual Report of 1876 sadly concluded:

> That there should be many fluctuations in the tide of opinion on so grave a question as the suitable employment of women, is only to be expected; and while some employments, in all respects suitable to their powers and tastes, such as glass-engraving, gilding, &c., have had to be abandoned on account of the difficulty of gaining admission to those trades, or securing sufficient employment in them. . .
>
> Though these arts must for the present be set aside, other openings have been found during the past year, which seem to promise remunerative employment. As ladies of good position and connections have started and are conducting them, it is hoped that the difficulties which the slender means of the glass-engravers and gilders were unable to withstand, may in these cases be overcome.

Decorative Art

The window of hope described in the last paragraph of this Report was probably a reference to the success the Committee was having in placing girls with one of these "ladies of good position and connections". The increasing determination of young women to find "something to do"[22] of which the Women's Movement was just one manifestation, had meant that quite a number of those with artistic talents whose parents or husbands were prepared to support them had managed to get training in the Art Colleges that were opening all over the country. Some of them then devoted themselves

The Female School of Art in 1868
(From The Illustrated London News, 1868)

to the decorative arts, beginning probably by carrying out commissions for acquaintances, but gradually building up a "connection" which allowed them to earn a substantial living. The Society's first encounter with one such woman came unfortunately a little late to prevent the disastrous venture into gilding, but it certainly showed the Society a better way to capitalise on any artistic talent that had been revealed during their clients' conventional "female" education. The minutes for the General Committee meeting on October 9 1874 reported:

> Miss Collingridge of 20 King Street, Baker Street, who had been a student at the Royal Academy, and followed the profession of artist & art decorator applied to the Society for a pupil. Miss Collingridge is employed by some of the best houses in designing and painting panels, cabinets, papers, &c. &c. And has more work than she can get through single-handed, and having formed a good connection she feels that she is able to give employment to one or two young ladies. She proposes therefore to take one or two girls who have a good knowledge of drawing and a little of painting as articled pupils for three years for a premium of £25 each engaging to pay them small salaries from the commencement according to their capabilities.
>
> As this appears to be a desirable opening it was resolved that inquiries be made for suitable pupils & that the Secy be empowered to advance half the premium, if required, for one girl.

Suitable apprentices were quickly found, and the Secretary reported:

> . . . that Miss Black of 101 Adelaide Road, N.W. who had been strongly recommended by Miss Buss had after a fortnight's trial resolved to be articled to Miss Collingridge . . . her parents paying her premium; that Miss Collingridge has a second pupil, a Miss Jones who had been a student for three years at the Female School of Art, and who had been recommended to her by Miss Gann. (MCM 30-10-74)

A third soon joined them:

> Read a letter from Miss Collingridge stating that Miss Dora Connolly had been on trial for ten days, that she thought she would succeed well in decorative art and was quite willing to receive her as an articled pupil
>
> Miss Dora Connolly is the daughter of a naval chaplain on half pay who is in very bad health suffering from heart disease. She has studied at the Lambeth School of Art, and has great artistic taste.
>
> Her eldest sister[23] who prepares pupils for the higher Examinations, undertakes to be responsible to the Society for the £15, which she desires to borrow for part of her premium. (MCM 27-11-74)

A further, rather more experienced client, Miss A. Seeley who had two certificates from the South Kensington art school, was sent for an interview with Miss Collingridge in April 1875. The Committee had been shown her jewellery designs and told that she had previously worked with her father, but since his death "had found it impossible to get regular employment in the trade, and had therefore been obliged to work a sewing machine". Miss Collingridge responded very positively, recommending her for stained glass work, volunteering to give her teaching for 3 months for 2½ guineas a month. "She urged her to commence at once as she has orders for stained glass windows in hand at present, she could also give her opportunities of drawing from the model which she might not be able to afford her later in the year." (GCM 9-4-75, MCM 28-5-75, 11-6-75)

Other girls were sent to Miss Collingridge during the next few years, some as regular apprentices, others who had already received some art training for shorter periods to receive lessons in specific areas. Among the regular apprentices were Ellen Gregory of Norwood, aged 14½, the youngest daughter of a draper's widow, who had obtained two certificates from the Norwood School of Art (a branch of the South Kensington school) and who was granted a loan of £20 for the premium and "Miss Wray . . . the daughter of a ship builder, lately dead. Her mother carries on the business, and pays her daughter's premium." (MCM 11-2-76, 9-6-76)

Miss Collingridge began almost immediately to act as mentor to the Society's clients, seeing it as part of her responsibility to place her pupils with commercial firms after they were trained. The Minutes reported that "Miss Seeley had through Miss Collingridge's introduction obtained regular employment in tile painting" with Mr Stacey, Duke St, Manchester Square, and a year later that she had "lately been made forewoman with a salary of £2 a week", that "Miss Jones, whose term of apprenticeship had very nearly expired has obtained a situation at Messrs Simpson, Decorators, in the Strand" (MCM 10-12-75, 22-12-76). In 1878 it was reported that "Miss Black, whose apprenticeship terminated in the autumn is now regularly employed by Miss Turck of Gower Street" (GCM 1-2-78). In the same year, to help Miss Nathan, a 20-year old orphan with some art training, Miss Collingridge reduced the cost of her life classes from 31/6 to one guinea (which the Society provided) for a course of eight lessons, and when they were finished "offered to receive her into her studio for a month for 27/- thinking she would be able to study at the Museum till Christmas, and then try for the Royal Academy". (MCM 7-6-78, 19-7-78, 25-10-78)

The Committee seem to have grasped very early that they had at last found a way into an occupation which could be set beside the various forms of teaching as suitable for the girls brought up as "ladies" but whose families had fallen on difficult times, for example, Ethel Nisbet, aged 18, whose "father has suddenly lost, through the death of his employers, a very responsible position which he had held for 24 years," Ellen Harnett (aged 25) "the daughter of a medical man who died some years ago after an illness of three years which consumed almost all his savings", and Sarah Freeland, "a nice bright girl of 18", whose father, a solicitor, "had had heavy losses lately" (MCM 14-2-79, 25-7-79, C&GL GK to OR 22-12-82). The Annual Report for 1876 commented:

> Art decoration affords suitable and remunerative employment for gentlewomen. It requires special study, careful training, taste, and some knowledge of architecture, ancient and modern. Art decoration includes the designing of stained glass windows, the designing and painting of panels, tiles, &c., the designing of patterns for embroidery, and for hangings of various kinds, and the harmonious arrangement of colours in rooms, &c. It is essential that the art decorator should have a good knowledge of the human figure, of flowers, and other natural objects.

Throughout the next decade the Society directed quite a number of young women into the decorative arts. The Secretary soon built up a knowledge of the various art schools where elementary training could be acquired, and further studios where girls could be apprenticed were found. Girls were apprenticed not only to Miss Collingridge, but also to Eliza Turck of Gower Street, and to Messrs. Cameron & Co's Stained Class and China Works, Duke Street, Manchester Square (MCM 27-2-80, 18-3-81, 27-5-81)

There were two other initiatives of the 1870s where the Society, though not the innovator, gave valuable support. In 1872 the Secretary visited Minton's Studio at South Kensington and reported that 15 women who had trained in the South Kensington Art School were working there as china painters (MCM 6-3-72), and in 1874 arranged for one of Society's clients, Maude Gardner, to be employed there. In October 1875 Minton's factory was burned down, and it was decided not to rebuild, leaving the female china-painters out of work. Maude Gardner and two other painters, Miss Spiers and Miss Welby, approached the Society for help in establishing a business for themselves. The Committee's response was extremely generous, over £70 being raised, with Lord Shaftesbury, who usually confined his help to his annual subscription, contributing £15 (GCM 29-10-75). The three established a studio at 68 Newman Street, and though Maude Gardner soon withdrew, the others persevered, taking pupils on occasion from the Society. In the Annual Report of 1883, it was reported that although there were complaints of a market glutted with inferior work, the studio was still operating successfully, in part because "they continue to give lessons in drawing and painting generally, as well as on china and tapestry".

In the Annual Report of 1908, in a retrospective account of the Society's achievements, credit was claimed for a development not reported in any of the earlier documents:

> Wood-carving is another branch of art to which the Society introduced several students. When the National School of Wood-carving was started in 1879 in a small room in Somerset Street, three of the first six women students were introduced by the Society. One of these was made manager of the school, which was afterwards removed to Kensington and became the large and important school still flourishing in Exhibition road in connection with the London County Council.

CONCLUSION

The Society's dealings with Miss Collingridge and the china painters foreshadowed a change in the emphasis of its activities that was to become more apparent in the next thirty years of its history. By 1880 the "wall of prejudice" was no longer as impregnable as it had seemed. During its first twenty years the Society had used its protégées to attack some of these prejudices, and awoken some employers at least to the desirability of employing women as book-keepers and clerks, both in commercial firms and in the Civil Service, and as typesetters, hairdressers and dispensers. Even more importantly the publicity surrounding its activities had aroused others to the possibility of doing the same. In 1871, for example, the Manchester Public Free Libraries began to employ young women as librarians, this possibility only occurring to them the Chairman later explained, because "at this time the subject of woman, her rights, duties and employment - particularly her exclusion from certain trades and professions - was engaging the attention of thoughtful people". Furthermore the wider Women's Movement was encouraging young women from backgrounds a good deal less disadvantaged than those of the

Society's clients to enter professions like medicine and the decorative arts where even when trained they needed resources to allow them time to "build a connection" before they could expect a regular income. Such women, as can be seen in the cases of Elizabeth Garrett and Elizabeth Collingridge, could open the path for women from less privileged backgrounds. As the new situation unfolded the Society seems to have moved its focus to having a Secretary who had a broad knowledge of the employment scene and could give informed advice, and to building up a loan fund to allow young women to train for these positions.

---

1   The office was moved to 23 Gt Marlborough St in 1867, and to 22 Berners Street in 1872, where it remained into the next century.

2   For its first three years the Society's income exceeded £600, but for the rest of the decade it fluctuated between a high of £550 in 1865-66 and a low of £320 in 1868-69.

3   There is some confusion about who actually passed on the skills. The Minutes of February 7, mention "Miss Martin, the daughter of a Law Engrosser" as running the class but in 1884 Jessie Boucherett described their teacher as "an invalided law-stationer's clerk" (Boucherett 1884: 172).

4   The census records of 1851 show her as living with her father, a "navy agent's clerk" aged 40, her mother aged 38, two older sisters, a younger brother and a domestic servant in Kings Rd, Islington. By 1861 another sister had been born and by 1871 the two older girls were no longer there. In this year Mary Harris Smith's occupation is recorded as "book-keeping" and that of her 20-year-old brother as "navy agent's clerk". In 1881 her occupation was given as "accountant", and her younger sister's as "clerk" with the family still in Islington, though the address had changed. We have not been able to find her details in later censuses.

5   The Annual Reports recorded that 13 women had undertaken this work on the Society's recommendation in 1875 and 16 in 1876.

6   Various accounts of the founding of the Victoria Press have been published, for example: Stone 1994: 42-8, and Tusan 2004: 103-126. The second of these contains a number of errors in its account of the Society and its relations with the Victoria Press.

7   The Victoria Press was eventually sold and the new proprietor approached the Society to allow the press once again to do their printing. The Minutes for October 22, 1867 noted: "The Secretary reported that in compliance with the request of the Managing Committee she had seen Mr Head, the present proprietor of the Victoria Press, and had been informed by him that he has in his employment 16 women, that the most skilled can earn about a guinea a week, and that he is willing to employ more if he can procure work for them. As since the last meeting of the Managing Committee it had been ascertained that Mr Head was printing a newspaper of a very low character, it was resolved that the printing of the Society should not be transferred to him."

8   See GCM 12-10-1900, 9-11-1900, 14-12-1900, 11-1-1901, 13-12-1901, 14-11-1902, 28-11-1902, 12-12-1902, 13-3-1903.

9   This printing business is referred to by a number of names in the Minutes, Women's Co-operative Printing Society, Women's Union Printing Office, Women's Printing Company, before the name stabilised. In 1877 it moved to 21b Gt College Street Westminster and was still employing women in 1908.

10 The publicity was apparently strong enough to inspire one of the many fraudulent schemes that exploited the charitably-minded: "The Secretary reported that she had had some correspondence with a member of the Charity Organisation Society respecting

the Ladies Home and Printing Office, 48 Hunter Street, and that she had received from the Secretary of that Society an account of the Institution which was then read - "From this it appeared that the Home and Printing Office was established in 1869 by Mr Colmer, by whom subscriptions amounting to between £300 & £400 a year had been raised, the only visible results of which were that his brother Mr William Colmer receives a salary of 36/- a week for teaching printing to six or seven girls residing at their own homes, and that at different times since the establishment of the office three or four girls had been boarded in the house for some time. The whole account showed a considerable amount of money had been raised and that very few ladies had derived any advantage from it." (MCM 12-5-76).

11 The census of 1861 recorded only 419 women (3.8% of the total) as hairdressers, though the Society found that at least four women were running their own hairdressing establishments in London: Madame Myers, 104 Mount Street, Grosvenor Square, W.; Mrs Davis, 44, South Street, Grosvenor Square, W.; Mrs Price, 3 Pont Street, Lowndes Street, S.W.; Mrs Paine, 44 High Street, Marylebone, W.

12 The Minutes for October 14th 1862 recorded: "A prospectus was submitted of a plan for establishing a shop for Ladies' Hairdressing, on co-operative principles; for which the sanction of the Society was desired; & Miss Emily Davies had an interview with the Committee, & explained the plan. After some discussion the Committee unanimously accorded sanction."

13 His actions were apparently prompted by a strike among his male employees (Faithfull 1871: 380).

14 It is possible that hairdressers' furnishings, having been designed with men in mind, were too high for some women. In 1871 Mr Atwell refused to accept one girl "because he considered her too young and too short to learn hairdressing".

15 The original premium asked was £5, but because of her medical connection the St Mary's Committee decided that "she would have to pay one guinea only to the Dispenser."

16 These three women all had successful careers as pharmacists. Isabella Clarke opened her own chemist shop in Spring St. Paddington, married a fellow pharmacist and became first President of the Association of Women Pharmacists. Rose Minshull became head dispenser at the North Eastern Hospital for Children, and Louisa Stammwitz, after her years as dispenser at the New Hospital for Women, entered into partnership with a woman pharmacist who had qualified in 1884, Anne Neve, and established a successful chemist shop in Paignton.

17 See GCM 13-4-77, 6-7-77, 19-10-77, MCM 22-6-77, 7-12-77, 15-3-78.

18 She became Mrs Müller, and a prominent member of the SPEW Committee. See Chapter 3.

19 See MCM 24-5-89, 19-7-89, 19-7-89, 4-10-89, 14-3-90.

20 This was probably the Alice Brain recorded in the censuses of 1861 and 1871 as the daughter of an ivory cutter. The 1871 census shows her still living with her parents in St Pancras, and gives her age as 22 and her occupation as governess.

21 The 1871 census records a J.O. Eisert as a 29-year-old glass-engraver, born in Bohemia, and lodging with a printers' reader's family in the St Pancras area.

22 Florence Nightingale's impatience with the restrictions of family life has long been documented, but she was not alone. This was of course the aspiration that drove Elizabeth Garrett into medicine and Emily Davies into political campaigning, but, one researcher has noted, even before this, in the 1850s the feeling manifested itself among the socially conservative readers of the High Church girls' paper The Monthly Packet (Sturrock 1999).

23 The Managing Committee minutes for 7-4-76 suggest that she was the principal mistress at Aske's School for Girls.

CHAPTER 3

Finding "suitable and remunerative employment": 1880-1909

Knowing how strongly the Society for Promoting the Employment of Women advocated thorough training in all branches of work, & how zealous it was in seeking suitable and remunerative employment for women . . . (MCM 18-6-80)

The Minutes from the first twenty years of the Society's history give the impression that members saw the over-riding object as opening more occupations to women. By the beginning of the Society's third decade, however, this object was not quite so prominent in the discussions. In part, the Committee were aware that the message had now gained its own momentum and was spreading without their intervention, but its members had also learned some salutary lessons about the dangers faced in over-confidently persuading young women to enter uncharted territory. A balance had to be struck between the needs and potentialities of individual girls, and the wider aims of the Society, and over time the needs of the individuals seeking "suitable and remunerative employment" (the phrase is used a number of times in the Minutes and Annual Reports) became the more significant focus.

THE SOCIETY DURING ITS NEXT THIRTY YEARS

During these thirty years the Society saw a number of changes in the Committee. New significant members who joined in the 1870s were Lady Knightley of Fawsley (1842-1913), Mrs Müller, (1845-1931), Lady Goldsmid (1819-1909) and Mr Mocatta (1809-1904). Louisa Knightley was the daughter of General Sir Edward Bowater and in 1869 married Sir Rainald (later Baron) Knightley, a Tory MP for many years. She thus spent much of the year in London, and as well as moving in political circles, could devote time to causes concerning women. Jessie Boucherett was her cousin, and through her she became committed to the suffrage movement and to the SPEW, whose Committee meetings she attended regularly from

Society for Promoting the Employment of Women.

UNDER THE PATRONAGE OF
HER MAJESTY THE QUEEN.
H.I.H. THE EMPRESS FREDERICK OF GERMANY.
H.R.H. THE PRINCESS LOUISE, MARCHIONESS OF LORNE.
THE LADY EBURY.
THE LADY ELIZABETH CUST.
THE LADY STANLEY OF PRESTON.
THE LADY ALFRED SPENCER CHURCHILL.
LADY ACLAND.
LADY EASTLAKE.
LOUISA LADY GOLDSMID.
LADY LOCH.
MRS. W. E. GLADSTONE.

President.
THE EARL FORTESCUE.

Vice-Presidents.
HIS GRACE THE ARCHBISHOP OF CANTERBURY.
THE DUKE OF RUTLAND.
LORD ABERDARE.
THE RIGHT HON. W. E. GLADSTONE, M.P.

Committee.

*Miss BAYNE.
*Miss J. BOUCHERETT.
Mrs. BULLOCK.
*Mrs. W. BURBURY.
Miss BUSS.
*Miss CROWE.
*Mrs. EARLE.
C. W. EARLE, Esq.
*Mrs. J. G. FITCH.
Miss GORDON.
*The Hon. VICTORIA GROSVENOR.
R. HAMILTON, Esq.

T. HARE, Esq.
Miss JAMES.
*Miss LOCKE KING.
*Lady KNIGHTLEY.
Mrs. LANKESTER.
Miss LEWIN.
F. D. MOCATTA, Esq.
*Mrs. MULLER.
*Hon. Lady PONSONBY.
*Lady ROBERTS.
R. SWAN, Esq.

* These form the Managing Committee.

Treasurer—The Hon. VICTORIA GROSVENOR.

Secretary—Miss KING.   **Assistant-Secretary**—Miss E. HARE.

Auditor—JOSEPH BIGGS, Esq.

Bankers—Messrs. COUTTS & Co., Strand.

Donations and Subscriptions are received by Messrs. Coutts and Co., or at th
Office, 22, Berners Street.   Post Office Orders payable to Gertrude J. King.

SPEW Officers and Committee Members (AR 1890)
(Girton College Collection)

1877 to 1900. She was also an early supporter of the Girls' Friendly Society (GFS), an Anglican youth group at that date directed primarily at young domestic servants. From 1885 onwards she kept diaries of her activities, but unfortunately these contain almost no details of SPEW meetings (Gordon 1999). Elizabeth Müller, who as Miss Crosby had begun the plan-tracing business (see Chapter 2), married the extremely wealthy research chemist, Dr. Hugo Müller, FRS, in 1879 and was a member of the Committee from 1879 to 1900. She left £500 to the Society in her will.[1]

When Sir Francis Goldsmid, who was listed as a member of the General Committee from 1859 to 1879, died, his widow, Louisa Goldsmid took his place. She had been an active supporter of Emily Davies's educational causes since 1862 and became a member of the Girton College Committee in 1872, as well as a member of various suffrage societies and a supporter of many Jewish causes (Crawford 1999: 247). She was a vocal member of the SPEW Committee and a strong supporter of Jessie Boucherett's concerns about industrial legislation. In 1891 she brought a deputation of female Chain and Nail-makers to London to protest against legislation limiting their work (MCM 10-4-91). In the mid-1880s David Mocatta, a retired architect most noted for his work with Jewish charities, began to attend the Committee regularly, the only man to do so since the 1860s. He left the Society £100 in his will.

There were also organisational changes. When the Assistant Secretary, Sarah Lewin (see Chapter 1), retired in 1889 her place was taken by Edith Hare who had "on several occasions been employed on temporary work in the office" at a salary of £50 a year (MCM 19-7-89, 1-11-89). There were also a number of holders of the position of President, a position that throughout this period involved little more than chairing the Annual General Meeting. The Earl of Shaftesbury died in 1885 having held the position since 1859. He was followed by the Earl Fortescue from 1886 to 1895, Lord Stanmore (who proved to have views on restrictive labour legislation at variance with those of the Committee, and had to be tactfully asked to resign) from 1896 to 1898 (GCM 11-3-98, 20-1-99), the Viscount Knutsford from 1899 to 1905 and Lord Stamford from 1906 to 1909.

The Committee meetings were usually confined to discussing cases where parents needed help paying for the training, but the Annual Reports give a more complete picture of the broader work of the Society. This description was given in 1889:

> The office is a centre at which inquiries concerning the various branches of women's work are constantly made, and the Committee are grateful for information as to work already going on, as well as for suggestions as to openings in new directions, which may enable them to help as efficiently as possible those who come to them.
> It often happens that parents are both willing and able to pay the fees for the apprenticeship or technical training of their daughters, but they

are in difficulty as to the selection of a suitable industry, and the means of obtaining the requisite training for it. For want of such knowledge serious mistakes are often made which cause waste both of time and money, and those who have had experience of the service rendered to them by the Society, and whose elder girls are happily maintaining themselves, almost as a matter of course bring their younger girls, when they leave school, to see what it will be best for them to try.

It is clear that the Society's ability to provide this service (throughout the decade over 3,000 inquirers a year came to the office) owed a great deal to the skills of Gertrude King. She had built up a personal knowledge of the work available and had by the 1880s a considerable network of contacts both among tradesmen and businessmen in central London and within a wider field of those with philanthropic interests.

From the time of her first appointment she had made a practice of visiting the businesses of employers who applied for workers and assessing their reliability. In 1878, for example, the Annual Report noted "During the past year 145 visits of inquiry have been made", that is roughly three a week, and the Minutes are strewn with records of such visits:

> The Secretary reported that she had visited the School of Telegraphy in the City Road . .
>
> Also that Mrs Craig, the Supt of the government female clerks in Telegraph St, had informed her that the government had established a school in Cannon Street for training their own clerks, & that no girl received any appointment until she was able to pass a difficult Examination in Telegraphy. . . .
>
> Resolved that it is not necessary to establish classes for telegraph clerks nor to send them to the School of Telegraphy.
>
> The Secretary was requested to ascertain if possible whether the telegraph clerks employed in small post offices were under government or not, and if not, what control the government had over them. (MCM 18-5-70)
>
> The Secretary stated that she had spoken on the subject [of copying play scripts] to a gentleman connected with the theatres and had learnt from him that at every theatre copyists are employed in copying plays & the various parts before any new play is put on the stage, that these copyists are well paid, and he considered the suggestion a very good one. (MCM 10-6-81)
>
> The Secretary stated that she had visited Mrs Feltham in her new office, that some of the girls [recommended by the Society] were correcting proofs for the directories others preparing the slips. Mr Kelly praised the work done by the girls very highly. Six of those at work there had gone to her from Miss Boucherett's school or were sisters of pupils. Their

wages are 8/- weekly during the first year, 10/- during the second, rising gradually to 15/-. (MCM 13-10-76)

> As it was thought desirable that the Committee should gain all possible information respecting the technical schools for women in Paris, and how the young women trained in them procure employment, Miss J. Boucherett proposed & it was resolved that the Secretary be requested to go to Paris immediately after Easter to get this information. (GCM 4-5-79)

Some of her inquiries prevented the Society becoming involved in hazardous ventures proposed by over-enthusiastic advisors. For example:

> The Secretary stated that in compliance with the directions of the General Committee she had made careful inquiries to ascertain whether cameo cutting would be a desirable employment for women, the Council of the City and Guilds of London Technical Institute having resolved to start a class for learning this art at their schools in the Kennington Park Road. There appears to be but little demand for cameos in England the few that are offered for sale being brought from abroad and sold at prices which would not prove remunerative to English Artists. Under these circumstances it does not seem advisable to persuade girls to learn this art. (MCM 2-2-83)

She also joined in the effort to expose frauds designed to prey on vulnerable women in need of work:

> The Secretary stated that she had answered an advertisement which she had seen repeatedly in various papers stating that persons of either sex could add £2 weekly to their incomes without interfering with their present occupation
>
> The reply was a proposition that the applicant should purchase from the advertisers a quantity of common jewellery, carry it about in his pocket and sell it to his friends and others at double the price paid for it.
>
> Having the papers she could caution the unwary against it. (MCM 15-10-80)

As wider interest in women's employment grew her expertise was called on by individuals and groups outside the Society. Her evidence to the Civil Service Commission has already been mentioned, and she gave advice to Mercy Grogan for her book on women's work (Grogan 1883), and to Louisa Hubbard who in 1875 began to publish a *Handbook for Women's Work* (later called *The Englishwoman's Year Book*) and who edited the *Woman's Gazette* (afterwards named *Work and Leisure*), from 1875 to 1893. In 1882 she wrote a short account of the Society for *Friendly Leaves*, a paper published for the members of the GFS (GCM 7-7-82).

There were organisations as well as publications that sought the Society's help. When Lady Mary Feilding established the Working Ladies' Guild to bring together "gentlewomen engaged in some remunerative employment, and other ladies who are willing to give time or money to promote their welfare" (MCM 24-11-76) the Society was approached for advice and support, and close contact with this group was maintained for the rest of the century, partly because Jessie Boucherett and Lady Knightley were members of both Committees (GCM 7-7-82).[2] When in 1892 Clara Collet, one of Sub-Commissioners for the Royal Commission on Women's Employment, wished to gain evidence from "dressmakers and milliners living at the houses of their employers, as to their hours, and the domestic and sanitary conditions under which they worked" in a place where "they might have no fear of speaking frankly to her", she used the Society's office for her interviews (GCM 1-4-92).

In the 1890s an annual Conference of Women Workers was held in various provincial cities and Gertrude King attended each year as the Society's representative. Out of this grew the National Union of Women Workers with which the Society had for a time strong links.[3] When the NUWW formed a sub-committee to find suitable employment for educated women, Gertrude King was invited to join it, which she did, telling the Committee "that as the work was the same as that which the Society had done for many years she thought it was most desirable that she should serve" (GCM 11-1-1896). The Society was also consulted by Sir Walter Besant on a proposal that the various women's employment societies should come together to create a Central Bureau "for general information on all subjects connected with Women's work" (MCM 17-7-96). During the next year the NUWW under the leadership of Louisa Creighton (the wife of the recently appointed Bishop of London) set about implementing this plan. Mrs Creighton invited representatives of the various societies (including the SPEW) to give papers at a conference, and then took the lead in setting up a Central Bureau with which the other societies were invited to co-operate. (GCM 30-4-97; MCM 19-3-97, 14-5-97) The Bureau was launched at a public meeting on December 10, 1897, an honorary secretary, Miss Bateson, appointed and the proposal to rent an office near Chancery Lane and appoint a salaried assistant secretary approved. The Bureau soon became dominated by another secretary, the redoubtable Miss Spencer, some of whose tussles with the Society are described in the next chapter.[4] Even at this early stage the SPEW had to put up a certain resistance to being co-opted into the Central Bureau. They refused to allow their loan fund to be amalgamated with that of the Bureau and rejected a request to become involved in the Bureau's plan for incorporation (GCM 20-1-99, 13-7-1900). Nevertheless the two groups exchanged information on available employment, and the Society was prepared to consider candidates proposed by the Central Bureau for its loans (GCM 29-4-98, 20-1-99).

The Society was not, however, simply concerned with establishing that the occupations being recommended were sufficiently remunerative. Members were equally determined that they should be "suitable", that they should not jeopardize the girl's femininity nor reduce her too far below the social level on which she had been brought up. One offer to take an apprentice at a small printing office was declined, because "the printer ... conducted & printed entirely by himself a small workman's paper, & that the girl would often be left by herself at a tiny office in the city, & would there have to see any rough men who might wish to put anything into the paper" (MCM 9.11.1883). On another occasion, when an apprentice to the decorative artist Miss Turck applied to take a situation on her own account, the Minutes recorded: "Resolved that Eleanor Garratt be allowed to accept the situation offered, and that as her home influence was not good, it would be better for her to live in one of the Homes for girls." (GCM 8-7-1887)

In an article about the Society, published in *The Quiver* in 1889 the journalist wrote: "Most of the new occupations found for women during this period have been either established or materially aided by this parent institution, which, unnatural as it may seem, casts off her children and bids them support themselves as soon as they are old and clever enough to find food and shelter" (Beale, 1889: 113). In practice, however, the Secretary and the Committee were not quite so prepared to cut all ties. While they did not claim guardianship of the young women, they seem to have felt themselves guardians of the good name of the innovations they had promoted. The 1870s Minutes contain the following:

> The Secretary stated that at Miss Buss' request she had read the last Report before a meeting of her old pupils and had discussed various employments with them. She had also had some conversation with four of the clerks in the P.O. Savings Bank who had protested first to Mr Thompson and afterwards to Lord John Manners against the appointment of Miss Smith as superintendent on the plea that her conduct was unmodest and unladylike. She had endeavoured to show them that such interference on their part was likely to do considerable harm to the increased employment of women in public offices. (MCM 9-6-76)

A few years later the Committee showed this same protective attitude towards an occupation for which the Society was only marginally responsible. Having received a report that the Postmaster General "had been obliged to dismiss two of the Counter women at the Post Office for incivility, and that complaints of this kind had become more frequent since women had been employed" Jessie Boucherett proposed "that the Committee should make an effort to gain some influence over the young women". As a result of this suggestion, the girls were to be

> . . . invited to tea at the office, [and] some entertainment in the way of music or readings should be provided for them, and that someone be asked

to urge upon them the necessity of punctuality, civility and earnestness in the discharge of their duties, and pointing out to them how materially the future employment of women as clerks in the Civil Service depends on the manner in which they fulfil their duties (MCM 14.3.1879).

. . . it was found that about 40 young women were employed at the various offices within easy distance of Berners Street - it was therefore resolved that these young women should be invited to tea on the 15th, 16th or 18th of July, that Mrs W. Burbury be asked to give them a short address, that the choice of the evening be left with her. That gentlemen & ladies be asked to sing, read, or recite and that a substantial tea be provided at about 1/- each, independently of hiring and attendance. (MCM 27-6-79)

A similar entertainment was later provided for more direct protégées of the Society:

The Managing Committee having decided to give a party to the book keepers who have been trained in the Society's classes, and who are creditably holding situations through the Society, the arrangements were discussed. Between 50 & 60 young women have been invited for Tuesday July 7th and promises of help in singing & recitations have been received from Me Isabel Fassett, Miss Sophia Smith, Mr Michael Sautley & Mr T. Watt Cafe. (GMC 26-6-1885)

This care and concern was of course made possible because the Society had its permanently attended office where applicants could be received and classes held, where casual copying work could be done under the Secretary's eye, where the Committee members could pop in and out keeping *au fait* with the doings of the office staff and the clients, and where the Committee and Annual General meetings could be held. Consequently it seems worthwhile to give some account of the office, its position, size and furnishings.

THE OFFICE AT 22 BERNERS STREET

In June 1869 the Society was given notice to vacate the rooms they had occupied for the last three years at 23 Great Marlborough Street, just south of Oxford Street. Although they were offered alternative accommodation at the same address they decided to move and "the Secretary was requested to look for rooms suitable for an office as near the circus as possible". (GCM 30-6-69) After a good deal of searching they finally settled on 22 Berners Street, once again north of Oxford Street but further east than Langham Place. The ground lease of the building was held by Messrs Nisbet & Co. who seem to have carried on their business on the ground floor while letting the rest of the building to the Rev. J. Kelly, who then sublet these rooms to

Houses in Berners Street similar to the one rented by the Society
(With the permission of the City of London Metropolitan Archives)

a number of different tenants. Kelly offered the Society "a large front room on the first floor" for £50 a year, which they accepted. The back room on their floor was occupied by the Ladies Sanitary Association, which had also rented rooms at Langham Place and had either accompanied or preceded them to this address.[5] The upper floors were also let, and a housekeeper for all the tenants was supplied by Kelly. By the beginning of February 1872 "a bell & click had been put up and a matting purchased", advertisements of the change of address had been placed in the *Times*, *Telegraph*, *Daily News* and *Guardian*[6], and the Society was installed in the house it would occupy for the next thirty-five years. (GCM 24-1-72, MCM 7-2-72, Annual Report 1907)

Kelly proved to be a difficult landlord, raising the price he charged for the housekeeper's "attendance", demanding that the Society lay matting on the stairs, insisting that they install a smaller brass plate to match that of the Ladies' Sanitary, and getting his way by threatening to give them notice. He also made difficulties for the Society by moving the housekeeper down to the basement and then insisting that the Society pay for moving the bell used to summon her to their office.[7] On the other hand the room soon became a source of income for the Society as a number of groups began regularly to hire it at five shillings a night for their meetings: the Library Committee of the London Association of Schoolmistresses, (MCM 18-7-73), the Association for the Help of Friendless Girls in London (MCM 12-6-74), the General Benevolent Association (MCM 28-5-75), and the Ladies' Debating Society (MCM 26-11-75). This led to the Society purchasing six more chairs, bringing the number provided for such meetings up to 22 (MCM 23-12-75).[8]

In July 1877 the Secretary reported that Mr Kelly had been given notice and "that Messrs Nisbet have offered to let it to the Society for £150 a year inclusive. They will pay all rates and taxes and put the house into thorough repair." The Secretary's account of the finances involved gives a picture of just how the house was occupied:

> At the present time the back rooms on the 1st floor are let to the Ladies' Sanitary Association for £45 a year, the whole of the second floor is let to Mr Such, a professor of medicine for £50. Both these tenants desire to remain if the house is done up and properly ventilated. The third floor is now let to a dressmaker but as the room underground, at present occupied by a housekeeper is unfit for a family to live in, two of the rooms on that floor must be set apart for the housekeeper, so that two only will be available for letting. These two rooms might be let for £15 or £20 a year. Supposing the whole house to be let the committee would gain rather than lose by the proposed change as they would receive £110 or £115 of the £150. There will of course be an increase in the expense of coal and gas, but it was thought that £5 would cover this. (GCM 6-7-77)

This arrangement seems to have worked admirably with the Society's efficient secretaries managing the tenancies and the housekeeper's "attendance", and thus making a modest annual reduction in the Society's expenses. The housekeeper, when moved up from the basement seems to have performed her duties adequately, and at one point her son whitewashed the basement for the Society (MCM 22-6-88). The secretaries put a good deal of effort into the maintenance of the house, persuading the landlords to repaint and repaper, and arranging for gas lights and heaters to be installed and replaced. Things did not go totally smoothly. Although the two rooms on top floor not occupied by the housekeeper were rented for many years to Sarah Lewin the assistant secretary (GCM 6-7-88, MCM 19-11-97), the second floor had a succession of tenants some of whom were less than satisfactory.

Residents of 22 Berners Street returned in 1881 census

One, summarily evicted in 1894, was a Mrs Watson, who after three years occupancy "married a man of intemperate habits, whose behaviour has caused considerable disturbance in the house", and who had "been to the house the worse for drink, & had had to be turned out by the Housekeeper's Son" (MCM 4-5-94, 18-5-94). These problems were compensated for by the steady income from the hire of the office for meetings in the evenings at between three and five shillings a night. Most of those renting the space were charitable societies like the Boarding Out Association, the Matron's Aid Society, and the Women's Employment League, but it was used on occasion for literary purposes. In 1880, for example, the room was hired by Miss Kellog, an American "reader and reciter" for her performances (MCM 13-2-80, 27-2-80, 10-12-80) and in the 1890s by a Shakespeare Reading Society (GCM 10-10-90). In 1902 the Committee were told that the Society "receive regularly £28 towards their rent by subletting the office, in addition to the occasional meetings which are still held there." (GCM 12-12-1902) Nevertheless the twentieth century saw an increase in the frequency with which concerns about the property were brought to the attention of the Committee, and finally in 1907, after an occupancy of thirty-five and a half years, the Society received notice from the landlord to leave in June. The office was transferred to 23 Berners St. where it remained until after World War I.

During these thirty-five years, however, an event had occurred that formed something of a watershed in the Society's first fifty years. In 1879, on the twentieth anniversary of the founding of the Society the early links with the National Association for the Promotion of Social Science were broken, and there was a change in the Society's constitution, the consequence a collaboration with the newly formed City and Guilds of London Institute.

THE CITY AND GUILDS OF LONDON INSTITUTE

In 1878, Emily Davies, who had resigned from the SPEW Committee in 1873 to act temporarily as Mistress of Girton College, once again intervened in the Society's affairs. She urged the Society to apply for funding to the various City Companies of London, most of which had large annual funds for charitable bequests, and she put Gertrude King in touch with the Secretary of the Clothworkers' Company, Mr Owen Roberts (MCM 7-6-78). This began an association that had a significant influence on the fortunes of the Society.

Gertrude King, after a number of discussions with Owen Roberts, reported to the Committee that the City Companies were on the verge of setting up a joint association to be called the City and Guilds of London Institute. This has become today a major accreditation body for vocational training, but the early intention was to improve industrial training by paying apprenticeship fees for deserving applicants who could not otherwise afford them and by setting up a College of Technical Instruction to supplement the training given by masters. Roberts, who was soon to become the first Secretary of the proposed Institute, had obviously realised that its aims and those of the Society were very similar, and Gertrude King reported his advice. His first suggestions were that the Society should become incorporated by Licence from the Board of Trade, as the Institute was proposing to do, and that letters should be sent to the various City Companies outlining the aims and achievements of the Society and asking for support.[9]

The SPEW Committee quickly set about the business of becoming incorporated. By early July Gertrude King had received advice from a solicitor on what was involved, and after some discussion he was asked to prepare these articles for members of the Society to sign. His draft was received in November 1878 (MCM 8-11-78) and after considerable discussion, and some suggestions for modifications from the Board of Trade, a final version was approved on April 4, 1879. The Articles of Incorporation were adopted on June 18, the twentieth anniversary of the Society's foundation (*AR* 1880). During this reorganization the Society's connection with the National Association for the Promotion of Social Science, which had played so significant a part in the Society's first few years, was broken. It was decided that, as its Secretary "had not replied to the letter sent in November last respecting the Memorandum and Articles of Association", all mention of the NAPSS should be dropped in the new draft of the Society's Rules that incorporation demanded.

While the incorporation was progressing, Owen Roberts was busy putting the Society's case to the committee of the new Institute, and on March 17, 1879, he sent the good news to Gertrude King

> The vote of £300 per annum in aid of your Society's operations has been carried subject to certain limitations and reservations, as I shall hereafter have to define and we shall nominate a Committee to act with a Committee of your Society in the disposal of the fund.

The "limitations and reservations" appear to have meant that the Institute's Committee expected to be informed of how the money was to be spent, and to have the power to veto grants to particular candidates or for particular occupations. A joint committee was set up with the Society to discuss these issues, the Society proposing as members "Miss J. Boucherett, Miss Crowe, the Honble Victoria Grosvenor, & the Hon Lady Ponsonby, as being the oldest members of the Committee, who were in the habit of attending the meetings" (MCM 30-5-79).

On Roberts's advice, the Society prepared a Proposal of 15 octavo pages (now held in the City and Guilds archives at the Guildhall Library in London) suggesting that up to £200 should be spent on establishing classes in wood-engraving, and £30 on classes for shorthand. It concluded:

> The Committee would be very glad if their means permitted it, to do more in the way of assisting deserving girls by paying their premiums as apprentices to various trades, or if they have marked talent by enabling them to attend the established art schools. They therefore venture to suggest that, should the Council consent to establish the classes above proposed, the balance of the sum kindly voted for promoting the employment of women in industrial pursuits, should be used in this way.

There is no record of whether or not the £30 was used for the second set of shorthand courses (see Chapter 2) run by the Society, but the City and Guilds agreed that £100 of the grant would be "used for paying the training or apprentice fees for young women selected by the Committee of the Society". The proposal for teaching wood-engraving was also approved by the Institute in a manner that involved the Society to a considerable extent with its new Technical College. Unfortunately this attempt to feminise another of the art-related trades, like the forays into glass-engraving and gilding, did not produce the desired outcome.

Wood-engraving

Wood-engraving, that is preparing blocks from artists' drawings for reproduction in books and magazines, had long been regarded by the

Women's Movement as a potential occupation for women. It had been advocated in the third issue of the *English Woman's Journal* (March, 1858: 165-177),[10] and was discussed by the Society's Committee a number of times in the early 1870s, primarily with reference to a Mr Paterson "the best engraver in Edinburgh" who had offered ladies' classes there for six years, and moved to London in 1876 (MCM 15-5-72, 27-10-76). The Society's proposal to the City and Guilds seems, however, to have been prompted by a recent development in training in the area. On May 16, 1879, Gertrude King reported to the SPEW Committee:

> Mr Sparkes, the head master of the Art Schools at South Kensington, informed her that an excellent class for wood engraving had been carried on at the Art Schools Kensington under Mr Charles Roberts of 188 Strand an engraver of very high standing; that this class is to be closed at the end of the present term, not from any failure on the part of the pupils but because the teaching is practical rather than scientific.

She also reported that she had received estimates from two possible teachers for teaching a class for two hours twice a week. Charles Roberts from the South Kensington art school would charge £200 a year, and Mr Paterson, who had now conducted a ladies' class in London for three years, would charge £125 a year. The rent of a room, light and heating would cost a further £50 a year.

The Institute members approved the plan in principle, and persuaded the Society to establish the class at the Institute's Technical School in Kennington Park Road in South East London, and to employ the more expensive Charles Roberts. The school opened in November 1879, with three pupils, and with one of the former Kensington pupils, Miss Moffat, superintending the pupils during their practice hours. (MCM 21-11-79). It was described in detail in the Annual Report of 1880:

> This School, established by the City and Guilds of London Institute, offers to girls, who have a good elementary knowledge of drawing, the opportunity of acquiring a thorough mastery of wood engraving. *Good English engravers are much needed*, and if the students will but persevere, they will ultimately earn good wages of from one to three guineas a week, or even more. The fees are very small, only £4 4s. for the year, and free Scholarships after the first year are offered to those girls who show a steady desire to improve and who work heartily. The comfort of the students has been most kindly cared for. A dining room has been furnished for their use, and a housekeeper provides meals at a fixed tariff, if required. A lady resides in the house as assistant teacher, who superintends the practice of the students, and the master gives his lessons twice a week. The hours of practice are from 10 to 4 daily, with a break for dinner, and the lessons are on Tuesday and Friday evenings from 6 to 8. Girls over 16 years of age are admitted, and the Committee wish

to impress on all who desire to enter the School the necessity of steady and earnest work for four or five years at the least. Students may earn a little during that time, but they must not expect to acquire excellence in what is essentially a fine art, unless they devote years to the work. Bad engravers are not at all wanted, but there is ample employment in these days of illustrated newspapers and books for all who can execute good work. The School was opened in November last; 5 students are at present attending it, and there is room for 8 or 9 more.

Numbers soon expanded. There were 13 pupils by May 1881, all that could be accommodated, and in December 1882 two girls, Alice Girdlestone and Annie Bates, won the first two of the prizes offered by the Institute for the best work done by present and former students. (MCM 15-12-82). Nevertheless there were problems. Gertrude King's recruiting area was inner London, and the distance to Kennington meant that attendance was not as regular as it should have been – sufficiently irregular to induce the SPEW Committee to offer £2.15s in prizes for regular attendance. There was also a swift turnover in superintendents of the girls' practice though they became easier to recruit after October 1881 when the City and Guilds was persuaded to provide a salary of £50. There were also concerns expressed year after year that the girls did not have sufficient art training when they began, and that they would not persevere with the long unpaid training until they reached a standard of professional competence.

On the other hand, provision was made for the eventuality that had plagued the earlier efforts to teach girls craft skills: employment when they had acquired them. Charles Roberts proposed to Gertrude King that if the Society would pay the rent of a room in which girls who had completed the Technical School course could work, he would employ them on projects that would allow them to build up their skills (MCM 21-11-79). Though some Committee members felt that the cost was rather high, it was generally agreed that, as it was later (MCM 18-6-80) clearly stated, "the plan seemed extremely desirable as it would give the girls a regular footing in the trade and lead to their permanent employment in it", and letters were sent out asking for contributions to a fund of £85 to pay the rent for two years (MCM 12-3-80). Leading Committee members contributed substantial sums, Lady Goldsmid, for example, promising £25. The project began in October 1881 "with four students from the School, Misses Mudie, Gowland, Girdleston and Harden". A fortnight later Gertrude King reported

. . . that Mr Roberts is well satisfied with the work done by the young women up to the present time. He had expected some opposition from his men but he had told them that the wages would not be at all lowered by the employment of women, as they would be paid exactly the same rate as they were, and that consequently he had had no trouble with them. (MCM 26-10-81)

The 1884 Annual Report noted that he was by then employing eight women and that "the more advanced of these are earning good wages".

For the next five years things seemed to be going swimmingly. It looked as if this "suitable and remunerative" occupation was opening to women, and the Society directed girls not only to the school but to Mr Paterson's classes as well (GCM 29-10-80). Then word began to spread that technological changes were threatening the kind of routine work for which the girls at Kennington were being trained. In March 1886 the superintendent of the classes at Kennington reported that "Mr Sparkes paid the school a visit on Friday prophesying the extinction of wood-engraving" and that he had on previous occasions discouraged the girls by similar speeches. Gertrude King discussed the matter with Charles Roberts and reported that he "thinks that the process work will probably in time take the place of the common work but that it is not likely to interfere with work of a high order".

Gertrude King nevertheless continued to recommend the class, and the Committee was given the heartening news that one of the earliest engravers, Miss Harden, was now earning £100 a year and wished to join the Society (MCM 24-3-89). (Her name appears as a subscriber of 10s in the Annual Reports for the next three years.) However, because Charles Roberts's business took commissions only for "work of a high order", it took a discouragingly long time for the girls to begin earning, and, realising this, the Committee instructed Gertrude King to write letters "to printers, publishers, engravers, & to various firms, stating that the Committee are anxious to procure easy engraving suitable for catalogues, magazines &c. for young women connected with the Society, that specimens of their work can be seen at the office, and that orders can be received there." This was successful and she was able to report that "the women engravers employed by Mr Roberts are now fully occupied and have been ever since Christmas" (MCM 28-3-90).

Nevertheless the Committee members became increasingly aware of the threat of the new technology, and in 1889 Gertrude King began making inquiries about photogravure, now increasingly replacing wood-engraving in the production of illustrated papers and magazines. Perhaps fortunately, it became increasingly difficult to find pupils for the class, and it was closed in 1892. There was an elegiac note in the account of the occupation that Gertrude King wrote to a member of the Institute Committee earlier in that year:

I went over to the wood engraving class last night, and had some conversation with the Master Mr C. Roberts. He speaks highly of the young women who are working for him, all of whom have been trained in the Technical Art School at Kennington. Though the various kinds of process work now in use for cheap publications have taken away the engraving which some years ago was done by learners, and which enabled them to earn a little in their second or third year of study, still there seems to be good scope for really skilled engravers, and there are few industries in which women are employed by means of which they can earn more when they are skilled. . . Wood engraving is a beautiful art, and we should indeed be grieved if it were again closed to women after some having been successful with it, through the training they have received through the liberality of the Council of the Technical Schools. (C&GL 05-03-92: GK to A.L. Soper)

Wood-engraving was in actuality rapidly ceasing to be the kind of skilled craft that the Society sought for its clients, and was becoming primarily an art form in its own right. Engravers were no longer routinely engaged by publishers for the reproduction of artists' designs, and although woodcuts continued to illustrate books throughout the twentieth century, these were illustrations in the tradition pioneered by William Morris and his followers, designed as well as executed by the engraver, using skills different from those taught even by high class engravers like Charles Roberts and Mr Paterson (Cundall 1895).

It became apparent in 1893 that the decline in routine work was permanent. In July Miss Harden reported that "orders for engraving are gradually getting worse & worse", and asked for advice on alternative work for the girls employed there (MCM 20-7-93). On June 29, 1894 Gertrude King told the Committee that Charles Roberts had suffered great losses and was behind in the payment of his employees' wages. Two of these she said were "very anxious to acquire skill in some other branch of art, one wishing to learn fashion-plate drawing, and the other the retouching of negatives". Jessie Boucherett gave a donation of £10 "for the purpose of helping Engravers", and it was decided that the two girls should receive £2 each to pay for instruction in the skills they had nominated.[11] On this occasion things improved, and they were in work again by mid-July (MCM 13-7-94), but by 1899, even Miss Harden "the best of the wood engravers" was "very much wishing to take up some other industry as that has so nearly died out". She was immediately granted a loan of £16.16.0 to study Chromolithography for a year at the School of Lithography and Art in Queen Square being run by Louisa Gann (MCM 20-10-99).

This was a disappointing outcome for the Society, in an area which initially seemed to suggest that they had learnt from past failures and had now found a viable strategy for introducing women into skilled crafts.

Grants for Individuals
If collaboration with the City and Guilds did little to open new areas of women's work, the Institute provided valuable support for what was increasingly becoming the Society's major function, organising loans that allowed girls to train for work in new and expanding areas. Its help was invaluable in extending the benefits, first revealed by Miss Collingridge,

of apprenticing women to female pioneers of the decorative arts. Within the first few years of the collaboration the Society found two new female artists prepared to take apprentices, Miss Gann who ran the Female School of Art in Queen's Square, Bloomsbury, which in about 1883 established a chromolithographic department, and Miss I.W. Bennet who ran the South Wimbledon Art College for Ladies. The Institute at first queried their appropriateness, Owen Roberts telling Gertrude King "that the Council required that grants should be for bona fide apprentice fees not school fees, that the apprentices should be bound to one following some trade a knowledge of which he or she could personally impart to the apprentice" (GCM 12-10-83), but some compromise was reached, possibly when it was pointed out that the schools executed commissions and sold their pupils' work, and the girls to whom grants were given were in consequence usually described in the Minutes as apprenticed to the schools' directors.

These ventures proved most successful, and in October 1883 Gertrude King wrote to a member of the Institute Committee:

> I am glad to be able to report favourably of the young people who have from time to time received help from the Technical Institute. The first, Miss Harnett has been working for herself for the last two years and has been fairly successful with decorative work, china painting and teaching. Her studio is at 131 Abbey Road St Johns Wood.
>
> Jessie Wood, who is with Mr Cameron, glass stainer has done some excellent work in painting and design both for church windows & for private houses.
>
> Miss Allen who learnt decorative work has married an artist and continues her painting.
>
> Ada Keeble who learnt art and fancy needlework with Mrs Hillier of Tunbridge Wells, is now holding satisfactorily a very good situation in Yorkshire.
>
> Miss Campbell who was articled to Miss Bennett of Wimbledon is getting on very well indeed with various branches of decorative work - especially china, terra-cotta and panel painting.
>
> Grace Warboys, the last girl helped is working under Miss Collingridge, and has made a very good design for a wall paper quite unassisted, and has painted some glass & panels very creditably. (C&GL 12-10-83: GK to Magnus)

Ten years later her report was equally positive:

> Since 1879 in the latter part of which year the first grant was made, 36 young women have been helped. Ten of these are still serving as apprentices. Three are at the Chromolithographic Art Studios in Queen Square and are making satisfactory progress there. Two are already able to take part in work for publication. These are earning a little.
>
> One girl was apprenticed to a printer, and will have completed her

apprenticeship in June. Though not a quick compositor, she is remarkably steady and careful, and in every respect trustworthy.

Two girls are learning fan-painting, decorative art, &c. under Miss Vasey and have done some designs for wall papers and groups of flowers which are very creditable considering the short time they have been at work.

One girl who is apprenticed to the Women's Gardening Association, shows great taste in arranging flowers, particularly likes the green house work.

Two students who are learning stained glass and decorative work under Miss Bennett of South Wimbledon have taken part in a memorial window which was executed in the Studio and put up in a church at Christmas time. One of these two shows great talent for ecclesiastical needlework and designs. The younger of the two has much improved in her drawing and has done a chalk head from the life very well. When she was first apprenticed her drawing was very weak.

The student who entered the school of cookery last autumn in order to gain a diploma as a cookery teacher has passed her first examination - the theoretical - satisfactorily and has to go up for the second examination - practical cookery - on Saturday. She has the promise of an appointment in the country if she gets her full diploma.

The majority of those apprenticed in former years are maintaining themselves more or less satisfactorily. I have lost sight of a few of them, which very probably means they are in work.

Three of them have studios of their own, and one of them has two apprentices herself. Four have become art teachers, and also paint various fancy articles. One gained a scholarship at the Slade School & is still studying there. Another who learnt chromolithography is still working for the master to whom she was apprenticed and is earning good wages. Two others are regularly employed as artists in houses of business.

Another whose apprenticeship ended last autumn got work in Farringdon Street immediately, but has gone to Sheffield with her family and hopes to get work there. Another is devoting her energies to drawing fashion plates. She has no regular engagement yet, but has had & has executed various orders.

One young woman who was articled in '83 to a chemist failed to pass the Pharmaceutical Examination, and I have not heard of her for a long time, two married, one died, the sight of one and the health of two others failed and they were unable to continue their work. (C&GL 09-02-1893: GK to Soper)

Though the Institute did not expect the Society to repay the money granted, the Society, continuing its established practice, passed the funds on to its clients as loans. This caused some confusion at one point, when Miss Bennet of the Wimbledon School wrote to a member of the Institute querying the Society's right to ask for repayment from one of her pupils. The confusion seems to have been sorted out, but the Annual Report of 1883 stated firmly:

> Being convinced that people value little what costs them little, the Committee have generally made it a practice to require the repayment in small instalments of apprentice fees advanced by them. They have thus been able to render assistance to a larger number of girls than they could otherwise have done, the sums thus returned being entirely reserved for apprentice fees, apprenticeships affording the best and most satisfactory introduction into trades.

In 1895, however, the Institute made a decision to devote all its funds to its technical schools, where some of the classes were open to women. The Institute had in the period between 1881 and 1895 provided funds for loans to 42 women, amounting in sum to £1,025, much of which was gradually repaid into the Society's apprenticeship fund.

TYPING

Although technological changes had destroyed one area for women's work, the increasing use of the typewriter in the 1880s and 1890s was opening another. As one commentator wrote,

> One of the most remarkable features in the revolution being brought by the type-writer is that it has done more to solve the women problem than anything else. ... [T]he demand for efficient operators at present exceeds the supply. ... Offices for type-writer copying are now being opened in the leading cities, and they are not only proving to be paying concerns, but they give employment to hundreds of educated ladies of limited means. (Harrison 1888:349).

Such a comment echoes the SPEW rhetoric of the preceding thirty years, suggesting that the Society may have played its part in preparing the ground for the feminization of this new technology. Certainly the Society responded very positively to the advent of the typewriter, giving substantial help to some of the pioneers of the female-run typing agency, and recommending the work to its clients.

The first commercial typewriter was developed in the United States and marketed in 1873 by the Remington Company. By 1878 the system of ten-finger touch-typing had been developed and the company began an aggressive marketing campaign (Davies 1974: 10). Almost from the outset the Remington Company saw the operator as female, claiming that "no invention has opened for women so broad and easy an avenue to profitable and suitable employment as the 'Type-Writer'." (Keep 1997:405) The

Remington marketing campaign transported this identification to the United Kingdom, and in many cases the company offered those businesses that bought the machine the services of a trained female typist (Martindale 1938: 67).

As early as 1881 Gertrude King reported that one of the businessmen to whom the Society had sent clerks suggested that girls should be trained as "type writers" (MCM 25-11-81), but it was not until 1884 that the Society became involved in promoting this new occupation. As had happened in the case of plan-drafting, the initiative came from someone outside the Society, with the Society's main contribution being to provide funds to start the business and young women to train for it. The Minutes of January 18, 1884 reported:

> Miss Garrett of 23 Poplar Grove, West Kensington Park applied for apprentices to learn typewriting. Miss Garrett has for some months passed undertaken to copy legal documents, M.S.S. &c, with the new typing machine. She has more work than she can undertake singlehanded, and a large connection, which would enable her to get a constant supply of work for four or five ladies if she had an office in the city. If she could get the promise of apprentices she would take an office at once. She will pay 1d per folio for all good work done by the apprentice. . . . Miss Garrett is able to earn 30/- a week working steadily for 4 or 5 hours a day & charging 1½d. a folio. (GMC 18-1-84)

The Committee approved the scheme[12] and promised help, Jessie Boucherett being particularly enthusiastic. They first approached the City and Guilds of London Institute, but were told that typing was not "sufficiently artistic or scientific" for their support, and so set about raising money for the scheme themselves. (MCM 1-2-84, MCM 14-3-84)

In the meantime Miss Garrett was joined by a Mrs (Marian) Marshall "who was well known to the late Mr Charles Reade & who had done a great deal of theatrical work". The two women believed they could command enough work between them to employ four or five women and proposed opening a typing office in October 1884 if the Society would lend them £60 for establishment expenses, including an extra typewriter, and the first year's rent. They already had three typewriters between them but they asked the Society to provide a fourth, since they did not believe the rent and other expenses could be covered unless there were four typists at work. A supporter giving only the initials D.M. donated £100 through Jessie Boucherett to the Society's funds and Jessie Boucherett herself donated £20 for the purpose, the Committee agreed to grant the loan, and the office was opened at Lonsdale Chambers, 27 Chancery Lane on October 6 (GCM 10-10-84).

The partners seem to have had no difficulty getting all the work they needed, though they had more trouble finding and training suitable apprentices (MCM 20-2-85; AR 1885). In July 1885 they asked for an extension of their loan for the next year and this was approved after they had signed an agreement that: "The said Marian Marshall and Ethel Garrett shall employ only female workers for doing the work which shall be sent to the said office and each efficient worker shall be paid for the work done by her one half of the sum which shall be charged to the public for the same work, each worker counting and correcting her copy," and that the fee paid by learners should be £2.2. (MCM 17-7-85) (Some of these "learners" received loans from the Society. For example a Miss Goatley, recommended by the Working Ladies Guild, who "had lately lost her father & is left entirely dependent on her own exertions", was granted £2.2 (MCM 17-7-85).) The next year was even more successful. Eight typists were employed who earned from 10s. to £2 2s. weekly, and they had had sixteen pupils, two of whom went on to open their own typing offices in other cities, also turning to the Society for help.

The early success of the Garrett and Marshall venture seems to have encouraged the Committee to look kindly on these appeals. In June 1885 the Secretary reported that "Miss Perkins whose father is the manager of some large chemical works at Liverpool, is learning typewriting at the office in Chancery Lane in the hope of being able to establish a similar office for the employment of women in Liverpool. She would be able to work up a good connection among merchants, shipping agents and others. Her father will be responsible for the rent of an office, but she is anxious to get a loan of £40 or £50 for the purchase of machines and furniture." (MCM 12-6-85) Gertrude King looked into her background, reported that she had "thoroughly satisfactory recommendations" and "bonâ fide promises of work from 10 or 12 sources" and was told by the Committee to make an agreement with her "similar to that made with Mrs Marshall and Miss E. Garrett" (MCM 17-7-85). The fortunes of this office were recorded regularly in the Minutes. Although Miss Perkins made only a small profit for a number of years she was able to repay her loan by May 1888, when she handed the business over to her sister "in partnership with a lady who had been with them from the beginning" (GCM 4-5-88).

In April 1886 a second pupil of the original office, Miss Burnblum, opened her own typewriting office in Bocardo Chambers, Oxford, and in October was granted a loan of £15 to purchase a second machine (GCM 8-10-86). Gertrude King reported "that when passing through Oxford she had called on Miss Burnblum and was much pleased with her energy & business-like manner. The office is in an excellent position though very small & Miss Burnblum has very good introductions." (MCM 22-4-87) Although Miss Burnblum had to ask several times for extensions to her loan, on one occasion giving the explanation that she had "so much difficulty getting in her payments at Oxford", she managed finally to pay it by June 1893 (MCM 22-4-87, GCM 29-6-93).

Meanwhile the original office went from strength to strength. At the end of 1885 the partners rented two further rooms in Lonsdale Chambers and the Society's Minutes reported that they were "getting on very satisfactorily, and have commenced an account at the Birkbeck Bank, and have a whole year's rent in hand" (MCM 18-12-85). In November 1886 Ethel Garrett married, and after a certain amount of negotiation[13] the business and the responsibility for the loan from the Society passed to Marian Marshall (MCM 19-11-86). A year later Mrs Marshall moved her office to premises on the ground floor at 126 Strand. The original rooms she told the Committee were "not sufficiently central for a type writing office as the greater part of their work comes from the theatres. The immense number of steps up to her present office is also a great drawback" (MCM 11-11-87).

The journalist who wrote the article in *The Quiver* visited Mrs Marshall's office and talked to some of the girls employed there:

> They say they like their work which is more easily done than by old and stiffened hands; but anxiety to live by it is tolerably apparent. Surveying the bright young faces in a pretty room adorned by pictures, fans, and artistic workmanship, it is difficult to realise that each individual inmate will have to struggle for her daily bread.

Mrs Marshall's Typing Office in 1889
(From The Quiver, 1889, p. 114)

Mrs Marshall, she reported, told her that "from thirty shillings to two pounds a week may be gained by expert typists and shorthand writers, but they should have a knowledge of one or more foreign languages". (Beale 1889: 114)

Mrs Marshall and those trained by her made strong efforts to have the occupation defined as one for educated women, and by 1887 the Society was endorsing this view. The Annual Report of that year noted:

> A large proportion of the MSS. brought to be copied are written illegibly, and unless the copyist has a good acquaintance with historical and geographical names, some familiarity with foreign languages, and at least an elementary knowledge of science, she will in all probability make such egregious mistakes as will disgust her customers. The Committee, therefore can only recommend type writing as a desirable employment for those who have had the advantage of a liberal education. (*AR* 1887: 13)

They also argued strongly that it was better for women wishing to be typists to undertake the kind of apprenticeship training they offered than to attend one of the new schools that were now opening. These schools, Mrs Marshall wrote in 1889, "advertise largely, and so attract learners who are taught more or less the use of the machine, but fail to acquire the practical knowledge to be gained only in an office where general copying is done, and where they have an opportunity of typing direct from MSS. Last month two ladies came to me in order, as they said, 'to improve themselves' on concluding a course of instruction at a 'School.' One of these ladies has since opened an office in Reading and is doing well." (*AR* 1889:15)

Mrs Marshall took the lead in a broader attempt to formalize and professionalize the occupation. In May 1889 she organized a meeting "of the proprietors of several of the chief offices" at the SPEW office where "it was resolved that an association be formed for the purpose of protecting the profession by arranging a standard scale of prices, regulating fees for tuition, & granting certificates of efficiency to pupils &c." (MCM 24-5-89) In her report to the Society in 1890 she announced that this group had set up "The Society of Typists, a union of employers, and the Type-Writer Operators Union, for Clerks" to cope with the constant under-cutting of prices and wages by the many new offices being established. The society set minimum levels of acceptable charges and salaries, and also, imitating the practice of the male professional associations like those of pharmacists and accountants, proposed establishing examinations to provide a "a wholesome check on the shoals of ill-educated girls who seek appointments". Twenty-seven employers, but so far only five typists had enrolled (*AR* 1890: 13-14).

Later in 1890 Mrs Marshall, claiming ill-health, sold her business (which now employed twelve typists) to a Mrs Callard (who was still conducting the business under the name 'Mrs. Marshall's Office' in 1908), and repaid the loan to the Society. She then seems to have moved to Cambridge and opened an office there at 33 Trinity Street in June 1892, asking the Society to distribute her cards. (MCM 18-7-90; GCM 17-6-92, *AR* 1908) She kept up her interest in creating professional standards for the typist, informing the Society in 1898 that the Union of Typists was holding examinations and issuing certificates, but her place as the main link between the Society and the profession passed to her fellow promoter of the examinations, the proprietor of another flourishing typing bureau, Mrs Constance Hoster.

Mrs Hoster (1864-1939) was guided into this business by Gertrude King in the early 1890s, and, as the next chapter will show, became a leading figure not only in the professional typing world but in various philanthropic projects concerning women's work, in particular the work of the Society. Constance Hoster also embraced Marion Marshall's belief that the ideal Secretary should be a woman with a secondary education who had been trained in a typing agency rather than a commercial school and seems, through her long contact with Gertrude King, to have confirmed this as the Society's policy. The Annual Reports for the next decade spelled this out clearly:

> The supply of girl clerks who can write shorthand and type after a fashion, but whose education has been very limited, far exceeds the demand for them. Consequently they are often out of employment, and the salaries offered to them are very low. The supply of liberally educated secretaries who have been well trained in good offices is by no means too great, and they receive good salaries.
>
> The best secretarial training is obtained in a good typing office, where pupils are carefully taught, and where they gradually get accustomed to work of various kinds—legal, tabular, theatrical, &c., &c.—and where they see how such work ought to be done and finished. This training takes about a year. At the ordinary schools of shorthand and typing girls can learn to write shorthand and manipulate the type-writer, but they have no opportunity of seeing the kinds of work sent out in good style. (*AR* 1902: 10)

The Society did not, however, restrict its support to these two prestigious typing agencies. Though the Minutes are sprinkled with records of girls given loans to train under Mrs Hoster, grantees were also supported at a range of other businesses and institutions: that of "Miss Mangan, shorthand writer and typist" (MCM 7-11-90), "Mr Waterman, 12 John Street, Bedford Row" (MCM 6-2-91), "Mr Cusack, of the Cusack Institute, Finsbury Pavement" (GCM 11-1-95, MCM 23-2-1900), "Mr Coulson of 19 Queen's Road, Lavender Hill" (MCM 3-2-99) and the Pitman Metropolitan School of Shorthand (MCM 23-2-1900, GCM 19-4-1901, 10-1-1902). Some of the grantees were young widows, trying to find a way to support their children, for example, Mrs Conroy of Battersea, "the widow of a Chemist whom she helped in his business" (MCM 3-2-99), and "Mrs Cross, of Albert House, Fleet, Hants, . . . the widow of a clergyman" (GCM 9-11-1900), and others were young women with the "liberal education" advocated by the Society. Two of these, both of whom were sent to Mrs Hoster, were Miss H.C. Gordon, "a thoroughly well educated woman" recommended by a clergyman and one of the Society's members (GCM 1-12-99) and Ruth Collard of Harpenden Road, West Norwood, the daughter of a deceased solicitor, who had been "educated at St Anne's Schools" (GCM 1-12-99, 9-3-1900). Even more detail was given about an Irish applicant, Gladys Apthorpe of Dublin, the daughter of a deceased colonel, who had "passed the Senior Oxford Examination with Honours in French, and English Literature" and was "strongly recommended by Miss White, Principal of Alexandra College, Dublin, at which she was a student for three years."

Nevertheless the Society was prepared to lend its support to promising girls from much further down the social scale:

> Mrs Maloney applied for a loan of £12.12 to enable her daughter Louisa to train as a clerk learning shorthand and typewriting, and Book-Keeping at Manton's School of Commerce in Chancery Lane. Louisa Maloney is well recommended by the Head Mistress of the School she has attended for the last six years and also by Mrs Cowper . . . Mrs Maloney is a widow and has a situation as office cleaner and is very respectable. She will repay the loan by Monthly instalments if it is granted. Mrs Cowper will guarantee the repayment. (GCM 26-6-1908)

THE PUSH FOR ACCREDITATION

The efforts of Marian Marshall and Constance Hoster to establish credentials for typists were in fact part of a wider trend to introduce accreditation as well as training into female areas of work, not only in the new fields but in traditional ones as well. The Society's records give something of a worm's eye view of how and where this was happening, and demonstrate that the Society's support for the trend was wholehearted.

The most striking and best documented of these developments was the transformation of girls' secondary education. By the final quarter of the nineteenth century, although there were still a great many untrained governesses and teachers in private schools, the wider Women's Movement had brought about a revolution in girls' secondary education with growing numbers of girls being educated at "public" high schools and boarding schools where most of the teachers had qualified themselves by passing the public examinations held by the universities, and even gained university degrees (Levine 1987, 26-50; Jordan 1999b, 199-219). Though not participating directly in this movement, the Society was kept informed of this trend from its inception. Two of the leading figures were members of the Committee at various times, Emily Davies, who began the campaign for university degrees for women in 1862, from 1865 to 1873, and Frances Buss, who founded the North London Collegiate School, from 1875 to 1888.

The Society, however, seems to have played a more significant part in promoting forms of training and accreditation that did not require the same outlay of money and time as those provided by the universities. Although throughout the 1880s the Annual Reports recorded that between six and twelve women had each year been found permanent appointments as "Governesses and Visiting Teachers", these were most likely women working within the old system of home schooling and the small private school. The Society's loans to such teachers seem to have been devoted to helping them improve their skills and qualifications for work within this sector. The Minutes reported, for example, that "Miss Tennant a musical governess at a school in Wales, being very anxious to prepare her pupils for the Senior Examinations, applied to the Committee for a loan of £3", and almost two decades later that "Miss Slacke, an Irish lady, who teaches singing and music, applied for a loan of £3 to enable her to get some good lessons in voice production. She is staying in London for a short time and wishes to utilise that time." (MCM 27-6-79, 8-11-95)

The Minutes also reveal that during the 1890s physical education training was beginning to be offered, though very much as a private enterprise, and give the names of several of the leading practitioners who were willing to take apprentices:

> Read a letter from Mrs Pass, saying that if the Committee can grant her £25 towards the premium of her daughter who wishes to be apprenticed to Miss Chreiman, she will pay off the remaining £27.10, by instalments, if Miss Chreiman will accept it in that way. Miss Chreiman's fee of 50 guineas was considered high, and it was suggested that Mrs Wordsworth should be asked what her fee would be. Miss Chreiman's system is rather different from that of Mrs Wordsworth, being especially directed to Hygienic exercises which are intended to develope [sic] the physique generally, exercising the muscles systematically and strengthening any that were weak, whereas Mrs Wordsworth's classes were specially for making her pupils graceful in dancing and movement generally. (MCM 9-3-94)

Dorothy Pass was eventually granted a loan of £10 for a two year apprenticeship with a Mdme. Piper-Rickman to train in Physical Exercises and Calesthenics [sic] (MCM 19-10-94), but in 1895 another young woman was refused help in obtaining a loan of £200 for training in Callessthenics [sic] at Mdme. Osterberg's Physical Training College at Dartford (MCM 6-12-95). In 1896, however, help was given to a Mary Whitewright to train under Miss Chreiman, and it was reported that she "likes it even better than she thought she would" (MCM 15-5-96).

There was also a whole layer of certification emerging for those who wanted to teach or practice even older and more traditional female skills. Here again there were Committee members able to keep the Society informed of developments. Mrs Burbury, for example, was also an active member of the Women's Educational Union, and reported on the courses being offered at the Working Women's College in Queen Square, Bloomsbury and the Brompton Evening College for Women, 1 Queen Street, Brompton (MCM 1-3-78), and Lady Knightley described the activities of the GFS and the Working Ladies Guild (GMC 5-7-78). Gertrude King seems also to have kept up to date with what she described as "the excellent classes now established in almost every district by the County Councils", on occasion advising bodies like the GFS that they had no need to set up classes of their own for things "like cooking, dairy-work, home-dress-cutting, hygiene, etc." (GCM 12-01-1893).

Throughout the 1890s the Society granted loans to women wishing to study cooking, laundrywork and dressmaking. Though many of the loans for dressmaking were for traditional apprenticeships to established commercial dressmakers, others, like those for cooking and laundrywork, were for study at training institutions.[14] The courses seem to have been particularly useful in providing the accreditation needed for older women to teach the skills they already possessed. The following are examples:

Read a letter from Miss Hingeston, of All Saints House, Lorrimer Square, Walworth, asking if the society would help her by paying the Fee for her to get a Diploma for Cooking at the National Cookery School with the view of getting a Lectureship. Miss Hingeston has been accustomed to work among the poor, and has taken classes and addressed Mothers Meetings &c. She has always been fond of cooking, and has, as an amateur, given lessons in it to poor people. If she can get a diploma she has the promise of an appointment. The sum she needs is £13..13/- for the first Certificate. This she would repay as soon as she began to earn. (GCM 7-10-92)

The Hon. Victoria Grosvenor desired to call the attention of the Committee to an application made by Miss Emily Pass for a grant of Two Guineas to enable her to obtain a Certificate of Plain Needlework from the London Institute for Plain Needlework. Miss Pass is about 40 years of age, & the eldest of a family of 18, 12 of whom are now alive. The Mother has very small means, which have been used for educating the younger members of the family. Emily Pass is a good needlewoman, and might, with a course of training, obtain a certificate which would enable her to advertise herself as a Certificated Teacher of Needlework. (MCM 6-4-94)

> Read a letter from Miss Florence Burwell of Colwyn Bay asking for a loan of 10 guineas to enable her to train as a teacher of needlework and dresscutting. Her father is an organist at Colwyn Bay and is much respected. Miss Burwell believes that if she can gain a certificate she will get technical classes in her own neighbourhood. Her father will guarantee the repayment of the loan. (MCM 23-4-98)

The Minutes also record the attempts to professionalize and raise the status of another traditional domestic servant: the children's nurse or nanny. In 1892 Emily Ward, née Lord (1850-1930), opened the since renowned Norland Institute for training children's nurses, and the Minutes suggest that this lead was followed elsewhere. Within a couple of years the Society was recommending this occupation and granting loans to girls wishing to qualify for it. Two young women, the daughters of a solicitor and of an engineer, were granted loans to study at the Norland Institute (MCM 14-12-94, 17-11-99), another was directed to St Mary's Hospital & Day Nursery at Plaistow (MGC 20-1-1899), and in 1905 the daughters of two army officers (one of them a general) were directed to Sesame House, St John's Wood (Miss Buckton and Miss Schefael, Principals) (MGC 10-11-1905, 24-11-1905). Though these were the only grants recorded, it is to be presumed that it became one of the occupations Gertrude King recommended to the parents of girls who could pay the fees of £22-£36 these institutions charged for a year's training (MCM 14-12-94, MGC 20-1-1899, 24-11-1905). The Annual Report for 1906 noted: "Gentlewomen as nurses for young children are now much in request, and those who have hitherto been helped by the Society to get the requisite training have had no difficulty in finding situations."

In the case of children's nurse there had been no "Chinese wall of prejudice" to break through, since the work had always been seen as suitable for women, with the introduction of training and accreditation raising its status in the eyes of middle class parents. The Society did, however, play a significant part in an occupation where training and accreditation were attempting to break down both sorts of barriers: the scientific practice of gardening and horticulture. The Society's interest was first engaged in June 1891:

> The Secretary stated that she was also making inquiries about gardening for ladies on behalf of Miss Harding, who has been teaching in Hungary but who, having no diplomas or certificates, finds it difficult to get an engagement. She has been accustomed to an active country life & would very much like to take up gardening. Miss Yates, Secretary of the Women's London Gardening Association, 62 Lower Sloane Street, employs gentlewomen who have been thoroughly trained in taking charge of conservatories, window-boxes, balconies by the month or year, & in attending to valuable plants in rooms, or to graves in cemeteries &c, and she thinks that there will be a considerable amount of work in this.

The training can be procured at the Womens Branch of the Horticultural College, at Swanley, Kent of which Mrs T. Chamberlain is Secretary, but the cost of the training has not yet been ascertained. (MCM 12-6-1891)

> Further inquiries having been made about the training for gardening, it was found that the expenses of the Training College, Swanley, Kent, were from £70 to £80 a year; that all the pupils there could learn all the work of a garden practically, both for fruit, flowers and vegetables, doing all the work themselves except digging or heavy carrying. There is also a place in South Derbyshire at which 36 ladies can be received, each of whom has a small piece of land placed entirely under her care and she receives a share in the profits on the produce of this land. The cost here is £100 a year. No candidate has, as yet, been found able to pay her expenses at either of these training colleges. (MCM 26-6-91)

It is to be presumed that Gertrude King thereafter recommended this work to enquirers at the office, but it was not until October 1893 that the Society actually sponsored a student, arranging for a grant from the City and Guilds for Constance Manville, of 254 Elgin Avenue "the daughter of a Surgeon-Dentist now paralysed, and quite unable to follow his profession" to be apprenticed to the Women's Gardening Association.

In 1893 the Swanley College made overtures that resulted in something of a partnership with the Society.[15] The Society agreed to publicise the college as widely as possible and was soon receiving applications both from those requiring female gardeners and from trained students from the College seeking posts, and was also recommending clients to apply for the scholarships to the College offered by Kent County Council. In June 1894 Gertrude King reported that "in accordance with the wishes of the Managing Committee she had attended the distribution of prizes at the Horticultural College, Swanley, had seen the Boarding House for the Lady-Students, and the gardens and hot-houses to which they attend. There are 21 women there at present: they all looked bright & healthy & seemed to enjoy their work. They grow fruit & flowers for sale, & work practically as well as theoretically, each one having charge of certain work. Altogether the College & Home seemed to be well-managed, comfortable & healthy." (GCM 29-6-1894)

This association continued untarnished into the twentieth century, the Annual Report of 1906 stating:

> The study of horticulture and practical work in gardening is a most healthy and useful occupation for women, as it gives them plenty of exercise in the open air. There are now several places at which gardening can be studied, but the Horticultural College at Swanley was the first to which women were admitted. The course of study there is both theoretical and practical, and is very thorough. Many of the students have taken good places in the Examinations of the Horticultural Society of Great Britain.

The full training lasts for two or three years. Short courses have also been arranged at this College for Colonial training, including cookery and laundry work, and other courses for dairy work, poultry keeping, bee keeping and fruit preserving.

The first female occupation to establish a regular form of training and certification had, of course, been nursing with the voluntary hospitals like Kings College and St Thomas's establishing training programs from 1856 onwards (Jordan 1999b: 136-142). From its early days the Society took advantage of this development, directing women they considered suitable into nursing (see, for example, AR 1865, 1870, 1877, 1880, 1887). In the 1890s, however, the range of paramedical work for women began to expand, and again the Society's Minutes give a worm's-eye view of this in progress. In the late 1880s and early 1890s women began applying to the Society for help in training as midwives, foreshadowing the formalising of their accreditation in 1902 (Donnison 1977: 213). In 1892, for example, Mrs Wigley of 53 Upper North Street Brighton, was granted a loan of £5 for three months training at a Lying-In Hospital at Brighton (GMC 27-5-1892), and in 1894 Miss Kate Taylor, a former governess, was granted a loan of £5, for training as a Monthly nurse at Endell Street Hospital (MCM 18-5-94).

Although the London School of Medicine for Women had opened in 1874 (Manton 1965: 240-44), it was not until the late 1890s that the Society received requests for loans for medical degrees. One of these was from a woman wanting to practise in India and the other from a woman halfway through her medical course whose father had "sustained heavy losses, which render a loan necessary to enable her to complete her studies". The Committee responded positively in both cases, though the first applicant soon withdrew her request. (MCM 20-3-96, 19-6-96) Two years later the Society provided help from the beginning of her studies to a student, Miss Henrietta Williams, who successfully completed her course (MCM 25-3-98). In 1905 the Minutes reported "Mrs Stephens, who as Miss Williams, was helped to study Medicine both from the Pfeiffer and from the C.A.B. Fund has repaid £20 to each fund." (Minutes 12-5-1905) The news that the Society would make loans for medical studies seems to have spread. In the same year Miss Dowie, Warden of the School of Medicine for Women, prompted two further students already at the School to apply for loans, both of which were granted (Minutes 9-6-1905, 14-7-1905).

Also interesting is the picture the Minutes give of the gradual emergence of what was to become physiotherapy. In 1905 the Society granted loans to three young women, Miss Gye, "30 years of age, the daughter of a retired Artillery officer," Miss L.C. Wilkinson, "aged 20, the daughter of a doctor who is dead", and Miss E.M. Harris, to study with a Mrs Coghill-Hawkes, M.D of 91 Cromwell Road (Minutes 27-1-1905, 10-3-1905, 14-4-1905). The course was variously described as "Swedish physical culture", "Medical gymnastics and Massage", and "Curative Physical exercises", and the

Annual report of 1906 explained the purpose: "Curative physical exercises, of which massage forms a part, used under the direction of a doctor, have been found so beneficial in certain cases of deformity or weakness that a moderate demand has arisen for well qualified women who can administer them." Other young women seem to have been directed to Mrs Coghill-Hawkes during the years that followed (Minutes 28-2-1908), and at the end of the Society's first fifty years, training with another practitioner, Dr Fletcher Little at 211 Great Portland Street, was approved for 34-year-old Mrs Young whose "husband lost all his money, and she wants to help keep the home together" (Minutes 23-4-1909).

It would appear that, by the early twentieth century, at the end of its first fifty years, the Society no longer saw its primary role as opening new occupations to women. Indeed the Annual Report of 1907 stated: "Since the foundation of the Society, so many new spheres of work have opened up to women, that it seems almost impossible now to find anything *new* for them to do." Gertrude King still devoted the bulk of her time to the other aim formulated in 1860, "collecting and diffusing useful information" through an office which was "a centre for inquiry", but during the 1890s an objective which had not been considered in the Society's earliest years came to play an increasingly significant part in the discussions of the Committee: providing loans to women to pay for their training.

THE LOAN FUNDS

In its initial phase the Society had not foreseen that the granting of loans would become one of its major functions. However, the Committee soon came to the conclusion that if young women were to take advantage of the opportunities found for them by the Society, many of them would need help with apprenticeship fees. In the earliest years, as was noted in Chapter 2, a number of small loans seem to have been made out of the general funds, and in 1867 the practice was formalised. In that year special donations to pay apprenticeship fees for the disastrous glass-engraving venture were requested, £85.14s was received and placed in a separate fund, and the conditions under which the loans would be made and repaid were laid down. The fund seems thereafter to have been augmented by donations from members for other special purposes, as well as being maintained by the trickle of repayments.

It is not easy to trace the progress of this fund, referred to variously as the Loan Fund and the Apprenticeship Fund, through the accounts published in the Society's Annual Reports, but it looks as if by the end of the first twenty years £15-£20 was being granted annually, and repayments of about £10 being received. When the Society's clients began to receive grants from the City and Guilds, the size of the fund increased substantially, and by 1895 when the grants ceased, £1,025 had been added to the total amount lent.

By this time, however, the Society had gained a reputation for the efficient administration of such funds, and other sums became increasingly available, primarily in the form of memorials for individuals. The first of these came from the will of Emily Jane Pfeiffer (1827–1890), a poet and journalist who was also a strong supporter of the Women's Movement. Her husband, who died a few years before her, had made it known that he would like the money he left to her to pass to women's causes when she died, and she left most of her estate of £63,611 10s. 8d to trustees to carry out his wishes (Hinings 2004). One of these trustees was J.G. Fitch, a one-time school inspector and Assistant Commissioner on the Schools Inquiry Commission of the 1860s, and a long time supporter of Emily Davies's projects, whose wife had become a member of the SPEW Committee in 1875. On his recommendation the trustees applied to the Charity Commissioners for permission to award £2,000 (yielding an income of £50 p.a.) from the bequest to the Society (MCM 6-4-94). They also wrote to the Society offering the funds "for the endowment of Scholarships, Studentships, Fellowships or Lectureships with the title of which the name Pfeiffer should be associated" (GCM 20-5-1894). The solicitor and the Secretary were required to sign "an affidavit respecting the work of the Society", and to promise "that the money should be devoted to the technical training of women". The Charity Commissioners then "sent a notice that the interest on the £2000 awarded to the Society from the Pfeiffer bequest to found Studentships for Technical Instruction would be paid quarterly to the Society's Bankers". The fund was thereafter referred to as the Pfeiffer Studentship Fund (MCM 15-6-94, GCM 5-10-1894) and in 1903 it was decided that, since repayments from the Pfeiffer Fund were being placed in the Apprenticeship Fund, the two accounts should be combined under the single title of the Pfeiffer Fund (GMC 13-2-1903).

The second of the separate funds to be administered by the Society was the Caroline Ashurst Biggs Memorial Loan Fund. Caroline Ashurst Biggs (1840-1889) had edited the Boucherett-funded *Englishwomen's Review* since 1871 and been a member of the SPEW Committee since 1876. After her death her family set up a small memorial fund to be devoted to loans for the training of young women. (The whole of this sum was available for loan and when loans were repaid the money was again lent out.) The committee administering this fund seems to have had trouble finding suitable grantees, and in 1898 an affiliation with the SPEW was proposed, with the conditions that the fund's name and separate finances should be preserved, and that a member of its original committee should be consulted before grants were made (MCM 15-7-98). By the end of the year negotiations were complete and a new affiliated committee took over the management of the £186.13.6 available for loan and the £68.10 waiting to be repaid.

In 1902 a third fund was entrusted to the Society, the Mrs Haweis Memorial Loan Fund. Mary Joy Haweis, (1852-1898), who was the daughter of an artist and wife of the rather disreputable incumbent of a fashionable city church, had made a reputation as a writer on artistic dress and interior decoration and as a supporter of the suffrage movement. Her family and friends collected £160 for a memorial fund, and then, like the Biggs family, had difficulty in administering it. They therefore invited two representatives from each of the "the three principal women's societies", the SPEW, the Women's Institute, and the Central Bureau to form a committee for the purpose (GMC 13-12-1901). Thereafter the Society usually had a candidate or two to compete with those put forward by the other Societies (see for example GCM 14-2-, 25-7-, 12-12-1902). The whole sum was used for loans, and the money was reloaned when repaid. Finally, in June 1904 the Society was entrusted with the sum of £250 raised as a memorial to Helen Blackburn (1842-1903), who had succeeded Caroline Ashurst Biggs as editor of the *Englishwomen's Review*, and been a Committee member since 1892. This fund was wholly managed by the Society's Committee, and again the whole sum was available for loan.

The Annual Report for 1908 stated that "The same form of agreement is used for all these funds. The serious illness of the grantee, which renders her unable to work, or her death, cancels the debt", and that "at the present time eighty-three grantees have loans from the various funds amounting to £1,211 19s. 3d." , while the 1909 Report was particularly positive about the chances of repayment: "Those who have had loans and gained certificates of efficiency in various occupations seldom, if ever, fail to get appointments … Some of these have paid off the whole of their loans [during the last 18 months], but the majority of them are still paying their instalments". Thus the Society entered its second half century with the basis already established for the function it serves, today, a hundred years later.

---

1   Her other charitable bequests were: £1000 each to the New Hospital for Women, Euston-road, the South London Hospital, Clapham Common, the Royal Free Hospital, and the Royal Alfred Orphanage, Camberley: £500 each to the Lawes Agricultural Trust, Bedford College for Women, and the Society for Promoting the Employment of Women; £200 to the English Folk Dance Society. Her husband's estate was worth £495,306 9s. 8d. One of her daughters left £100,000 to the National Trust in Cornwall in 1976.

2   Like the SPEW, this Society has survived to the present day, though it too has changed its name – to the Mary Feilding Guild.

3   There was a proposal in 1895 for the Society to sub-let the second floor of the Berners St house to the NUWW. Unfortunately the sitting tenant demanded longer notice than was convenient. (MCM 8-11-95, 6-12-95).

4   In 1941 the Central Bureau was wound up and all its records were transferred to the SPTW and are now housed with the Society's Girton archive. The last Chairman attributed its decline to the retirement of Miss Spencer and its successes to her "energy, enthusiasm, graciousness, and, if I may say so, . . . beauty". (GC/R2.3 Central Bureau Minutes).

5   Until the Ladies' Sanitary Association gave up their rooms in 1900, the Society was able to borrow their office and their chairs for its Annual General Meeting. Presumably a partition between these rooms was opened for the occasion. (GCM 11-1-1900, 10-5-1901).

6   This was a High Anglican weekly, not the *Manchester Guardian*, possibly selected because

a number of the Committee (e.g. Grosvenor and Knightley) were strongly committed to this church.

7   See MCM 10-7-72, 24-7-72, 18-12-72, 27-11-74, 11-12-74, 12-6-74, 28-5-75, GCM 9-5-75.

8   Not all organisations were considered suitable. The 1879 Minutes contain this entry: "Mr Henry, treasurer of the Benevolent Association which meets monthly at the office having asked whether the Committee would let the office for the weekly meetings of a gentlemen's bicycle club, it was resolved that it would not be desirable to let the office for such a purpose." (MCM 28-2-79).

9   Roberts warned that, when drafting these letters, "it is advisable not to raise the question of the admission or non admission of women to the classes at the Technical School about to be established by the Companies and Guilds of the City of London, but to take it for granted that they are to be admitted" (MCM 6-12-78).

10 In Charlotte M, Yonge's *The Clever Woman of the Family* (1865) the headstrong heroine, influenced by ideas picked up from the *English Woman's Journal* and the SPEW, chooses wood-engraving in her imprudent attempt to find an alternative occupation for the little girls employed in lace-making.

11 One of these women, Miss Greville, "declined the offer from the Committee as she is going to be married very shortly to a professor of Science who edits the publications of the Geologists Association, and she will find her wood-engraving very useful in illustrating these". (MCM 13-7-94).

12 Lady Goldsmid, however, "cautioned the Committee against spending much money on a scheme the success of which she considered doubtful. She had herself tried the typewriter but had found it extremely troublesome to manage and slower than ordinary writing. This she attributed in great measure to her being very shortsighted." (GCM 25-4-84).

13 This negotiation was not particularly friendly. The Managing Committee minutes of 17 December 1886 reported: "The Secretary stated that Mrs Comyns [formerly Ethel Garrett] had refused to sign any agreement with Mrs Marshall which bound her not to set up another type-writing office when and where she liked, unless Mrs Marshall would pay down £25 before Christmas and a second £25 by weekly instalments after Christmas. Mrs Marshall was unable to do this herself but Miss J. Boucherett had most kindly lent the sum of £20 so that there is every prospect of the matter being settled in a few days.
"A vote of thanks to Miss J. Boucherett for her kind help was passed.
"A draft of the new agreement to be made between Mrs Marshall and the Society was submitted. In this it is proposed that Mrs Marshall shall bind herself to give to the Society six months notice if she wishes to dispose of the business and shall agree to pay the £60 due to the Society by weekly instalments of £1 each, the first instalment to be paid on the 2nd of January 1888, after she has paid Mrs Comyns and Miss J. Boucherett."

14 See for example MCM 6-2-91, 6-11-91, 13-4-93, 7-6-95, 10-5-95, 17-4-96, 25-2-98, 4-11-98, 6-1-99, 17-2-99.

15 The College was founded in 1889, originally for 50 male students, and accepted its first five women students in 1891. After 1902 it ceased to take male students, and the name was changed to Swanley Horticultural College for Women. By the 1930s it was offering B.Sc. degree courses, and after bomb damage in 1944 moved to premises in Wye, near Ashford Kent.

CHAPTER 4

"An association for lending money": 1909-1939

ORGANISATION AND ADMINISTRATION

The first years of the twentieth century saw the replacement of the 'old guard' – the pioneers who had helped shape the Society since 1859 – by a new body of equally dedicated personnel. After Jessie Boucherett's death in 1905 and Gertrude King's official retirement in 1915 a 'new guard' began to emerge within the Society's administration. Committee members invariably still served for many, many years; and the Secretaries who succeeded Miss King continued to provide effective and dedicated management. Although she retired in 1915 after fifty years of active secretarial duties, Miss King remained on the Committee in an 'advisory' capacity for almost another thirteen. Gertrude King was succeeded as Secretary by Edith Hare who in turn was followed in 1934 by Mary (Moya) Cane. Mrs Winifred Golding (of whom more in the next chapter) took over from Miss Cane.

During the Society's nineteenth-century years the role of Chairman of Committee had been rotated amongst members - each member chairing one meeting at a time. By the beginning of the next century, however, it seemed that the chair was occupied by one of only three of the 'senior' members: Jessie Boucherett, Mr Frank Mocatta, or the Hon. Victoria Grosvenor. In 1905, by which time the first two had died, Victoria Grosvenor was elected Vice-Chairman of Committee (that is, second-in-command after the President) and she generally presided over meetings until her own death in 1913. Separate Minute books were kept for the General and the Management Committees from 1870, with the former taking place monthly, and Management fortnightly: a practice which continued until June 1902. Only one Minute book recorded meetings from then onwards; and after 1920, those books were simply labelled 'Executive Committee'. During the twenties and thirties the Committee usually met between 20 and 24 times each year, a pattern which lasted until the Second World War (see next chapter). In 1920 the Society met for the last time at 23 Berners Street. The Annual Meeting explained the change:

We have to change our quarters, as our rent has been raised and we do not feel justified in paying the extra amount. Miss Hare, our admirable secretary, looked about and has found us a room on the second floor at 251 Brompton Road. The quarters are smaller, and we shall have to sell some of our furniture. … (AM 4.11.1920)

The Hon. Victoria Grosvenor's roles during her 50 years' service to the Society had included that of Hon. Treasurer as well as Vice-Chairman.[1] Her death made it necessary for the bankers, Messrs. Coutts, to act as custodian trustees for the Society's funds which had previously been invested in the names of Victoria Grosvenor, the Secretary, and Miss Constance Plumptre (*Quarterly Report* 24.6.1913). At this point the Committee formalized the position of Chairman, as the Presidents did not regularly preside over Committee meetings; and it was Mrs Julia Spring Rice, the Vice Chairman, who became the first 'permanent' Chairman of Committee. She remained in that role until 1934 and presided over virtually all meetings during those twenty years. The Minutes do not contain references to any formally-agreed change in the appointment of chairmen: rather, it seems to have been a natural progression. It would not be until 2006 that the Society decided that the Chairman's appointment should be for a term of five years (with re-election for a further term within the rules).

The resignation of the Auditor, Mary Harris Smith, FCA whose links with the Society are set out in an earlier chapter, was regretfully received in 1928 as "she has accepted a very advantageous offer to move her offices to the country. For 37 years [she] has had charge of the Society's accounts, and for 14 of those years gave her services gratuitously". She was succeeded as auditor by Miss M M Homersham, MA, FSAA.

SOME COMMITTEE PERSONALITIES

It is not possible to profile all the individuals who have contributed to the success of the Society during its history, but a few have been selected for mention. During the First World War the Committee consisted of a larger proportion than usual of titled members. In addition to the number of women whose titles were hereditary (Lady Susan Fortescue; three 'Honourables': Constance Russell, Mrs Robert Grosvenor and Mrs Trevor Bigham) there were others whose husbands had been knighted, such as the wife of Sir Owen Roberts (he who had played so large a part in the Society's early history). Many other members were long-serving and loyal supporters, attending meetings regularly, contributing informed knowledge and opinions towards decision-making, and combining as a pressure group via their links with influential figures.

Mrs Constance Hoster (1864-1939)

This Society "was the one Society to help to promote the employment of women and it will now help to reduce the unemployment of women."
(Address to Annual Meeting, 4.11.1920, by Constance Hoster, Hon. Secretary)

When Jessie Boucherett died Gertrude King seems to have looked elsewhere for inspiration, and she appears to have found it in a one-time protégée of her own, Mrs Constance Hoster (née Kalisch, 1864-1939). Mrs Hoster did not serve as a Committee member until 1913, although a close reading of the Minutes and Annual Reports (both written by Gertrude King) suggests that, from 1900 on, her vision of how the employment of women could best be promoted was increasingly adopted by the Secretary and so informed the advice the latter gave to the Committee. She also introduced three new members to the Committee: the Countess Dowager of Desart, the Viscountess St Cyres and Lady Bertha Dawkins. Lady Dawkins subsequently played an important role in the Society.

Mrs Hoster also played an important part in the Society during the first three decades of the twentieth century. Clearly possessed of a strong character, she was involved in a wide range of interests which brought her to the notice of the public, as were detailed in a lengthy Obituary published in *The Times* on 3rd June 1939. Her influence on the Society's activities was clear for many years even before she became a member of the Committee, through her friendship with Gertrude King. These two women had met at a time when Hoster was faced with a choice of either "dependence on others, or making her own way" after apparently being widowed at an early age. The word 'apparently' is inserted here as it has been found impossible to verify her marital status from Census records, in spite of her having been referred to as a widow throughout the archives, as well as in her obituary. The 1901 Census records her as 'M' (i.e. married), but Court reports in *The Times* of 10 August 1895 and 6 and 10 February 1896 list details of an undefended divorce between Constance and Albert Bertram Matthew Hoster. It would have been entirely in keeping with the times that a woman in Hoster's business position would find it preferable to be considered a widow than either divorced or separated. There were no children of the marriage.

The meeting with Gertrude King at that vulnerable time in Mrs Hoster's life led to a close friendship between the two women which lasted for over forty years. Mrs Hoster said that Miss King had "encouraged, advised, helped and strengthened" her in her desire to be independent. She did not become a subscribing member of the Society until 1902, but her connections with it had begun as early as 1894. Through her friend, Mrs Hoster was kept informed of the Society's activities, many of which coincided with her personal sympathies and business interests. She had established her own typewriting office in 1893 which shortly afterwards expanded into a secretarial training college;[2] and it followed that she encouraged some of her potential trainees to approach SPEW for assistance if they were unable to afford her fees. Gertrude King's entry in the Minutes for 1ˢᵗ December 1899 records a loan of £6 being granted to a Miss H C Gordon (referred to in Chapter 3) who had been accepted for training at "Mrs Hoster's ... one of the best city typewriting offices" and when settling this debt a few months later the young woman's accompanying letter to the Secretary said that "through Mrs Hoster's kind interest she has obtained a Secretaryship to a literary man for 3 months, which may possibly lead to a permanent engagement". The Minutes went on to record that Miss Gordon "writes in the highest terms of Mrs Hoster's office and is very grateful to the Society for enabling her to go there" (*Minutes* 13.7.1900). In these ways Mrs Hoster's name and activities became very familiar to the Committee. Another entry mentions that Hoster had reduced her "normal fee of £30 to twenty guineas" for similar applicants who were in receipt of loans from the Society (*Minutes* 9.3.1900). Such a gesture was likely to have been calculated to reassure the Committee that Hoster was prepared to sacrifice some of her profits, in keeping with the Society's own values.

Mrs Hoster's links with the Society coincided with the period when many of their applicants were finding that shorthand and typewriting, and in due course 'secretaryship,' could provide a most suitable route to financial independence. As this was the field in which her main business expertise was centred, the relationship was a mutually beneficial combination. When she addressed annual meetings, or made reports to the Committee, she was quick to stress the importance of the high standards which she had always advocated, and she was critical of a perceived erosion as demand for office workers increased. She would not have approved of the upsurge in semi-skilled office work which would become available to a future generation nor the erosion of the "accomplishments" which she considered essential for secretaries to possess. In an address to the Society's members in 1920 she deplored the lowering of standards which had followed a surge in demand for office workers after the First World War. Her own former trainees had enjoyed much entrepreneurial success, but she felt that more recent applicants "think they are going to pick up things. ... I have a great many University girls, and they especially seem to think that looking at a machine will teach them how to type." She complained that there were now "very few women in London who know French ... or any other language as well as they know English. There is one lady in this room, Miss Kerr Sander, one of my former pupils, who claims to know three languages as well as she knows English, the result is, she has been able to make a position for herself and has now started a school of her own".[3] She was also able to claim that "at the close of the War, when it came to the Peace Conference, there was only one expert ready and able to attend the handing over of the Peace Terms and to take down the German speeches.

I am proud to say it was one of my pupils." (Hoster's address to SPEW *Annual Meeting* 4.11.1920)

Constance Hoster stands out not only as one of the first people to take advantage of the paths opened up through such employment, but also as someone who was prepared to be a trail-blazer for other women. In spite of an apparent difference of opinion with the Committee during 1917, Mrs Hoster never ceased to support the Society's aims and its work. She was always grateful for its endorsement of her secretarial college and it is apparent that she gave much back to the Society. Amongst the warm tributes to her appearing in the Report were these extracts:

> Through the death of Mrs Hoster we have lost one of our truest and most valued friends and supporters. ...Nearly fifty years ago she had the vision to foresee the future opportunities for trained women. She founded the College, Typewriter Offices and Appointments Bureau which bear her name and spared no effort to make the training as complete and comprehensive as possible, and to widen the field of openings for women. ... Her life's work, summed up, is the record of a woman of undaunted courage, clear vision, great tenacity of purpose, immense capacity for taking trouble, wide sympathies, and a very stimulating and withal a very lovable personality. ... We shall remember her as a woman of great gifts of heart and mind who used those gifts in pioneer work for her own and succeeding generations. May the torch she lit in 1893 be carried on with unfaltering hands. No greater tribute could be paid. No greater tribute could she ask. (*AR* 1938-39)

Mrs Julia Spring Rice [later Lady Monteagle] (1855-1936)

Julia Emma Isabella FitzGerald was the sixth daughter of the 19th Knight of Kerry, First Baronet Sir Peter George FitzGerald. At the time she joined SPEW in 1892 she was the widow of Stephen Spring Rice, whose family had an inherited connection with the FitzGeralds. She resigned the chairmanship in 1934 after suffering an accident, but agreed to become a Vice-President. She married again in 1935, at the age of eighty. Her new husband was Commander Francis (Frank) Spring Rice, RN (4th Baron Monteagle of Brandon) a relative of her first husband; he had also once been her brother-in-law (Frank was the widower of Julia's older sister Elizabeth). Lady Monteagle continued her association with the Society until her death in 1936, a year after this marriage.[4]

According to statements in the Annual Report after her death, Julia was a well-respected and very competent Chairman and Committee member whose personality endeared her to her fellow members. From the very beginning of her membership she also supported Jessie Boucherett's wider interests and soon became involved in a number of other committees, amongst which were both the Parliamentary and the General Committees of the Women's

Lord and Lady Monteagle leaving the Registry Office
after their wedding in 1935
(From an unknown newspaper, courtesy of the FitzGerald family)

Industrial Defence Association.[5]

The family's tribute to Julia after her death (*J.S.R. – Sketch of a Background*) offers almost the only direct reference to her involvement as a supporter of women's suffrage, although her name is included on at least two occasions amongst those of many well-known women who wrote to the Editor of *The Times* newspaper on the subject: they included Dr. Elizabeth Garrett Anderson, Dr. Anderson's sister Millicent Garrett Fawcett, Lady Frances Balfour and Louisa Twining. One letter in October 1900 regretted the "disabilities imposed on women by the Act of 1899" (that is, the London Government Act 1899) and suggested successful local council candidates should petition Parliament to restore to electors the right to choose women representatives on those councils; and the Committee also discussed sending a representative to a meeting in the Albert Hall (*Minutes* 22.5.1908). The newspaper photograph of Julia after her wedding to Lord Monteagle seems to depict her as quite a formidable figure; and according to the '*Sketch*' produced by her family, she was not averse to making forthright comments when the occasion demanded, as in this extract:

In the rigid world as it then was of the Civil Service hierarchy it took some courage to advocate Enfranchisement of Women under the numbing influence of [the 'establishment'], but J.S.R. managed to fight a strong battle without ever losing her social influence and authority. An infuriated man once told her that if she persisted in her advocacy of Women's Suffrage he would no longer open the door for her, to which she replied that if he did as he said, she would no longer pour out his tea. But it was characteristic of her that when enfranchisement had become law she was quick to discern that certain classes of women were being put into a privileged position, and that though certain classes of men had previously been in a privileged position it did not excuse the new inequalities of the law. A joy of her last days was to have overheard one of her grandchildren say "Black's black and white's white and silly's silly."[6]

Her forthrightness is also apparent from a Minute dated 1916, when after representing SPEW at a meeting of the Central Bureau's 'Pensions and Homes Sub-Committee' after which she "stayed on" for a meeting of their 'Relief Committee', she expressed the view that she "did not feel that the Committees were very helpful or that they were run in the way she liked, but said she would continue to attend for the present if desired to do so by the Committee" (*Minutes* 3.2.1916).

Miss Constance E. Plumptre (1848-1929)
Miss Plumptre was a long-serving member of the Committee, having joined in 1906, perhaps as a result of being one of the referees for a loan applicant, Miss H C Gordon, who wished to train at Mrs Hoster's in 1899 (see Chapter 3). Miss Plumptre scarcely ever missed a Committee meeting, and in addition to chairing two sessions (in 1908 and in 1913) she was appointed to be the third signatory on the Society's cheques from April 1909. Educated by a governess, Miss Plumptre was a prolific author in her later years, publishing many books and articles on "philosophical subjects", most of which enjoyed numerous reprints.[7] Official censuses between 1881 and 1901 list her as an author, as well as living 'on her own means'. Her father Charles Plumptre, as well as her two brothers, were barristers; her father also lectured at Oxford and at King's College London on public speaking and elocution, publishing a number of books on those subjects.

Lady Susan Fortescue (1848-1919)
An active member of the Committee, Lady Susan Fortescue was its Hon. Treasurer from 1913 until 1918. The eldest daughter of Earl Hugh Fortescue of Filleigh, a previous President of the Society, she was clearly a compassionate woman, who was involved in a range of charitable concerns – even, it seems, becoming the victim of a fraud. This occurred in 1909, when a woman was charged with "obtaining charitable contributions by

fraud and false pretences" from Lady Susan and others - the woman was convicted and sent to prison for four months "with hard labour".[8]

Lady Susan was also a keen supporter of Boucherett's Freedom of Labour Defence group and served on that Committee. She played a key role in placing a number of women into the Civil Service during the First World War. In December 1915 the Admiralty decided an additional 500 women were required "to help with war work", which would include opportunities for about 25 "well-educated, intelligent women" to be given higher-grade appointments. Lady Susan wrote a personal letter of introduction to Sir Graham Green, the Permanent Secretary to the Admiralty, as a result of which she and Mrs Hoster met Sir Graham to bring to his notice the suitability of some trainees from Mrs Hoster's 'Bank Book-keeping Classes' (see 'Mrs Hoster's Scheme' below). The Minutes mention that she ran a successful jumble sale during 1913 in the grounds of the home in Tewkesbury of one of her sisters, to raise more funds for the Society.

After her death in 1919 her sisters, the Countess St. Aldwyn, Lady Mary Bridgeman and Lady Frances Gordon-Duff donated £200 to the Society in her memory. This money was later combined with loan funds donated for Mrs Hoster's Educated Women Workers Loan Training Fund (see below) as well as those for a memorial to Miss Annie Seppings, dating from 1913.

Lady Bertha Dawkins (1866-1943)

Lady Susan was succeeded as Hon. Treasurer by Lady Bertha Dawkins who had joined the Committee in 1915. Bertha Mabel Wilbraham was the third daughter of Edward, first Earl of Lathom, who was for many years the Lord Chamberlain. Bertha had married Major Arthur F. Dawkins, Fifth Fusiliers, in 1903 but he died only two years later. Lady Bertha was subsequently appointed Woman of the Bedchamber to the future Queen Mary, a position she held for 18 years, until 1935.

Lady Bertha became interested in the Society through her friendship with Mrs Hoster, but when she was first invited to join the Committee she had to decline, saying that "the Queen does not want me to belong to it as another of the Queen's Ladies" was already on the Committee.[9] Lady Ampthill, Lady of the Bedchamber, had been on SPEW's Committee since 1896. However, Bertha was able to join the Committee in 1915. After terms as Hon. Treasurer and Chairman she accepted the role of President in 1932 when Lord Leigh resigned[10] - a position which she retained until her death in 1943.

Whilst Lady Bertha Dawkins was Hon. Treasurer the Society was facing a serious shortfall in its funds, so she launched an appeal which included making a broadcast on BBC radio on 30th December 1928. As a result donations of over £230 were received. Through a number of other activities (not specified in the records) she was responsible for collecting a further sum of £861 11s so, happily, the Committee "were able to face a new financial year with courage, and hope..." (*AR* 1929-30). This was a most welcome addition to the Society's funds, coming as it did at a particularly lean time. During 1931 they decided to have 5,000 copies of an appeal pamphlet produced which, according to the balance sheet, cost £192 0s 4d; but as only £112 7s was received in donations this appeal to the public was not financially successful.[11]

A later appeal for funds was made in a BBC broadcast, on 6 March 1937, on behalf of the Society and three other co-operating societies: the Women's Employment Federation, Women's Service and the Soroptimist Club of Greater London. Mr Desmond McCarthy made the appeal, although Mrs Oliver Strachey, Organising Secretary of the Women's Employment Federation, was responsible for the initial arrangements. As a result of this broadcast, the Society's share of the proceeds amounted to £110 6s.

Lady Catherine Cushendun (1888-1939)

Catherine Cushendun was the daughter of Sir Mortimer and Lady Isabel Margesson: one grandfather was the sixth Earl of Buckinghamshire, the other the Rector of Blendworth in Hampshire. Catherine ('Kitty') Sidney Louisa Cushendun was the second wife of the Rt. Hon. Lord Cushendun, Chancellor of the Duchy of Lancaster, whom she had married in December 1930. He died at the family seat in Co. Antrim in October 1934, his wife "not having left his side" throughout his last illness.

Kitty had always been "an adventurous spirit, travelling gaily and travelling far along the ways of life". In her earlier days she had been a passionate supporter of the suffrage movement; but she had many other interests including the Church in England and Northern Ireland, nursery schools, women police, hospital libraries, and the activities of the Carnegie Trust. In April 1938 Catherine had responded to an article in *The Times*, her letter offering a witty endorsement for the need to take steps to prepare for a possible war. She wrote:

> As I was one of those who could not, or would not, believe in the likelihood of the last War, and who therefore found themselves in 1914 without even a modicum of Red Cross or V.A.D. training, I feel it the more incumbent on me not to be caught again. I can only hope that others who too made this miscalculation will follow the lead given by [yesterday's] Correspondent and join the A.R.P. Reserve, so that before long we may be among those described by her as practising on Lord's Cricket Ground. And what more suitable place could the authorities have provided for those who do not want to be caught out! (Letter to *The Times* 5.4.1938, p.17)

Lady Cushendun was a member of the Society from May 1937 and took over the Chair in February 1938; but she served in that capacity for only two years, as in December 1939 she died suddenly, after an operation. The next

Annual Report paid tribute to her service:

> By the sudden death of Lady Cushendun, member of the Committee since May 1937, and Chairman since February 1938, the Society suffers an irreparable loss. We shall miss, sorely, her kindly and serene judgment, her wise leadership, her infinite patience and her untiring energy. Above all we shall miss the inspiration of her wonderful personality. That her great gifts of mind and heart were given so abundantly in its service is something for which the Society must be for ever grateful. (*AR* 1940)

The Society was represented at her memorial service by Committee members Miss Dorothy Selby (who was a partner in Mrs Hoster's business) and Mrs F W Ogilvie. Mrs Ogilvie then replaced Lady Cushendun as Chairman.

"OUR ADMIRABLE SECRETARIES"

The Society has always been particularly fortunate in the calibre of its salaried secretaries. After Gertrude King's 50 years of employment came to an end, the Committee took the opportunity to re-examine their employees' working conditions. From time to time the clerical aspects of the Society's work had come under discussion, as for example in 1916 when

> ...it was proposed by Mrs Wilfred Lloyd and seconded by Mrs Henriques that some help should be given occasionally to the Secretary in starting a Card Index, and the Sec. was desired to get catalogues and price lists in regard to setting up a Card Index for consideration at the next meeting of the Com. Also to enquire about the price of a second-hand Typewriter for the office, and that Mrs Hoster be consulted about this. (*Minutes* 1916 etc)

The record-card system was duly adopted, and now forms part of the archive at Girton. Many entries provide researchers with an additional insight into the lives of individual women in the middle years of the twentieth century. The cards were maintained until the 1980s.

Miss King although officially retired by 1916 was still being called upon to "cover for the Secretary" during staff holidays. She had "kindly offered to go to the office three mornings a week to see to the letters and Miss Brown promised to go any morning Miss King was unable to attend. It was also decided that a notice should be put on the office door to the effect that the office would be open in the morning only three days a week during August; and that interviews could be arranged by letter, between 2 and 4 o'clock, if the matter was urgent" (*Minutes* 12.7.1916).

At the next meeting it was recorded that the Society would be buying the second-hand typewriter "offered by Remington's for £14" (*Minutes* 26.7.1916). This typewriter, Model No.10, served them well. A second machine "a built-up No.12 machine" was purchased in 1932, after

Early Remington Typewriters, Models 10 and 12
(Courtesy of Marjorie McNinch, Reference Archivist, Mcpts & Archives Dept.,
The Hagley Museum and Library)

Remingtons had sent one on approval for which they asked £13 10s. They would "allow £1 for the old machine". The Committee agreed to the purchase price, but subsequently sold "the old one" for 30 shillings! (*Minutes* 25.5.1932 and 8.6.1932). This was not the last time they had dealings with the Remington company, as it is recorded that "the Chairman and Managing Director of the company would like to make a gift to the Society of a more up to date machine to replace the old office Remington typewriter which was over 30 years old". This offer was gratefully accepted by the Committee (*Minutes* 10.3.1960); and that year's Annual Report made their thanks more public:

> The Committee would like to record their gratitude to Messrs. Remington Rand, Ltd. who presented the Society with a more up-to-date typewriter to replace the office Remington machine which had given sterling service for over thirty years. Messrs. Remington Rand Ltd. were most interested to have extracts from the Society's Annual Reports of 1887 and 1888 commenting very favourably on Remington typewriters in connection with the Society's pioneer work in training and promoting employment for proficient typists. (*AR* 1960)

Miss Edith Hare (1859-1951)

Gertrude King's successor as Secretary was Edith Hare, whose period of service to the Society was not quite as long-lasting; yet she remained in the Society's employ for over forty years until she had to retire. She had been appointed in July 1889 as the Assistant Secretary at a salary of £50 per annum, prior to which she had "on several occasions been employed on temporary work in the office" (*Minutes* 19.7.1889). She was appointed Secretary in 1915 and retired in 1934.

After 1926 Miss Hare shared her home with a severely crippled niece, whom she helped to support. At the time of Jessie Boucherett's death[12] her address had been given as the Society's Berners Street office (her predecessor, Sarah Lewin, had also lodged at those premises) but the aunt and niece later rented rooms in a hostel. When Miss Hare retired, in 1934, times were very hard for people without independent means, and the pension of £2 per week awarded to her by the Society must have been a welcome addition to her State old-age pension of about 10s a week. Some months after her retirement the Committee gave her an oil stove from the office, as it appeared that she and her niece had no heating in their room. Edith Hare died in May 1951 in her 92nd year "after a long and distressing illness", having worked for the Society from the age of 29. She bequeathed £500 to the Society (*AR* 1951).

Lady Bertha Dawkins (at that time Hon. Treasurer) paid tribute to her work during a speech to the Society's 61st Annual Meeting in 1920, calling Miss Hare "our admirable secretary". Typical of many letters of gratitude from grantees, extracts of which were frequently published in the Reports, was the following: "I should like also to thank you personally for the great kindness and helpfulness you have shown me from the beginning. Your thoughtfulness has made it very much easier for me to straighten my finances" (*Secondary school teacher*, 1927-28). Another extract is also typical of the letters received by the Secretary: "I enclose the last instalment of £6 to complete the repayment of my loan. Later I hope to send a donation to the Society. I would like to express my very real gratitude, in the first place for the grant which was made to me, and also for the fact that pressure has not been brought to bear upon the speedy repayment of it. Normally I should have repayed (sic) the £180 within six years, but having had two operations and one other serious illness since 1924, when I started my job, I am very glad to have been allowed to pay back more slowly." (*Sunday School Organizer*, 1934)

After receiving Miss Hare's resignation, the Society recorded a warm tribute to her in the 1934-35 Report, saying:

> Few could carry out the work of the Society with more sympathy and understanding than has been shown by Miss Hare over these many years. She succeeded in making those who were seeking the Society's assistance feel that in her they had a real friend who had the capacity to appreciate their difficulties at all times. In their letters of thanks to the Society grantees seldom failed to make special reference to the courtesy and kindness they had received from the Secretary, and after she had resigned many wrote to express their very deep and sincere regret. (*AR* 1934-35)

Miss Mary (Moya) Cane (1900-1939)

Moya Cane had begun her employment with SPEW when the Society decided that they needed to appoint an assistant to Edith Hare and they recorded that one applicant, Miss Moya Cane, "will finish her secretarial training at the end of March" and could start on 8th April (*GCM* 13.2.1929).

There is no indication as to where she had received this training. Moya's mother, Mary Lucy Cane[13] had been connected with the Committee, as indicated in a letter from Edith Hare to Julia Spring Rice after Mrs Cane had died in 1926: "I cannot tell you <u>how</u> sorry I am about Mrs Cane. She was a real helpful addition to the Committee" (*CF* 28.4.1926).[14] It may well have been this connection which led to Moya's application for the post, to which she was duly appointed in April 1929 as Assistant on a month's trial, mornings only, at 25s. a week. She was promoted Secretary when Edith Hare retired in 1934. What had prompted Moya to take up employment at the comparatively late age of 28 is a matter for speculation, but as her older sister was already married at the time of their mother's death in 1926, Moya may have remained at home to care for her barrister father; and it could be that after two years she felt ready to take on some 'outside' employment.

An exchange of correspondence between Moya and Edith Hare around Christmastime in 1937 was prompted by the receipt of a letter at the Society from Hilda Martindale, OBE.[15] Martindale was planning to write a book about women's entry into the Civil Service and had asked the Secretary about the extent of the Society's involvement (*CF* 22 and 27.12.1937) Martindale was "anxious to know whether the Society took any part in the early battles! I have so far been unsuccessful in tracing any activity in this direction. I feel you could tell me whether this is mere stupidity on my part or whether the Society really did not interest itself with regard to women entering the Civil Service" (*CF* 22.12.1937).[16] Miss Hare's reply said that "the Society <u>was</u> interested in women entering the Civil Service … I cannot remember dates, but there should be some mention … in the old (Brown) Minute Book, and those following – all in hand-writing! Many members of the Committee were very much interested in the matter" (*CF* 27.12.1937).

As a result of the approach, the Committee hoped that they would then be able to get Miss Martindale to prepare a publication about the Society, but this came to nothing. By 1939 Moya had to write to her saying that "in these uncertain times" the Committee could not risk money for the publication of a brochure about the Society's history, but she hoped that "eventually" Miss Martindale would write it for them "when the time comes" (*CF* 29.6.1939). The reply of 30th June says "When the time comes you will get someone better than I to write it!" Unfortunately, the next opportunity for a more wide-ranging celebration of the Society's achievements would not arise for a further 20 years, by which time Miss Martindale had died.

Moya's employment with the Society continued for only a short time beyond the years covered by this chapter. She was given leave of absence from her post as Secretary after being conscripted into the London Auxiliary Fire Service early in the Second World War but, tragically, she was killed at the height of the London Blitz whilst on fire-fighting duty during the night of 25 September 1940. The Annual Report for that year carried the following:

The London Fire-Fighters Memorial, St Paul's

The tragic death of Miss M O Cane in an air raid on September 25th is a loss to the Society which leaves us stunned. Miss Cane was Assistant Secretary to the Society from April 1929 until June 1934, when she became Secretary. No words can express the debt we owe to her for all her devoted work during the past ten years. We shall miss her at every turn of the Society's activities and our grantees will deeply deplore the going from among them of this strong personality who was always so ready with help and counsel to those on the threshold of their career.

At the Committee's next meeting Mrs Golding (who was by now the Secretary) recorded their appreciation of Moya for the Minutes:

> Miss [Dorothy] Selby spoke of the great loss sustained by the Society by Miss Cane's death. She was more than an efficient and competent Secretary, unsparing in her efforts on the Society's behalf; she was also a very loyal and true friend who had endeared herself to all who came in touch with her. As a tribute to her memory the Committee rose and stood in silence. It was unanimously agreed that Miss Selby should write a letter of appreciation and sympathy ... to Mrs Rawson, Miss Cane's sister, and also a letter of thanks to the Women's Employment Federation in reply to one they had written to Mrs Golding offering their condolences to the Committee on the Society's great loss... (*Minutes* 11.12.1940)

The Blitz lasted from September 1940 to May 1941. During one of the worst episodes St Paul's Cathedral was damaged in the midst of a major attack from 11,000 firebombs which began to fall from 6 pm on 29 December 1940. There is a memorial to London's firefighters, situated alongside St Paul's Cathedral, on which Moya's name appears (see illustration opposite).

The archives include a letter (dated 31st August 1939) from Moya to Mrs Golding, in which she makes reference to her fire-fighting duties: "The Fire Brigade is becoming a little more organised but I never seem to have the time to learn up my part. It will be nice to see you again. Yours in haste. (M.C.)".

"AN ASSOCIATION FOR LENDING MONEY"

"Spheres are open to women now almost universally, and we have become very greatly an Association for lending money, loaning money to women in order that they may be able to pay for their training." (President of the Society, Lord Leigh[17] chairing Annual Meeting 1920)

As had been the case from the Society's earliest years, at the start of the twentieth century the Committee continued to believe that "the power of helping applicants to get technical training is by far the most useful branch" of their work, pointing out that in many cases "the training is long, generally two or three years, for medical students it is five – so that the loans are necessarily out for a long time" (*AR* 1906). Individual loans advanced during the first years of the century did not, in fact "as a rule, exceed £30" although "special applications" were considered sympathetically where "a whole career might be marred for want of a few pounds extra" (*AR* 1907).

During 1914 the Committee considered the future direction which the Society would take. They considered that the Employment Register and office bureau were beginning to outlive their usefulness, and although certain changes were recorded in that year's Annual Report, it was felt that they should continue to take on commercial work:

> The Committee ... now devote their attention almost exclusively to the professional or technical training of their applicants. ... In addition to those who have been helped from the loan funds towards the expenses of their training, several others have received information and advice about women's work in general. The office has always been a centre for collecting and diffusing such information, and this has proved a very useful branch of its work, though no definite record of its usefulness can be furnished. ... Owing to the number of employment agencies for gentlewomen which have sprung up in all quarters of late years the Committee have considered it advisable to devote their attention and the funds at their disposal almost entirely to helping their applicants to acquire such skill or such knowledge as will enable them to do well the work they undertake to do. ... Nevertheless the register which is still kept at the office has proved useful to many, chiefly in procuring temporary work, though a few good permanent posts have been obtained through it. ...Orders for writing, addressing, arranging papers, sorting, arranging, and pasting out Press cuttings, making alphabetical lists, &c &c are undertaken at the office. (*AR* 1914)

The Society was always careful to maintain its original intention to provide financial assistance to its grantees on an interest-free basis; but by the 1920s the focus was changing from facilitating technical training to the provision of loans for professional qualifications. Although in the very early years of the twentieth century SPEW was still recording financial help for grantees training in "technical needle-work, dressmaking and millinery ... upholstery, cookery and secretarial work" (*Minutes* October 1902 and February 1903) in the 1920s help was being sought by a different type of applicant from those who had been the 'trail-blazers' during much of SPEW's first forty-odd years. SPEW no longer had to provide basic education for the applicants by running its own classes: many young people were now able to acquire additional skills at school, or for through evening classes. The Education Act of 1902 (the Balfour Act) created Local Educational Authorities which could organize funding, employ teachers, and allocate school places –

and it provided for state-aided grammar schools as well as municipal or county secondary schools. The Fisher Act of 1918 made school attendance compulsory for all children up to the age of 14; and then the 1926 Hadow Report identified a number of priorities for the school curriculum. These forerunners of the major 1944 Education Act combined to revolutionize British State-run education and ensured that applicants to the Society during the early part of the twentieth century were much more 'employable' than were previous generations of young women, with many more of them taking advantage of a wide range of the trainings on offer.

SPEW's Annual Reports during the 1920s and 1930s recorded the professions which grantees had trained for and which were now including medicine, teaching and managerial posts. In addition there was considerable demand for secretarial training, and the Society's increasing involvement in this specialism can be linked not only to Mrs Hoster's connections with the Committee but also to the massive expansion in the recruitment of women by the Civil Service and a number of City commercial institutions. The trickle of women into such positions initiated by the Society in the 1860s and 1870s had now become a flood. The new focus of the Society's assistance was summed up by its President in his speech to the 1920 Annual Meeting, when he said that "we have become ... an Association for lending money". In seconding that speech Constance Hoster emphasized that SPEW was "one of the oldest Societies and one of the very first to help women to help themselves". She recognised that although the First World War had opened up many new employment opportunities for women, she was aware that post-war conditions were once more disadvantaging them, adding that this "was the one Society to help to promote the employment of women and it will now help to reduce the unemployment of women." (*AM* 4.11.1920)

MRS HOSTER'S SCHEME

In 1908 when she was well-established in the secretarial training field, Mrs Hoster together with her friend Ellen, the Dowager Countess of Desart,[18] had conceived a scheme to raise funds to assist "educated girls" to receive professional training, which - unlike loans under SPEW's rules – could also be used towards the costs of maintenance, not just fees. Their plans to set up a loan training fund were announced in a letter printed by the *Telegraph* newspaper in November 1908, which brought forth an immediate response from the Secretary of the Central Employment Bureau, Miss M G Spencer.[19] She accused Mrs Hoster of appropriating the Bureau's own ideas for setting up a loan fund to aid women; what is more, she implied that Mrs Hoster was in danger of being seen to be launching her scheme in order to boost her own student numbers. At this time[20] not only were many women finding it difficult to find appropriate work but families were likely to have been reluctant to pay fees for their daughters to embark on expensive training courses. An entry in the Minutes in May 1909, for example, indicates that a two-year course of training as "a teacher of Physical Exercises and Games in Schools" cost £150, and one applicant's father – a vicar – had an annual income of £225, on which he had to support his family of seven (*Minutes* 21.5.1909).

Even though Mrs Hoster enlisted the aid of Gertrude King in an attempt to get the backing of SPEW's Committee for her scheme, the Society was initially reluctant to allow its name to be linked to it. Their response had been similar when, in 1905 (whilst Jessie Boucherett was still alive) Miss Spencer of the Central Bureau had approached SPEW with a suggestion that the Society should collaborate with her committee in "raising and managing a large Loan Fund for the South of England" (*Minutes* 13.1.1905). As the Bureau had once before attempted an amalgamation with SPEW, which had been rejected in 1901 (*Minutes* 13.2.1901) the Committee again spurned the approach, recording

> If the Bureau should succeed in raising a fund and should then wish to take advantage of the experience which we have gained to dispose of it, we should, I am sure, be willing to give any advice, or, if they wished it to form a mixed Committee, to consider the best way of spending it. ... But until the fund is definitely raised by them there is not much use in discussing how it is to be spent. We should be very foolish to join with them in raising a fund as we could raise one much better by ourselves if we required it. (*Minutes* 13.1.1905)

Mrs Hoster was undeterred by the dispute with the Central Bureau or with SPEW's lack of enthusiasm for her scheme, and the Educated Women Workers' Loan Training Fund (EWWLTF) was duly launched in December 1908, operating successfully for several years. By 1913 Mrs Hoster was Hon. Secretary on SPEW's Committee, and at that stage it was agreed that the EWWLT Fund would be transferred to SPEW, although the moneys were to be kept in a separate bank account. No early records have survived regarding the initial sums raised; but at the time of transfer to SPEW its grantees' debts amounted to a little over £740 – with the ongoing repayments no doubt a welcome source of additional money which could then be lent to new applicants. There were some bad debts: one of the earliest recipients had been granted £20 on 12 January 1909, but when the accounts were transferred to SPEW on 9 April 1913, the grantee still owed the whole sum. The column headed 'Remarks' explained it thus: "A bad debt. Home troubles and illness have prevented her working; want of grit too." Another earlier grantee was advanced £96 13s. on 23 March 1909 to train in 'Swedish Physical Culture'.[21] But after the grantee had repaid only £3 12s of this, the notes record that "the Committee has remitted all but £20 of Miss C's loan owing to family trouble. The total amount still due is therefore £16 8s." Happily, of the remaining 30 women who had been granted money, 28 were either still repaying, or had settled their debt at the time of amalgamation with the Society. The remaining two included one owing £32 15s whose repayments were "doubtful, owing to ill health" and one deceased, whose debt of £65 10s was written off.

A year after the EWWLTF had been transferred to SPEW's control, the outbreak of the First World War prompted Mrs Hoster to realise that many mature women were being displaced from the jobs they had held abroad, so she devised a fresh scheme to help them which was very similar to the earlier one. Firstly, she organised a 'Free Register'[22] to help place such women in suitable vacancies; but on interviewing many of them she realized that some were difficult to assist as their work abroad (as governesses or journalists for example) meant that they lacked the formal qualifications or skills which were now being demanded in this country. Many of them were also older than the usual trainees or applicants for office work. However, she persuaded some of the City bank managers to consider employing these women, if their competence could be demonstrated; and she set about arranging to equip them with the necessary skills.

She was invited to explain her fresh plans to the Committee. These involved setting up training sessions for suitable applicants in book-keeping, or alternatively in shorthand and typewriting. She felt that the fees for maintenance and training should be *given*, not *lent*, "because the elder women would feel a debt too great a burden" (*Minutes* 6.5.1915), and she hoped that £500 from a recent legacy from Miss Harker Smith to the Society could be used for the purpose. Hoster's plans were discussed sympathetically by the Committee although the suggestion about using the legacy was refused: perhaps because many members still recalled cases during 1909 which had involved older applicants: Isabella Maxwell, aged 55, had hoped to obtain a loan of £5 to help her to train as a journalist. She had been a governess in Russia and other countries, but could not get a similar situation in Britain "owing to her age". The Committee had turned down this request, as "it was thought that the training asked for would be useless, and journalism being such a very precarious employment no loan has ever been granted for it" (*Minutes* 26.3.1909).

Nevertheless, perhaps influenced by the fact that Mrs Hoster had persuaded Queen Mary to support her scheme (Her Majesty had sent a £50 donation through Lady Bertha Dawkins) the Committee did agree to back it. The balance of donations (£57 10s 6d) was duly transferred to SPEW, although the Committee made it clear that in line with the Society's usual rules, SPEW's own loan funds could not be used to help supplement the trainees' *maintenance* costs: these would have to come from other sources. As with the earlier EWWLT Fund the money was placed in a separate bank account with Mrs Hoster as "Hon. Treasurer and Organiser" and was known as the Educated Women's War Emergency Training Fund (EWWETF). The classes Mrs Hoster had already set up in arithmetic and book-keeping were relocated from her office to the Society's premises and the scheme operated successfully until, in 1919, it was wound up as being deemed to have served its purpose. The remaining balance of £52 17s 1d was used to enable two grantees who "had suffered through the war, to complete their training, granting fees to one and maintenance to the other" (*AR* 1919).

Mrs Hoster provided regular reports on the successes of this Fund to the Committee as well as in speeches at Annual Meetings. She was particularly pleased to report that she had persuaded the banks to employ so many older women after they had completed their training; she had also consulted "several of the important banks in the City" as to whether the classes should continue, receiving encouragement to do so, as many vacancies "for ladies will certainly occur" should National Service be introduced. She told her audience that "fifteen of the applicants who are now in posts after having attended the Bank Classes are from 36 to 40 years of age, while nine are over 40" (*AR* 1916). During 1915 she had interviewed and tested 344 applicants for the bank book-keeping classes, some requiring no further tuition before being deemed suitable for employment in a bank; and whilst some were unsuitable for further training in her classes, 177 subsequently attended them. Not all of the applicants retrained as bank clerks: the Fund supported three women who trained as technical tracers, and many others took secretarial courses. The women's former professions were listed as: 48 governesses or teachers; 11 artists; 10 companions/housekeepers; nine teachers of music; five hospital nurses; four actresses; two clerical workers; two elocutionists; and one each sanitary inspector, beauty specialist, milliner, decoder, electrolysist, teacher of dance, lady's maid. Seventy of the women had no former profession.

THE IMPACT OF THE FIRST WORLD WAR

It has already been noted that one of Mrs Hoster's special interests was the situation facing older women during the First World War, particularly with regard to office employment, so it is possible that her campaigns on their behalf influenced Committee members to take a more sympathetic approach when the more mature applicants applied for help, although after that war the Society again focused on the needs of their younger applicants. But it was not only ageism which could affect some individuals. During the First World War there was considerable anti-German feeling expressed both in the British Press and by the general public. The archives indicate how certain people faced discrimination as a result of having the 'wrong' surname, and the Committee felt that they needed to offer advice on this issue. Two examples from a number which can be found in the Minute books illustrate this. Margaret Hirschler, who had been educated at St Paul's Girls' School, applied to SPEW in 1915 when she was aged 19 for a loan of £63 to pay her fees for secretarial training with Mrs Hoster, as her father – a merchant – had lost his income as a result of the war. Mr Hirschler had lived in England for over 30 years, having come from Vienna at the age of 17. He was a naturalized British subject. His son – Margaret's brother - was an officer in the British Army. Shortly after sending in her application, Margaret said she had been unable to find a guarantor for the loan, but Mrs Hoster had advised her to take the Bank Classes (under the EWWETF scheme), and she was "now attending the Morning Class three times a week" (*Minutes* 26.11.1915). On the completion of this training, Margaret was "successful in obtaining a post at the Commonwealth Bank of Australia" but sadly "it was decided later by the Manager that he could not retain her services owing to her German name" (*Minutes* 12.1.1916).

The next month the Minutes recorded a discussion about another applicant, and no doubt Miss Hirschler's case was on members' minds, as this woman "though English-born herself" but "having married a German, was now of German nationality" and was refused a loan. The Committee felt that "in spite of this lady's not having heard from her husband for two years, it would be undesirable to admit her to the [Bank] Classes and the Hon. Secretary was instructed to write to her to this effect" (*Minutes* 3.2.1916).

Nevertheless, the Committee members were anxious not to make premature assumptions about other foreign-sounding names, so when in March 1916 they received an application from one of their former grantees[23] Mrs Schiodt, for a loan to enable her 17-year-old daughter to train as a shorthand-typist, they discussed the matter at length. The Secretary "was desired to make enquiries" (*Minutes* 8.3.1916) subsequently reporting that Mr. Schiodt "was of Danish nationality", so the loan of six guineas was granted (*Minutes* 22.3.1916). The same year another application to join the bank class was received from two girls whose surname was Derenburg. Their deceased father had been naturalized 40 years earlier, and their brother was "fighting in the British Army" but the Committee, clearly recalling the other cases recommended that the girls "should be advised to change their name" so that the loan could be granted – which the girls apparently agreed to do (*Minutes* 10.5.1916).

On a lighter note, the British public's anti-German attitude was demonstrated by an entry which recorded that whilst the Government was to be urged to employ more women in higher Civil Service posts such as in the Home Office, there was said to be "a strong trades-union prejudice in some of the Civil Service departments against the employment of women [where some women] were spoken of as the 'Huns'[24]..." (*Minutes* 24.5.1916).

ADMINISTERING THE SOCIETY'S LOAN FUNDS

The EWWETF aid, specifically targeted at older women, was meant to be only a temporary measure. The first three decades of the 20th century contained many occasions when older applicants had been turned away by the Society, as it was considered that women over 40 would be subjected to additional prejudice by employers, as well as within the Society itself.[25] For example, when a vacancy for an Assistant Secretary to Edith Hare arose in 1929, the Minutes noted that one applicant was "too old" at age 41 to be considered for such a position (*Minutes* 13.2.1929). Forty-plus was for long the watershed: correspondence between the Secretary and Pitman's College in 1935 mentions a 42-year-old Oxford graduate "who has had a rather chequered career" and that the "Committee do not care to recommend a secretarial training to anyone as old as she is" as it would "not be easy for us to get her an appointment at the end of the training" (*CF* 21.6.1935 to 5.7.1935). Amongst earlier examples, a Minute records that "it was considered doubtful whether any hospital would train a woman over 50 years of age for midwifery", so the Committee felt that the 54-year-old applicant for a loan should instead apply for training as a "lunacy nurse" as it was believed that "there was no age-limit for these" (*Minutes* 12.7.1916).

The situation regarding bad debts was also considered periodically. For many years, outstanding debts of grantees who died or suffered long-term ill health were written off (although such instances were still rare early in the 20th century). In 1907 the Annual Report had noted that "in two instances only during the last ten years have the Committee lost sight of grantees before their payments were completed"; and reiterated that "the serious illness of a grantee which destroys her power of earning, or her death, cancels the debt". Nevertheless, poor health would often cause a grantee to delay repayments. For example, Miss O. had to suspend instalments on her loan from September 1916 when she was ill for seven weeks with typhoid fever, followed by a further four weeks' convalescence (*Minutes* 27.9.1916).

It is clear that grantees in genuine difficulty met with only sympathetic understanding from the Committee, channelled through the Secretaries: "The relationship of the Secretary and the Committee on the one hand, and the applicants on the other, is helpful, intimate, and very human. When securing the repayments every consideration is given to the circumstances of the grantees who have completed their trainings. This can be done because of the Secretary's personal knowledge of the grantees." (*AR* 1927-28) However, there were times when members of the Committee felt bound to offer advice to certain applicants. The case of Miss F., being considered in 1938, illustrates their willingness to question her judgment:

The application from Miss F. for a loan of £50 to enable her to meet the fees for the Spring and Summer terms at the Froebel Institute was considered but the Committee did not consider they were justified in granting the required loan for the following reasons (a) That in their opinion as she was a qualified nursery nurse she should have remained in work until her sister had completed her training for the teaching profession and so avoided the necessity of her mother having to pay for two trainings simultaneously; (b) that Mrs F. in using the loan of £100 from the Bournemouth Corporation to meet the expense of moving to London and sending her other daughter abroad instead of reserving it for the applicant had shown a lack of foresight; (c) her inability to procure a guarantor. (*Sub-Committee Minutes* 4.1.1938)

The practice of cancelling certain debts was operating in 1910, when it was reported that "one grantee died of consumption and another, who was studying a new system of teaching music in schools, has completely broken down. Consequently there will be a loss of £10 to the Pfeiffer Fund and £10 10s to the Mrs Haweis Fund..." (*AR* 1910)[26] However, before the middle of the century, this 'unwritten' rule was being questioned, and the records indicate that efforts were subsequently made to recover debts in such circumstances. Miss Armstrong, a grantee who at the age of 19 had begun a three-year BSc course at Swanley Agricultural College in 1941, was killed in a bombing raid at that college on 2nd March 1944. Her father wrote to say that he would repay the loan as soon as possible. The Committee suggested that the *College* should repay the loan; but unfortunately they refused to do so. At this point the Committee said they would split the cost with her father, but he apparently felt that he wanted the matter settled at once, and sent a cheque to the Society for the full amount.

There was some correspondence between the Secretary Moya Cane and the retired Edith Hare in 1937, concerning bad debts. Cane wrote: "[A] point on which I should like your advice is with regard to the practice of cancelling a debt in the event of death of the grantee. I notice in many of the reports it is mentioned that this automatically happens. I think, in ordinary circumstances, legally we have full right to claim from the guarantor. I am therefore anxious to know whether you can remember if money was left to the Society with this proviso or the reason, if any, why this theory has grown up" (*CF* 22.12.1937). Edith Hare replied:

When the Loan Fund Rules were first drawn up there was a clause inserted to the effect that the death of a grantee cancelled the loan, or any balance outstanding, and Miss King always made that quite clear to intending grantees. Later, when the Rules were revised, its 'propriety' was questioned, as the Loan Funds were small, and in those earlier days there was C.A. Biggs' Committee's Loan Fund, whose members had different views when the question arose. There was never any proviso of the kind attached to any money left to the Society. The Rule was made by the Committee. I am not sure whether Miss King took any legal advice in regard to this: if so, it was unofficially from a friend, Mr Rayner Neate, long since dead. (*CF* 27.12.1937)[27]

There was a later occasion when the Secretary needed clarification, this time regarding the EWWETF scheme. In 1939 Moya Cane was asked by the Chairman (Lady Cushendun) if she could clarify the terms under which money had been lent to applicants under Hoster's scheme. After again checking with Edith Hare, Moya was able to report that as far she knew, there was no correspondence on the subject, although Mrs Spring Rice (who had died in 1936) had seen the officials "several times". Miss Hare added that "no one was to be pressed for repayment" (*CF* 14.4.1939).

Occasionally a debt would be settled through the generous actions of Committee members or friends of the grantee; and there were also examples of other kindnesses extended to individual young women. On one occasion a grantee's employer paid off the remaining £22 15s when the girl was confined to a mental hospital (*CI* 28.4.1938). Another, Miss L., a 27-year-old grantee whose sister was her guarantor eventually gave up the struggle to succeed as a shorthand-typist, and moved to Poland as a temporary governess. The guarantor ended up repaying virtually all the debt; and in 1939, shortly before the war broke out reported that the grantee "is still in Poland, just earning her keep" (*CI* 31.3.1938-4.3.1939)[28]. Early in the century a member of the Committee "kindly offered to give Miss C a holiday if a suitable home could be found for her at some bracing sea-side place", as she thought it would be desirable for the girl to have a holiday before taking up another post. The member had heard that Miss C wanted to "retrain as a Physical Trainer" in spite of having "a compound curvature of the spine", as Miss C had "found the Bank work distasteful to her" (*Minutes* 12 and 26.7.1916). Sometimes, too, if the rules precluded offering assistance for a particular course of training, Committee members present during a discussion would have a 'whip-round' and make a donation to the applicant.

Links for the collaborative administration of loan funds were formed in 1935 between the Society and five other organisations. This Co-operating Loan Committee included the Women's Employment Federation, the Fawcett Society, the Union of Jewish Women (of which Mrs Hoster was a Vice-President), the Soroptimist Club of Greater London and the Girls of the Realm Guild. These arrangements made provision for pooling *applications* when necessary, and "handing them over to whichever fund was suitable or had sufficient money available so that an applicant in search of financial assistance may be saved much tedious repetition if the first Society to which she applies is, through lack of funds or for any other reason, unable to help her" (*AR* 1935-36). However, after twenty-five years of sporadic collaboration this joint sub-committee was dissolved "as conditions and circumstances had changed and the organizations participating felt the co-ordination no longer served any useful purpose"(*AR* 1961).

Whilst the Treasurer and the Secretaries had a constant battle to keep the Loan Fund accounts in balance, conditions attached to some of them prevented the transference of money to the General Fund, which was used to meet administrative expenses. For example when the Mrs Haweis Fund was transferred to the Society in 1902, care had to be taken to use the money only in accordance with the founders' intentions, which was to assist 'poor working girls'. If there were no conditions attached then donations were used where they were most needed. Certain bequests were offered to applicants as *gifts*, not loans: one such was the Gertrude King Scholarship endowed in 1929 by Constance Hoster in memory of her great friend.[29] A similar arrangement had applied to fees for another scholarship administered by the Society which had been created in memory of Mrs Spencer Munt "covering free Secretarial Training at St. James' College [available only to a non-graduate aged between 17 and 25] in need of advice and financial assistance."[30] (*AR* 1938)

Variations in the type of training for which applicants required a loan began to appear in the Minutes during the years covered by this chapter. Loans for training in cookery, confectionery, poultry-farming or millinery, still being recorded up to the 1920s, were by the thirties virtually absent from the records. Laundry managing and sanitary inspectorship had ceased to appear in the lists by 1916; and between 1914 and 1938 massage and remedial exercises (the forerunner of physiotherapy) accounted for only six loans, with domestic economy and physical culture courses each receiving seven. Although there were five grantees taking cooking courses in 1914, the number had been reduced to one by 1937. In contrast, nursery nursing was still popular during those years, with eighteen successful applicants. The popularity of secretarial and shorthand-typing courses continued, with 26 grants being awarded between 1914 and 1937. After the War higher education or professional qualifications dominated: medicine, dentistry and veterinary science, as well as honours or post-graduate degrees in a range of other subjects.

By far the most sought-after courses were for teacher-training: 58 students were given financial assistance between 1914 and 1939. During the 1930s some of these included "the student daughters of Welsh miners who were suffering from the distress in the Coal Fields; subsequently some of these were granted loans from the Society to enable them to train for the teaching profession". However, it was clear that at that time employment in teaching was becoming hard to secure:

> Applications for loans from teachers have greatly exceeded those for any other training. The profession is, however, at present going through a period of transition owing to the reorganisation necessary for implementing the Hadow Report[31], the raising of the school leaving age[32] and forecasts as to the probable decline of the population. All these factors must have a

> bearing on the power to absorb trainees ... and the Society foresees that in many cases there may be a time-lag between training and the securing of a post which must necessarily delay the repayment of loans. (*AR* 1937-38)

Such a situation would, of course, affect the Society's income levels. The earliest rules stated that once grantees began to earn a salary they were expected to make regular monthly or termly instalments "of three shillings in the £1" (*AR* 1904). Later the phrase was added: "In the case of Grantees who have to form their own connections after training, the repayments must begin at the end of three months after the training is completed, and must not be less than 4s. a month" (*AR* 1930-31). A few years after that, this changed to "the amount ... shall be at the discretion of the Committee and ordinarily not less than 20 per cent of the salary for a Grantee in a resident occupation and 15 per cent. for a Grantee in a non-resident occupation" (*AR* 1934-35). (Today, grantees are usually expected to repay at the rate of 20 per cent of their salaries.)

THE SOCIETY'S NAME CHANGE: FROM 'EMPLOYMENT' TO 'TRAINING'

It was necessary for this Society, as with other charities, to conform to official regulations regarding its operations. The Society had been granted its Certificate of Incorporation in 1879, after which it became a limited liability company, subject to the requirements of the Board of Trade as well as the Charity Commissioners. In 1926 the latter questioned whether SPEW was in fact an *employment agency* - as implied by its name – or was genuinely a charity. The Commissioners also required clarification regarding the use to which certain funds were being put, such as from accounts set up in memory of individual women subsequently transferred to the Society's administration (for example the Pfeiffer and Mary Haweis Funds), which had certain provisos attached.[33]

After lengthy correspondence with the Secretary the Commissioners and the Board of Trade were satisfied of the charitable status of the Society, but required that its name be changed to make this more apparent. Although, in the end, only one word in the title was substituted, nevertheless the process involved a considerable amount of discussion in Committee as well as correspondence between the official bodies and the Society's solicitors.

The extended discussions prior to the agreement on the name change had caused some distress to Gertrude King, who although retired was still very much involved with the Society's affairs at that time. Edith Hare had received "an agitated" letter from Miss King expressing her deep concerns. Miss Hare passed on some of King's comments to the Chairman, Julia Spring Rice, which included these words:

It is difficult to change the name of anything and yet retain the prestige of that which had the original name. If the Society has a new name in alluding to its early days and early supporters it will be necessary to say that it was founded in 1859 under the name of the Society for Promoting the Employment of Women etc. You could not say Educated Workers' Loan Training Fund (or whatever new name is decided to give it) founded in 1859 Incorporated 1879. You must guard against the idea of its being a new Society just started; the Central Bureau would then get the credit for all our dear old Society has done and all those dear people who signed the Articles of Association will be quite forgotten. Of course I quite see that the old name does not suit the present work and it is very difficult to find one that does and yet retains the high tone of self-respect and self-help which was the characteristic of the Society in the old days.

Edith Hare agreed with these sentiments, adding:

I feel Miss King is quite right in what she says ... If the Board of Trade accepts the name of 'Society for Promoting the Training of Women' then 'Founded in 1859 as Society for Promoting the Employment of Women and incorporated in 1879' might be added in brackets. It will not do to overlook the number of the Society's years. I have had no further communication from Messrs Hewlett [solicitors]. You may think it right to refer to Miss King's letter at a later Meeting when the matter is in a more settled state. (FF 28.4.1926)

Subsequently, Edith Hare wrote to Mrs Hoster confirming that "in compliance with Miss King's urgent suggestion" the Board of Trade had been asked to approve the new title (see illustration below, showing Annual Report 1927-28). She added that her Committee "desired me to send you these particulars as you were instrumental in placing the Educated Women Workers' Loan Training Fund in the hands of the Society in 1913 and in November 1917 it was agreed by the Committee that the above should be used as a supplementary title to the original..." (FF 7.5.1926)

The official change took place, and SPEW became the Society for Promoting the Training of Women (SPTW). This recognised what had become a natural progression towards a specialization for the provision of loans to needy young women, and away from its careers advisory service and employment agency activities. The anticipated alteration in the title was announced in the Annual Report for 1926:

Since the publication of the Society's last Annual Report, the Committee have had to consider the advisability of changing a word in the Society's name. In order to recover Income Tax as a charitable institution, it became necessary to show that the Society was mainly concerned with the *training*, rather than with the *promotion of the employment*, of women. This involved alteration in the Memorandum of the Articles of

Association. The Committee, after taking legal advice, have drawn up a clause to show the altered purpose of the Society, and the name has been slightly changed with the approval of the Board of Trade. The Society will henceforth be known as the 'Society for Promoting the Training of Women (Women's Loan Training Fund),' … The Committee are very anxious to assure their friends – past and present – that the work will be carried on in accordance with the best traditions of this old-established Society, which started on its pioneer work in 1859. (*AR* 1926)

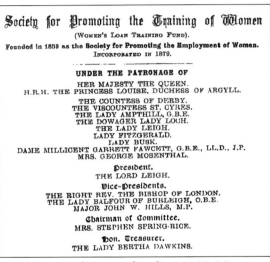

Annual Report heading 1927-28

It was still not quite the end of the matter. Miss Hare wrote to the Hon. Treasurer Lady Bertha Dawkins that she had "some rather tiresome news … which I feel will not please you" (*CF* 4.9.1926). This related to the solicitors wishing to draw the Committee's attention to the wording of the relevant Act of Parliament, which required that the necessary Extraordinary General Meeting should have been held *after* the 14-day statutory period of notice, and not *on* the fourteenth day, as had occurred. The matter was finally settled by re-convening an EGM on 11th November 1926, the same day as the next Annual General Meeting.

There was a return to the topic of the Society's name during the latter stages of the Second World War, but it is pertinent to include mention of it here. The Secretary at that time, Mrs Winifred Golding,[34] wrote to the solicitors in April 1945, asking what procedures would be needed if SPTW were again to change its title, wondering whether it would be possible "to adopt 'Women's Loan Training Fund' as our only title and to drop 'Society for Promoting the Training of Women'". Mrs Golding may not have checked the early records as she went on to state that "the Society was founded in 1879" (*CF* 9.4.1945). The solicitors' reply said that it was "not open to the Society ... to change its name without the sanction either of the Board of Trade or the Court" (*CF* 11.4.1945) and in a later letter they said that they were still having some difficulty in tracing copies of the Society's earlier (1926) papers on the matter because "unfortunately some of our papers were burnt during the War and these may well have been amongst those" (*CF* 28.5.1946). Nevertheless, two years later the papers had been traced and returned to SPTW, with the added comment:

> I note that the question of the change of the Society's name has arisen once more, but in my opinion you are not in a position to change its name without passing a Special Resolution and filing it in the Companies' Registry and advertising it in the *London Gazette* and possibly *The Times*, but I am not quite certain as to these last two items in view of the new Companies' Acts (*CF* 6.10.1948).

A couple of months later Mrs Golding wrote to the solicitors to the effect that "after a great deal of discussion it was finally agreed that the Society's name should not be changed" (23.12.1948). The name survives to this day, although the subject is aired periodically in discussions between members of the Committee.

OVERTURES FROM THE PITMAN ORGANISATION

A great deal of thought, discussion and investigation went into some of the decisions which faced committees. One example is illustrated by the lengthy negotiations during 1931 between SPTW and Mr Isaac Pitman. Pitman's college had been recommended occasionally to the Society's applicants from the 1880s onwards (see Chapters 2 and 3) yet by the 1930s it was still viewed with some reservation by Committee members who were more familiar with Mrs Hoster's 'genteel' training establishment which enjoyed a high standing in the secretarial field. Mr Pitman approached Mrs Spring Rice in February 1931 regarding a "scheme" relating to his new "Intensive Business Course" which he believed "would be helpful financially" to the Society. SPTW's Secretary Edith Hare was then instructed to approach other bodies for their views on Pitman's course, one of which was the London & National Society for Women's Service.[35] Their reply to Miss Hare's enquiry stated that that particular course

> has not yet been in existence long enough to enable a judgment to be formed as to the success of its efforts" and moreover "we consider that ... the existing establishments offer excellent opportunities for secretarial training at various levels of cost, and we should be very sorry

to divert pupils from the schools which have earned general confidence and have done so much service in helping women into good posts. (*CF* 18.2.1931)

The letter went on in more critical terms because it was felt that the Pitman Committee which took the decision to offer the Intensive Business Course consisted "entirely of business men, heads of men's colleges, and headmasters". The writer of the letter, Philippa Strachey[36] (Secretary) remarked that in consequence she "cannot help feeling that ... the outlook about women's employment must be somewhat old fashioned. In short we are not yet convinced that the women students will receive the best possible help from Messrs Pitman in the very difficult process of pushing into business" (*CF* Ibid. 18.2.1931).

Some members of SPTW's Committee expressed strong opposition to a link with Pitman's: Mrs Gore-Booth asserted that she was "strongly opposed to the scheme and that the Society should be in any way connected with Mr Pitman's College" (*Minutes* 30.3.1931) but negotiations continued, and reached the stage where a draft agreement was drawn up, finally being signed in June 1931. Committee voting in favour of accepting his 'scheme' was very close and the resignation of Monica Geikie Cobb was seemingly triggered by her recorded reservations about the outcome. The great fear of some members was that he "would use the Society's name, directly or indirectly, in advertising his course" (*Minutes* 6.5.1931). Discussions such as these underline the Committee's intention always to provide informed advice to their applicants, as this extract from the Minutes demonstrates:

Miss Alice Frances Ashley applied for a loan of £30 for the 3 months course at the Intensive Business College, 3 Marlborough Gate [*i.e. Pitman's College*]. Miss Ashley wishes to be trained for Industrial Welfare Work, or Employment Management. She holds the BA Honours Degree, Cambridge, and the London University Teacher's Diploma, and has had some experience as a teacher, but her great desire is to take up Social Work. Letters were read from her referees – Mrs Palmer of Peile Hall, Newnham College, Cambridge, and the Warden of the Women's University Settlement where Miss Ashley is living. The Committee considered these were quite satisfactory, but the Secretary was desired to ask Miss Ashley whether the remark in the Warden's letter, that she wished to become a Factory Inspector, was correct, as the training given at the Intensive Business College would not be adequate for the Civil Service Examination which all prospective Factory Inspectors have to take. Also enquiries were to be made of the Industrial Welfare Institute as to whether they recognised the training given by the Intensive Business College, as some of the Committee were under the impression that to obtain Industrial Welfare posts, it was necessary to hold either the Bedford College or London School Economics Diploma for Industrial

Welfare. It was agreed to grant the loan subject to these enquiries being satisfactory. (*Minutes* 28.10.1931)

Links with Mr Pitman continued despite the rocky start, so that by 1934 he was suggesting that it might be time "to consider whether our joint work could not be further extended" (*CF* 26.2.1934).

THE 'DEPRESSION' YEARS

Teaching in a range of subjects remained popular in the 1930s, but posts were not easy to obtain. Miss B. from Leeds was given a loan of £25 towards the cost of her two-year teacher training course in 1929. She qualified in the summer of 1931 but she was unable to obtain a teaching appointment until November 1932. For the next two years she could get only temporary posts, although in November 1934 she reported that she had at last obtained a permanent position. Her debt was finally settled in October 1937. In a second example Miss J. who qualified in 1933 (and who had borrowed £50 to help with her training fees) was also unable to find a teaching post for a number of years: in fact not until January 1937, as a result of the over-supply of teachers. Her 1937 post lasted only six months, and subsequent employments were on temporary contracts. However, she did succeed in paying off her loan by October 1939. There are no further details of the ongoing careers of these two grantees, but other cases in the record cards suggest it is likely that their employment prospects improved after 1939. By the end of the 1930s so many aspiring teachers were in receipt of partial financial assistance from their local authorities that the Committee decided that they could

> only grant loans to those [teachers] who were already in receipt of part financial assistance from their local education authority, or who had outstanding qualifications. This policy has naturally resulted in a reduction in the number of teachers to whom grants have been given, although inquiries have been as numerous as ever. It is apparent that the effect of the falling population on the teaching profession is not fully realized by the general public (*AR* 1938-39).

Many families in the country suffered in the throes of 'the Great Depression'[37] and were looking for ways of riding the downturn, and the Society was not immune to the problems, as noted in the Annual Report: "As in the case of many other Societies the acute depression has not left this Society untouched" (*AR* 1931-32). The effects for the Society were felt in the small or intermittent repayments grantees were able to afford, as well the length of time many of them were without work at all and therefore could not send any instalments.

The index cards which were in use by the secretaries from 1916 onwards reveal details of the personal and economic difficulties which could lie in wait for some women. Unmarried daughters were often left to support a widowed parent, their subsequently-reduced circumstances being in sharp contrast to the more comfortable lifestyle and status they had previously experienced.

One grantee - perhaps less typical than others - took 28 years to settle the debt she incurred. She experienced a succession of problems, which led her to try to change her career a number of times. Katherine J. was born in Yorkshire in 1896, the youngest child (but the only daughter) of a Church of England clergyman. The 1901 Census indicates that at that time the household also contained her parents, three brothers, a cousin, her maternal grandmother, and one servant. We have no information concerning any occupation for Miss J. before 1919 when she would have been aged about 23, but in that year, by which time the family was living in Worthing, she was given a loan of £30 from the Society in order to train as a Montessori teacher. (One of her brothers who was teaching at a Worthing preparatory school acted as guarantor for her.) Card entries indicate that she experienced many setbacks even before her father died, as is apparent from the following selected extracts:

1919:   Loan of £30 to do Montessori training. Gave up after two years for health reasons.

1921:   Further loan of £12 to buy uniform – being trained as housekeeper-pupil at St. Thomas's Hospital, but develops acute appendicitis after three weeks. Finally finishes training in 1923.

1923:   Takes post as under-matron in a school – can't repay yet as had to pay an agency fee as they were responsible for securing her the job.

1927:   Has moved to similar job in another school.

In May 1928 her father died. At that point Miss J. still owed the Society £6 2s. Worse was to follow, as in November of the same year the brother who had guaranteed her loan also died. Mrs J. was too ill for her daughter to leave her to take up another job, so repayments ceased. The entries continued:

1930-1935:   Still no repayments

1935:   Now learning cake-making (she and Mother have been living on tiny pension)

1939:   Still no payments, but sends 2s. in March

The outbreak of the Second World War caused further upheavals, as Mrs and Miss J. moved home five times after initially being evacuated to Devon in 1939, and they were living on a pension of only £125 per annum. An instalment of two shillings was sent in March 1939; in 1941 Miss J. promised to send one shilling per month. The final instalment was received on 12 July 1947 – which must have been a great relief to everyone!

CONCLUSION

These 'middle' years in the life of the Society demonstrate how it was able to survive by transforming itself. Members were quick to recognize when change became necessary in order to balance the work of the Society with grantees' needs and the employment market. Strategies were devised which would ensure not only survival, but development, and considerations regarding the advantages which could accrue from closer cooperation (even amalgamation) with other bodies were carefully examined. Although at times some organisations had been perceived as a 'threat' by Committee members, they came to recognise that a degree of co-operation could be advantageous for the grantees and for the continuing survival of the Society itself.

By the end of the 1930s the structure of British society was on the verge of major socio-economic change. The next generation would not experience such clear divisions between 'rulers' and 'ruled'; the servant class was already dwindling, and had virtually disappeared after the Second World War; and by the 1960s changes in the educational and occupational structure were leading British society towards what came to be called a 'meritocracy'.[38] Against such a background, SPTW once again adjusted its own focus and made the transformations outlined in the next chapter.

---

1   Victoria Grosvenor wrote a number of books, whose titles include *Business Habits in Ordinary Life;* and *The Head of a House: How to Live on £100 a Year.* She also wrote articles on amateur church music.

2   Business address St Stephen's Chambers, Telegraph Street, E.C.2.; she opened her Secretarial Training College in 1893, later moving it to 29 Grosvenor Place, S.W.1. The College finally closed down due to "lack of premises" in 1970, but the Employment Bureau was kept open (Letter from Mrs Bloncourt, Principal of the College at that time). She said that as a result of the College's closure they couldn't keep up the membership of SPTW, but she sent a personal cheque for three guineas "towards the Society's excellent work" (*Minutes* 12.11.1970).

3   Kerr Sander did indeed found a successful secretarial training college, initially sited at 21 Collingham Road, Earl's Court in London. These premises were requisitioned and the College moved to Grosvenor House, but when that was bombed they evacuated to the country (Stanway, in Stanton, Gloucestershire). The London branch reopened after the war under a new Principal, Miss Judson, when Kerr Sander retired; and in 1947, after qualifying at the Stanway residential course, one of her students, Ann Templer was appointed private secretary to Miss Judson. As a further link in the chain, Ms Templer reported that her own godmother had been one of the teaching staff at Mrs Hoster's College during the 2nd

WW. Ms Templer said that "the elite of the London Secretarial Colleges in the immediate post-war period were: Mrs Hoster's, Miss Kerr Sander's, Queens, and St. James's" *(private communication).*

4   At about this time, Julia's surname and that of her children began to be rendered with a hyphen. Julia's son Dominick also served on the Committee for a short time, then as Vice-President; his first wife Margaret (known as Margery) Spring-Rice, M.A., was the author of a book *'Working-Class Wives'* published in 1939 by Pelican. Margery's heritage was also firmly rooted in social reform: her two "intrepid" paternal aunts were Dr Elizabeth Garrett Anderson and Dame Millicent Garrett Fawcett, whose names are linked with SPEW's early activities. She was the daughter of Samuel and Clara (née Thornbury). Margery's first husband (m.1911) was killed on the Somme in 1916. She had married Julia's son Dominick Spring-Rice in 1919; they divorced in 1936.

5   See Chapter 1 for a description of Boucherett's central role in the founding of this movement.

6   The extract is reproduced with the kind permission of members of the Monteagle and FitzGerald families who provided the author with a copy of the family's booklet *'J.S.R. Sketch of a Background'*, privately printed by Charles Skipper & East Ltd. , 49 Great Tower St., E.C.3.

7   For example, *Studies in Little-Known Subjects* was reprinted as late as 1995, having been first published in 1898.

8   From *The Times* 16.10.1909, p.2.

9   This was Lady Margaret Ampthill, C.I., G.C.V.O., G.B.E., third daughter of Earl Beauchamp, who had married Arthur Oliver Villiers Russell, 2nd Baron Ampthill, in 1894. She was appointed Lady of the Bedchamber to H.M. Queen Mary in 1911. She had been a close friend of the Queen since 1891, when Mary was still Princess May.

10   Lord Leigh had been President since 1912, having succeeded when Col. Wilfred Ashley, MP resigned on being elevated to the peerage as Lord Mount Temple.

11   On a more positive note - in 1979 appeals sent to approximately 300 charities (selected from the Directory of Grant-Making Trusts) resulted in almost £14,000 being added to the Loan Training Fund Account. *(Mrs Golding's notes for correspondence with the Charity Commissioners).*

12   In her will, Jessie Boucherett bequeathed £200 to Edith Hare.

13   Mrs Cane was an Assistant Director of the WRNS during the First World War, and was awarded the C.B.E. in 1919 by King George V "in recognition of valuable services rendered".

14   According to press announcements of Mrs Cane's death, she had died "prematurely" at the age of 59, following an operation.

15   Hilda Martindale (1875-1952) "of H.M. Treasury" *(AR* 1934-35) was active in the Women's Liberal Federation in 1898; was a senior lady inspector of factories and also author of *Women Servants of the State 1870-1938. A History of Women in the Civil Service.* London: Geo Allen & Unwin Ltd, 1938; and *From One Generation to the Other* Geo. Allen & Unwin Ltd, 1944.

16   See Chapter 2 for information regarding the part the Society played.

17   Lord Leigh resigned the Presidency in October 1931. He died in May 1938.

18   Hoster was joint author with Ellen Odette Cuffe – Lady Desart – of a book published in 1924.

19   Full title at this period: Central Bureau for the Employment of Women; later known as the Central Bureau for the Employment of Women and Students' Careers Association. The Bureau had indeed approached SPEW at the beginning of the century, but Mrs Hoster may not have been aware of this. There was an exchange of correspondence between Mrs Hoster and Lady Caroline Grosvenor in 1916, in which Lady Caroline writes critically

of the Bureau's "making all access to the Government Committee (on elderly educated women) as difficult as possible". She added "Still, the Central Bureau is not the whole world and we are quite willing to work with them, so long as they are not going to work against us!" (*Correspondence File* February 1916).

20 The 1911 Census returns indicate that well over eleven million women but only about two million men were "unoccupied" at this time. The Census also recorded that "roughly one out of every three occupied single women is still a domestic servant", so the opportunity for 'training' which Hoster's scheme offered was naturally popular with better-educated women who wished for an alternative means of earning a living.

21 The 1905 Annual Report noted the growing popularity of systems for physical training being used in Sweden, Denmark and Germany; applicants variously referred to the one-year training as 'Swedish Medical Drill' or 'Swedish massage' at that time. During the following few years many grantees were listed as taking 'Physical Culture' courses and the earlier descriptions may well have applied to the same training.

22 It could be that she was influenced by SPEW's own Register, which they had 'inherited' from the *EWJ* in 1859.

23 She had trained as a domestic economy teacher.

24 Younger readers might appreciate the dictionary definition for 'Hun': "a German, especially in military contexts". During both World Wars the term was used by the general public when describing Germans in a derogatory sense.

25 An entry in the Annual Report for 1904 mentions that "the limit of age, which is generally 35 or 40 at the most" sometimes made it difficult to place women in employment.

26 The Pfeiffer Fund's origins have been documented in a booklet prepared by Basil Herbertson, Hughes Hall, Cambridge, published in 1993, celebrating the centenary of the awards. This booklet details the ways in which Jürgen Edward and Emily Jane Pfeiffer's legacy was distributed to a number of institutions, including SPEW. It was probably due in no small part to this generous bequest that the Society was able to survive until its own 150th anniversary. During 1938 the Minutes recorded that approximately one third of all the loans advanced by the Society came from the original £2,000 of the Pfeiffer invested fund (the Society received annual interest of £50 from this). The much smaller Haweis Fund continued to dwindle.

27 Note the date of this letter. There are a number of items in the archives from the 19th and early 20th centuries which are variously dated just before or after Christmas Day, which to a 21st century reader may seem a little strange in view of the length of public holidays now observed in Britain at this time of the year.

28 This does not seem to have been a particularly auspicious time to be living in Poland. One wonders what became of Miss L. after the German invasion of that country.

29 Years after Mrs Hoster's death, the Principal of the College offered two 'Jubilee' secretarial Scholarships in memory of Mrs Hoster to mark the 50th anniversary of its College's founding (CF 29.11.1943). Hoster's Secretarial College, which had kept its name after her death, finally closed in 1970.

30 There was great rivalry between Mrs Hoster and Mrs Spencer Munt, to the extent that Mrs Hoster had set up a branch of her own college a few doors away from that of Mrs Munt in Grosvenor Place (near Buckingham Palace). The dispute was eventually settled. (This information has been communicated to this author in private correspondence by a descendant of Monica Spencer Munt).

31 Sir Henry Hadow (1859-1937) chaired a consultative committee responsible for producing three important Reports on education: in 1926, 1931 and 1933. He stressed the need for a balanced approach to the curriculum, attaching major importance to the needs of individual pupils and their interests, but also the claims of society as a whole. He believed the latter function was to equip pupils for service as workmen and citizens. Years later,

Bridget Plowden's Report (1967) urged a similar balance for the needs of primary school pupils. (See Ch.5).

32 This was to be raised from 14 to 15.

33 See Chapter 3. The next Chapter will explain that these constraints were overcome as a result of the Charities Act 1985.

34 Mrs Golding's long years of service to the Society are featured in the next Chapter.

35 This was formerly known as the London Society for Women's Suffrage, and was affiliated to the National Council of Women.

36 Philippa Strachey, C.B.E. (1872-1968) was highly respected. One of ten brothers and sisters, she was the third daughter of Lieut.General Sir Richard Strachey, R.E., G.C.S.I., F.R.S. and his wife Jane. She was Secretary of the London Society for Women's Suffrage and later of the Fawcett Society, having been the latter's Hon. Sec. since her retirement from formal office in 1951. Living until the age of 96 she was able to see the passing of the Sex Disqualification (Removal) Act in 1919 and acceptance by the Civil Service of the principle of equal pay for women in 1955.

37 The Great Depression was the phrase used to explain the years when many millions of people were suffering hardship in the wake of the American stock market crash. In Britain in 1932 unemployment peaked at 22.5 per cent; but it never fell below 10 per cent during the 1930s. In contrast, unemployment fell to one per cent in 1955.

38 See Michael Young's dystopic science fiction work, *The Rise of the Meritocracy, 1870-2033: an essay on education* (Penguin 1961).

CHAPTER 5

"The constructive nature of the work": 1939-1988

THE GOLDING YEARS

"Winnie Golding __was__ the Society" (Committee member's words, 2008)

Mrs Winifred Golding

The 'middle' years of the Society's life saw far-reaching changes for the whole country, changes which fundamentally affected the business of the Committee. As had happened during previous years however, the members were quick to recognize when changes to the Society's activities were necessary, and they were proactive in their responses. This Chapter will indicate how the Second World War dictated some of those changes, but that educational reforms, the Welfare State, and major technological advances – especially for white-collar workers - prompted other adaptations.

The tradition of Royal patronage ceased after Queen Mary's death in 1953. That event brought to an end a time when the Committee had included many women closely connected with Royal and Government circles. During the 'modern' phase – the Society's next fifty years - the Committee was made up of many women who were successful in their own right, having had influential careers themselves; and when vacancies occurred efforts were made to fill them with new volunteers who would balance the range of expertise reflected within its composition. Such changes serve to underline the ways in which women's circumstances have altered fundamentally since the pioneering days of Jessie Boucherett and her band of dedicated supporters.

Economies made during the war meant that Annual Reports ceased to include names of Committee members, although retiring and new members were recorded within those Reports. A useful addition for future researchers is that from the 1930s, when Minutes began to be typed rather than handwritten (the typed pages pasted into Minute Books), many of the books contain a paginated Index of the names mentioned throughout. Some outgoing correspondence was preserved as the use of carbon copies gained favour: previously, few of the letters dispatched by the Society were duplicated for the files, apart from occasional rough notes which formed the basis of letters, announcements or speeches.

The Second World War had a number of effects on the way the Society operated. The first of these was that in September 1939 the Committee agreed that in view of the outbreak of hostilities they should close their London base and suspend further lending to applicants, as a temporary measure. However, after three months the situation was reviewed and they felt that "in view of the constructive nature of the work, the Society should function as far as possible normally and that new loans should be granted, but only to those applicants who had outstanding qualifications and were definitely training for the future" (*AR* 1940). Additionally, applicants were apparently finding it more difficult to find suitable people to act as their guarantors, so the Committee agreed to offer "as an alternative" a scheme whereby the Society would take out a short-term endowment insurance policy on the life of the grantee, for the amount of the loan. Of course the grantee would be responsible for the payment of premiums, and the policy would be assigned to her when she had completed repayments on the loan. The Committee reserved the right to accept or refuse this form of guarantee in individual cases.

Nevertheless the temporary closure of their London office did go ahead. This decision was precipitated by two events: firstly the conscription of the Secretary, Moya Cane, into the London Auxiliary Fire Service and the resulting promotion to Secretary of her Assistant, Winifred Golding, and secondly the severe bombing raids in London. The Committee decided that the new Secretary should "work from [her home in] the country" which at that time was in Gerrard's Cross, Buckinghamshire, but that monthly committee meetings could continue to be held at the London premises (*AR* 1940). But in 1941 they "regretfully decided to give up their lease of office premises at 251 Brompton Road, SW3,[1] as these have suffered from enemy action", although the Brompton Road building continued to be used for meetings until the end of the war "by kind permission of the Working Ladies' Guild".[2]

The London address was always going to be at some risk from bomb damage, and the inevitable had occurred when the office was hit during the Blitz late in 1940 and some of the Society's records were lost in the resulting fire. So it was considered expedient to move the meetings and the records to Mrs Golding's house, at least for a time. A note for the Minutes dated 28 November 1940 says:

> In view of the air raids the Acting Chairman, Miss Vansittart, decided to cancel the Com. Mtg. arranged for Wed October 2nd and to accept [Chairman] Mrs Ogilvie's offer to take full responsibility for granting or refusing loans to the five pending applicants after going through their papers with the Acting Secretary. An Emergency Meeting was, therefore, held at Jordans, Bucks on Friday Sept 27th between Mrs Ogilvie and Mrs Golding... (*GCM* 28.11.1940. This date was at the height of the London Blitz).[3]

Little did anyone envisage that the files would remain at Mrs Golding's home until 1989! As a further consequence of the disruption caused by the war, the Society suspended its Annual Meetings in 1939, 1940 and 1941, resuming in 1942; and perhaps because of those gaps the Chairman included a brief outline of the Society's history in her address to members during the meeting held in June 1944.

It has been well documented elsewhere that the population of Britain carried on their personal and business lives with very little fuss during these difficult years. Nevertheless, exchanges of letters between the Secretary and the Society's solicitors give some insight into what life must have been like in London during those days. Mrs Golding wrote to Messrs Hewlett & Co in Grays Inn during October 1940 asking for some guidance about the Society's having missed holding the Annual General Meeting. A reply was dated 28 December 1940, and contained the reason for the delay: "Your letter had been lost when we had to evacuate our office in October last on account of a large time bomb in the immediate vicinity..." (*CF* 28.12.1940) A short time later a reply to another letter recounted a further episode: "We will try to ascertain if we hold a copy of the Lease of 251 Brompton Road but on the night of 1st/2nd January a land mine fell within 150 feet of our offices and we are, at the moment, experiencing difficulty in tracing papers in our damaged office." (*CF* 13.1.1941)

Mrs Golding's Buckinghamshire home continued to be the Society's 'headquarters' address for more than forty years. She had been Assistant Secretary, on a part-time basis, since 29 August 1935, at a salary of twenty-five shillings (£1.25) a week. She wrote to the Committee on 6 May 1940, saying that she would be resigning as she wanted full-time work, but offering to carry on until she had found a new post. She was subsequently appointed to the full-time post at a salary of £3 per week "exclusive of out-of-pocket expenses" from 1 January 1941. The Acting Chairman added that "we should like to take this opportunity of expressing our appreciation of your work and interest, and not least during these last sad and difficult months. Yours very sincerely. Sibell Vansittart".[4] (*GCIP* 4/1) In September 1941 Mrs Golding's salary was raised to £3 10s per week and the Society would also "pay her a rent of 10s per week whilst the office is at Gerrard's Cross". As the years passed, her salary increased in line with the changing times. From the £3 10s of 1941, by 1982 she was earning £1,352 p.a.; she was awarded a further £250 per month in 1985 plus an extra £50 p.a. towards the costs of heating, telephone and so on, as at that date her home was still being listed as the Society's official base. Mrs Golding held the post until her death in November 1988, having served the Society for more than fifty three years.

Trying to get regular repayments from grantees had always involved a lot of time and trouble, and Mrs Golding apparently even settled some small sums herself. One recorded example concerned a loan of £40 which had been taken out in 1952 by Miss JB for teaching dance, but on which the last £2 11s 4d was still outstanding by 1966. After many, many attempts to have this bill settled, the Secretary had paid it herself, noting on the record card that she had decided to do so "rather than bother any more ... with the fruitless chasing of that sum" which she had been doing for 13 years.

Mrs Golding had a good understanding of financial affairs, including the stock market, and she kept a close eye on the invested funds as well as proving to be very capable and knowledgeable about the legal responsibilities. Her competent dealings with the Public Trustees, the Charity Commissioners, with lawyers handling bequests to the Society and with the organization of meetings or publicity, are well demonstrated by correspondence held in the archive, by entries in the records and from the tributes paid after her death (and see note 11). It was inevitable that the responsibility for most day-to-day decisions was left to the Secretary, as meetings of the Committee were now far less frequent than they had been pre-war. Mrs Golding was particularly successful in securing the support of the Chase Charity which inaugurated a trial scheme whereby it would make an annual donation of £3,000 to SPTW providing the money would be used exclusively for students wishing to qualify as Conservators of any part of the heritage, or as speech therapists, teachers of the deaf, social workers or dancers. They especially wished the Society to use some of the money to assist "risky applicants" who were not to be pressed for payment or part repayment if circumstances warranted writing off the money involved as a bad debt. Any repayments could then be absorbed into the Society's own Loan Training Fund and subsequently used entirely at the Committee's discretion. This generous funding continued until 1988. (*GCIP* 4/22)

The files contain a number of letters of appreciation from grantees of the work of all the Society's secretaries, but in the post-war era the practice of including extracts from those letters in the Annual Reports was discontinued; nor do the Committee's Minutes during those years include the biographical details about grantees' circumstances which added so much 'colour' to Gertrude King's entries - details which are of such interest to social historians.[5] On the other hand, summaries of applicants' personal details and repayment histories had been entered on record cards after 1916, continuing until

Mrs Golding's death and those cards were later transferred to the Girton archive where they offer insights to researchers into the range of jobs (or poor health and unemployment history) of grantees. Modern records are currently retained by the present Secretary, and stored electronically.

FIGUREHEADS 1939-1988

After the death in 1943 of the Society's President Lady Bertha Dawkins the Committee appears to have made no attempt to fill that office, possibly as a result of wartime conditions. Instead Chairmen assumed the leadership, and Annual Report cover pages recorded only the names of the Chairman of Committee, the Hon. Treasurer and the Secretary. The illustrations show the differences between the 1920s and 1930s cover pages, and the style used from the 1950s onwards (see p. 147).

During these 'middle' fifty years, the role of Chairman became more important, as she was now the 'figurehead' presenting the public face of a small Society which might otherwise have dwindled to obscurity within what was increasingly a bureaucratic Welfare State. Brief profiles are included here of some of those dedicated members of SPTW, many of whom were able to use their own personal prestige and public influence to further the Society's aims.

Lady Ogilvie, MA (Oxon) (1900-1990)

Mrs Mary Helen Ogilvie (née Macauley), MA (Oxon) had joined the Committee in 1938, possibly as a result of her friendship with Lady Cushendun, and continued her association with the Society until 1989. Between 1940 and 1942 she accepted the roles of Vice Chairman and then Chairman of Committee in spite of having many other commitments.[6] A well-respected speaker and lecturer[7], Lady Ogilvie was elected Principal of St Anne's College Oxford in 1953, and accepted an Honorary Fellowship from that College in 1966. Her other awards included Honorary LL.Ds from Wilson College, from Leeds University and from Queen's, Belfast. She served as one of the Society's Vice-Presidents from December 1949 until 1989.

In one of many attempts by SPTW to gain wider recognition of its work an overview of its history was prepared by Mary Ogilvie. Later, she used her notes as the basis for an article which was published in *International Women's News* in 1943, which concluded:

> During the last 48 years the Society (now known as The Society for Promoting the Training of Women) has been able to train 1,466 girls. The training chosen covers practically every career now open to women. War conditions have naturally governed the Society's work since 1939,

but the Committee have continued their policy of granting loans to those candidates most likely to make the fullest use of their training. The Society considers the question urgent both for the immediate war effort, and also for dealing with the problems that must arise in the post-war world. (Ogilvie 1943:121)

Lady Plowden, DBE, JP (1910-2000)

Another of the Society's higher-profile members during the latter years of the 20th century was Bridget ('Biddy') Plowden (née Richmond), wife of the life peer, Edwin Plowden. Biddy Plowden was the daughter of an admiral, naval historian and master of Downing College, Cambridge (her middle name was Horatia). Because of her father's profession, Bridget was educated at a variety of schools and by governesses in England and Ceylon. She did not take up a profession while her four children were growing up as she said she "wanted to cherish them." Lady Plowden's obituary reported that it was not until she was in her fifties that she became a national figure, but that "public service was in her bones".

Mrs Plowden had taken on the job of Hon. Treasurer during the early years of the War, although she attempted to resign that function in 1942, as she had begun "some nursing at a London hospital"; however she was persuaded to continue with the Treasurer's duties until 1947. She took over as the Society's Chairman in July 1947 and remained as such until 1962, at which point she said she did not wish to stand for re-election (Minutes 9.5.1962). She was created Dame of the British Empire in 1972, continuing her association with the Society as one of its Vice-Presidents from 1962 until December 1988 but her other responsibilities claimed even more of her time at that point, as she had achieved national fame for her work as Chair of the Central Advisory Council for Education (England) which culminated in the influential 'Plowden Report' on primary education.[8]

Lady Plowden was equally influential in the field of broadcasting. She was Vice-Chairman of the BBC from 1970–75, taking an interest in programming and was Chairman of the new Independent Broadcasting Authority (commercial television) from 1975–80.

It was during Lady Plowden's SPTW Chairmanship that the Society found itself in the unusual situation of having a particularly healthy balance in the Loan Fund. This led to efforts to publicise the 'surplus' (see below) and this was another time when the Society felt they could include older women in their target group for loans "as it was felt that there must be those who, faced by unforeseen difficulties or freed for the first time from family claims on their time and energy, or wearied by monotonous unskilled work, find themselves, at an age which renders them ineligible or unqualified for grants, eager to fit themselves for some worth while and interesting career" (*AR* 1955).

It was with great regret that the Committee accepted Lady Plowden's resignation from the Chair in 1962, and stated that they wished "to place on record their appreciation and gratitude for her untiring efforts and most valuable work on behalf of the Society for so many years. The Committee will miss Lady Plowden's sympathetic understanding and direct approach to the many angles of the Society's work." (*AR* 1964)

Lady Crowther
(1907-1977)

Margaret Crowther (née Worth) was born in Pennsylvania of a Quaker family. She met her husband Geoffrey at Yale University, whilst they were both post-graduate students (he was on a Commonwealth scholarship). They married in the USA in 1932 but then moved back to England. Geoffrey Crowther was an outstanding economist, journalist and educationist: as Chairman

Lady Crowther

of the Central Advisory Council for Education 1956-60 he published the '*Crowther Report: Fifteen to Eighteen*' which made a number of important recommendations concerning the education of children of 'middling ability'.[9] Sir Geoffrey Crowther was knighted in 1957 and created a life peer in 1968.

As was common for her generation, Margaret Crowther (a highly intelligent and well-educated woman) did not seek a career for herself in Britain. She and her husband raised a family of six children: two boys and four girls. She felt strongly that her daughters as well as her sons should be encouraged to do well both academically and in career terms. Having been invited by her friend Lady Plowden to join SPTW in May 1946 she was pleased to support an organization whose aims matched her own firm belief in the value of women's education. For the last few years of her life, Lady Crowther was in poor health, but she continued to be a member of the Society until 1972.

Present-day researchers have Lady Crowther to thank for her initiative in having some of the Society's records preserved in a more accessible form. In March 1960 she had arranged for the Society's Annual Reports up to the year 1896 to be microfilmed and suggested that "when the Committee had seen the copies they might consider it worth while having a second copy made which possibly could be lent to universities and reference libraries for research purposes, and perhaps benefit the Society financially by copyright royalties" (Minutes 10.3.1960). The Committee subsequently arranged for the next batch of Reports (from 1897 to 1959) to be microfilmed.[10] Members were asked to contribute to the cost, which was £25 (Minutes 16.6.1960)

Mrs Joan Cooper

Mrs Cooper was a member of SPTW's Committee from 1936. She was Hon. Treasurer from 1951 until 1962 when she became Acting Chairman, following Lady Plowden's resignation. She accepted the post of Hon. Treasurer for a second time until taking over the Chair in 1983; but as there were then some complex issues to resolve concerning the administration of commemorative funds being administered by the Society, instead of appointing another member of the Committee to the Treasurer's job, Mr J.S.C. Chandler, FCIS was temporarily co-opted to serve as Investment and Financial Adviser. He was able to provide expert guidance regarding the changes which would be necessary as a result of the forthcoming Charities Act 1985 - this came into force on 1st January 1986. This Act was to assist trustees of low gross-income charities, who might wish to pass a resolution that the whole property of a charity could be transferred to another charity, provided it was agreed "that the objects of the transferee charity were not so far dissimilar in character to those of the original charitable gift that the proposed transfer would constitute an unjustifiable departure from the intentions of the founder of the transferor charity or violate the spirit of the gift". As a result, the Pfeiffer, Haweis, Pioneer and Central Bureau funds were transferred to the Society's Loan Training Fund, bringing its total up to nearly £37,000.[11]

In recognition that the number of trainees offered interest-free loans during the previous 83 years had passed the 2,000 mark in 1981, Joan Cooper "very generously gave a donation to the 2,000[th] trainee who was delighted to receive this unexpected gift" (*AR* 1981). Joan remained on the Committee until 1993; in 2002, after her death, the Society benefited from a very substantial legacy which she earmarked for the General Fund – an important proviso because that Fund, as so often before, was then badly in need of additional capital.

Miss Daphne Sidebottom

Miss Sidebottom whilst never Chairman of Committee, played a key role in her capacity as Hon. Treasurer for more than eighteen years. In all, she was a member of the Committee for 26 years, resigning only after she and her husband prepared to leave the country in 1978 to live in France (she married in 1976).[12] Her resignation was "accepted with very great regret and [the Committee] wished to place on record its gratitude and sincere appreciation of the work Mrs Buckney has done for the Society since she joined the Committee in 1951 and in particular since 1960 when she was appointed Hon. Treasurer. It can be said that the greatly improved condition of the General Fund Account is due largely to Mrs Buckney's handling of the Society's finances during her term of office." (*AR* 1978) During the 1950s and 1960s Miss Sidebottom, who was a journalist, accepted responsibility for collating much of the Society's early history (see below).

Mrs Colette Maitland-Warne

Mrs Maitland-Warne joined the Committee in January 1970 and was appointed Vice-Chairman in 1973. Six years later she became Chairman, resigning that role in 1989 but remaining on the Committee until 2004. The members were warm in their praise of Mrs Maitland-Warne's "devoted service" when she resigned. It was during her chairmanship that the Society benefited from a donation "towards office equipment" from the Thomas Wall Trust, some of which was spent obtaining an Olivetti adding machine for the Secretary's use. Mrs Maitland-Warne died in 2008.

Mrs Patience Thom

Patience Thom joined the Committee in 1971, having been introduced to the Society by Lady Crowther. Lady Crowther felt that Mrs Thom's recent experiences in Nigeria would be helpful as at that time SPTW was receiving numerous applications from Nigerian girls who wished to train as nurses in England. This coincided with a period when it was becoming harder to find British candidates in need of help, so applications from overseas students were being considered. However, Mrs Thom had to suspend her attendance on the Committee the following year, as her diplomat husband was posted to Dublin "for a few years", but she was welcomed back when they returned to London in 1974. She became Vice Chairman in 1987 and was elected Chairman when Mrs Maitland-Warne resigned in 1989.

During this period the Society was faced with a difficult situation concerning a defaulting grantee, which dragged on for many years, and which necessitated the Committee having to instruct their solicitors "to take whatever legal action was necessary" to recover the bad debt (*AR* 1974 and *GCIP* 3/31). Happily, during this period Mrs Thom oversaw fresh donations totalling £3,700 from four organizations: the Alan Cadbury Trust, the Hambland Trust, the Robert McAlpine Foundation, and the Mercer's Company. Mrs Thom summed up her involvement with the Society in these words: "I have really treasured the contact with the candidates, young women who are confident, ambitious, and full of hope."[13] She retired from the Chair in 1993 and was succeeded by the Vice Chairman, Mrs Burgess. (The next chapter features Mrs Burgess's term of office.)

EMPLOYMENT ISSUES

Just as had happened during the First World War, the second major conflict opened up a number of fresh career and earnings opportunities for many women, even if some of the benefits were short-lived. Not only were women from 1939 onwards again required to take on a wide range of work previously only done by men – in factories, on the land, in offices - but they were also serving in the Armed Services, which presented many with opportunities to learn new skills. For example 16-year-old Georgina Andrews had embarked upon a year's course in agriculture in 1938 with the help of a £23 loan from the Society and £55 from her local authority, and although on the completion of her course she was employed on a farm (earning ten shillings a week) for a few weeks, she then became unemployed for months. The records show that she was drafted into the WRNS in September 1941 (earning 13s a week) where she served until her demobilization in April 1946. She then decided to change her civilian career, and became a journalist on a local paper, finally paying off her debt in June 1948. Perhaps her service in the WRNS had offered the chance of adding shorthand and typewriting to her accomplishments - which at that time were considered essential tools for journalists – and lower-paid outdoor work no longer appealed.

One additional consequence of the ways that the war impacted on the world of work meant that people began to re-think traditional attitudes regarding women's physical capabilities. In the nineteenth century the Controller of the Post Office Savings Bank had said that he "did not wish to employ [women] on the Ledgers, which in any case were likely to prove too heavy for them to handle"; but in a recent interview when asked about her experiences as a shorthand-typist in a City bank prior to the outbreak of war, one woman recalled that "when the men left" [to join up] she "took on the ledgers ... and they were great big books ... [but when] the men came back they needed their jobs back". She was then returned to her secretarial functions. (Bridger 2003)[14]

The Committee noted that there were fewer applications for loans as the war neared its end. The decrease was "thought to be due partly to the Conscription Act, and partly to the fact that many young women are waiting to see how the various Government plans for post-war training materialize. When demobilization commences the Society anticipates a heavy demand on its resources and looks forward to playing its part in the programme of reconstruction." (*AR* 1944/1945)[15]

Post-war differences in the type of training which applicants sought were also apparent. For example, the Annual and Financial Reports for 1952 and 1953 noted that "there have been no applications for the Civil Service and Agricultural loans for several years; the Society would welcome enquiries". Instead, twenty-eight new applications in 1954 included sixteen for degree or teaching courses, nine for medicine and health-related professional qualifications, one solicitor and only two secretarial. In 1956 the trend towards teaching courses continued: of the 51 careers chosen by that year's grantees, 15 were for some form of teaching: eight intending to teach in State schools; a further two for PNEU[16] (ie independent preparatory) schools; two teachers of the blind; and one each for the teaching of commercial subjects, music and Froebel. Ten of the 51 were embarking on a variety of degree courses; and six others chose medicine, with a further three training in dentistry. The remainder consisted of six secretarial trainees and one each for radiography, physiotherapy, public health nursing, speech therapy, child psychotherapy, almoner, educational psychology, personnel management, institutional management, barrister and horticulture. A year later the Annual Report added the details of the different degree paths being chosen by grantees: Bachelors of Arts or Science courses in Art, Economics, English and History, History and English, Geography and Industrial Relations as well as a Master's Degree in Political Science; for 1960 the list also included degrees in Biology, Mathematics and Russian.

Throughout this period, acquiring a qualification in shorthand-typing was still popular, with some applicants wishing to acquire those skills even when they fully intended to follow a completely different career path. It was widely considered that secretarial qualifications were 'something to fall back on': a secure job opportunity even if other ambitions were not. Parents and even members of the Committee encouraged young girls to learn those skills as 'insurance' against future unemployment in more precarious occupations. This was a very different attitude from the status which secretarial work had had for the well-educated women at the turn of the century. A typical example was that of Miss B., who had taken a law degree at Oxford, but was given a grant to study for a shorthand-typing qualification in 1954 at Mrs Hoster's college whilst she waited to be called to the Bar.[17]

THE SOCIETY'S FINANCES

That the loan funds were still in a "satisfactory state" at the end of the war was attributed in part to "the smaller number of new grantees on the Society's books during the last few years, and also to the fact that during the same period women have commanded higher salaries and so our grantees have not found it difficult to repay their loans in regular instalments" (1946 Annual Meeting). From SPTW's point of view, grantees who qualified as teachers were usually able to repay their loans promptly, though not all under quite the same circumstances as in this case:

> One of the chief reasons that the Society has been able to spare ... money is the fact that repayments from grantees now in employment have been exceptionally good during the last two to three years and, in a large proportion of cases, well above the percentage stipulated in the rules. To

give one instance of this – a week after a certain grantee had completed a 3 years' P.T. Teacher's training her father called at the office and handed the Secretary £150 in very dirty £1 notes which wiped out the whole debt. This, of course, is not the usual course of events but, while naturally it is necessary to find out the cause for arrears in repayments, it would also be very interesting if reasons for sudden repayment of large amounts were given. (*Treasurer's notes for speech at Annual Meeting 1942*)

As the economy gathered strength after the war, there was a big rise in the number of women seeking work. Between 1961 and 1981, the country's working population increased by over two million, largely due to a rise of 70 per cent in the number of employed married women. There was an explosion in demand for office workers, gaining momentum as technology advanced (electric typewriters, adding machines, and in due course computers). Many local authorities set up schemes during the 1960s and 1970s to equip older women with the new skills through a wide variety of 'return to work' courses and in preparation for entry to higher education as 'mature' students. All this had a beneficial effect on the Society's financial situation: as demand for employees outstripped supply, grantees found it easier to get well-paid jobs, and were therefore able to repay their loans more quickly.

At Committee meetings members discussed the changing circumstances of older women in the workplace. The post-war expectations of many young girls had been that marriage and home-making would supplant any intentions of pursuing a long-term career: jobs were viewed as temporary and would be abandoned once the girls married and started a family. But from mid-century many older women were considering a return to work as their children became less dependent upon them; and as this change in attitudes coincided with a time when the Loan Funds were - for once! - in a healthy state, SPTW's Annual Report drew attention to these circumstances:

> The very high repayments received from grantees has (*sic*) ensured that the Loan Funds have maintained healthy balances, but the Society would like its work more widely known so that its funds may be of maximum use. With this object in view the Committee agreed to join with the Women's Employment Federation[18] and other co-operating loan funds in making known their work to older women. …Whilst the loan funds are primarily for younger students, it was felt that there must be those who, faced by unforeseen difficulties or free for the first time from family claims on their time and energy, or wearied by monotonous unskilled work, find themselves, at an age which renders them ineligible or unqualified for grants, eager to fit themselves for some worth while and interesting career. It is too early to report any result of this new policy, but applications from older women who are genuinely desirous of training for a recognized career, but cannot finance a course, will receive sympathetic consideration from the Committee. (*AR 1955*)

Soon after this *The Lady* magazine agreed to print an article about societies which could provide help for women wishing to take up new work. This appeared in their edition of 12 January 1956 (p.41) entitled 'Funds Go Begging'. As well as the SPTW they listed other "sympathisers" such as the Fawcett Society and the Women's Employment Federation, who were also inviting applications from older women requiring help with the costs of training. In the exchanges of correspondence between the secretaries representing these three organizations, in which they assessed the reaction to the forthcoming publication of the article, Irene Hilton, Organising Secretary of the Women's Employment Federation told Mrs Golding that she felt that it was "dangerous to give a list of careers open to older women because conditions are fluctuating all the time. In many cases where the official maximum age limit is 45, people of 50 are now being employed. The Civil Service is about to appoint clerical workers up to 60 on a pensionable basis …" (*CF* 3.11.1955).

After the article had appeared Mrs Golding wrote to Miss Hilton again, saying: "Of the thirty-odd replies that I have received to date, none of them seem to be very bright – the impression gained from the article seems to be that the organisations concerned give some training for older women which will enable them to earn money, regardless of whether they have any qualifications or even leanings! My prize effort is a lady of 73 from Bude who wants to know where she can get 'braid' for making point lace handkerchiefs; she has written me two long letters on the subject" (*CF* 20.1.1956)

A further letter to Miss Hilton included a request, indicating that the Society was still being used as a source of informed advice:

> One application for a loan has actually materialized – this is from a woman of 45 who has only had an Elementary School education … She is separated from her husband and receives National Assistance … She wants to take a secretarial course, but has no idea where to train. Could you let me have a list of suitable colleges? One of her employers has written saying she 'has intelligence and capabilities above the average' so it might be possible to make a secretary out of her. Anyhow she is coming for an interview with my Committee when they meet next (*CF* 31.1.1956)[19]

The archives contain various references to Committee members' reluctance to commit loans for training which might not lead to settled employment. Although no formal rules are cited, there have always been discussions regarding applicants whose ambitions seemed risky to members, with the result that the Committee could be reluctant to grant a loan. Examples ranged from disapproval of a particular *place* of training (the 'wrong' music college, or typewriting instructor) to the *type* of work selected. An early entry in the Minutes had reported that an application had been received for a loan to assist a 39-year-old woman to re-train as a shorthand-typist at the Temple Academy, Chancery Lane; but the Committee thought that the training at that establishment would not be suitable for her

> as it would be only the training for an ordinary Shorthand Clerk in a shop or business. At Miss Hunt's age and with her education she could not take such a post and, judging from her letters she would be too sensitive for that sort of training or position. Unless she can get really good secretarial training it would not be wise to go in for that...The Secretary was desired to write to her [suggesting that] at 39, Miss Hunt would be better suited to be a Matron, or the Superintendent of a Girls' Hostel as she had passed the Senior Local Examination and knows French and German (*GCM* 23.5.1913).

Occasionally, an exception was made in spite of their mistrust such as when they supported a candidate who wished to train to be an opera singer. In that instance, they felt that she would always be able to earn money to repay her debt, as she had already qualified as a shorthand-typist and could fall back on that if the opera career foundered. The case of the opera singer is mentioned in correspondence between the Secretary, Daphne Sidebottom (Hon. Treasurer) and the Cornmarket Press in the 1960s, as the latter were preparing to re-issue a book on careers for married women[20] and had asked Mrs Golding to check the manuscript for accuracy. Mrs Golding wrote to Ms Sidebottom expressing her concerns: "The part about the Society would appear adequate, except I don't like the reference to the opera singer although no one is to know it refers to us. Possibly this should come out, as Miss A. might happen to see it and would probably immediately jump to conclusions that we had told Miss Brown [viz. *R. Simon, the co-author*] about her when our work is supposed to be confidential...." (*CF* 1.9.1966)

Sidebottom agreed, replying: "I don't like the Opera Singer reference at all from any point of view. I will do my best to draft a reply to bring on Thursday. Other things apart we don't want a lot of married women applicants for training in the performing arts." (*CF* 4.9.1966) In due course the Cornmarket Press received a strongly worded letter from SPTW, saying in part:

> The Society always emphasizes that it only gives loans for trainings leading to a qualification for a recognized profession which should ensure a reasonable steady income. We hardly ever lend money to applicants wishing to train for the arts because the prospects are so uncertain; the case you mention of the opera singer was an exception as the trainee in question is a fully qualified and experienced secretary, who could always return to this profession if necessary. (*CF* 10.9.1966)

Some twenty years later, the Chase Charity's provisos (see page 132) would mean that the Committee could take a more accommodating attitude towards applications from performing artistes, including opera singers.

During 1956 the Society had decided to take further steps to encourage more applications and asked the Hon. Treasurer, Daphne Sidebottom, to produce a publicity pamphlet on behalf of the Committee. She prepared a small four-sided leaflet setting out the Society's Purpose, Conditions, Finance and Application Procedures. After outlining its History, it concluded:

> **The Society Today.** It is sometimes asked, is the Society's help necessary in these days of the Welfare State? Our answer is that every loan is proof that it is, for a girl comes to us only when she has failed to obtain all or part of the cost of her training from the State or elsewhere and cannot pay for it herself. The reasons differ and are little realized. Some trainings are not eligible. Counties vary in their awards policy. A grant may cover only part of the cost, or cover fees and not maintenance. A girl may have saved part of the expenses. Only rarely does an authority pay for more than three years' training. Girls come to the Society in anxiety, disappointment, full of ambition or as a last hope. With details that always vary, the Society's loans enable ambitions to be fulfilled, disappointments overcome, qualifications obtained to support a family in unexpected loss, or to lead to a career for life in a chosen field.

> **Membership.** Wider membership of the Society would be welcomed. The annual subscription of 10/- entitles members to a copy of the Annual Report and to attend the Annual Meeting.

There is no record of the circulation list, but one of the letters received in response, dated 27 April 1956, suggested that Mrs Golding should contact Winifred Carr, Deputy Editor of the Woman's Department on the *Daily Telegraph*. Ms Carr was interested in the story, and an item appeared in that paper on 21 June 1956, entitled 'Money That Nobody Wants: It Can Mean Fresh Start For The Middle-Aged Woman' and included the following passages:

> It is strange in these days when everyone is complaining of being hard up, to hear of £5,000 that nobody wants. The Society for Promoting the Training of Women has this much money going begging. They want to lend it to women who need money to pay for tuition fees or maintenance expenses[21] while training for a career. But they can't find any applicants. … The society already has about £6,000 out in loans to women who have borrowed to train as teachers, secretaries, doctors, psychotherapists and social workers. One woman of 36, an ex-Wren, is using her loan to take a dental course. A woman barrister, an architect and three girls who went into dress designing and the theatre are among those who are now launched in their careers and repaying their loans. …

> *But the society won't be happy until all their money is being used. The lack of loan-takers has got them worried. … [Grantees] can get loans*

from the Society on the security of a guarantor or a short endowment policy and pay back without interest.

But many parents are unwilling to accept a loan, and some of the girls are afraid it might mean no marriage until they had paid the money back. "Supposing I gave up my training half-way to get married: I'd be taking a debt for my dowry," is how one girl put it. So the Society is now hoping to interest other groups of women who need help this way – women in middle-life whose families are grown up or whose homes are broken. And here, it feels, it can do a lot of good because most of these women are completely untrained for anything but running a home and looking after a family, and few can earn a living on that. But again there are snags. The standard of education needed to-day before anyone can qualify to begin training is too high for many of these women, and very few of them are prepared to settle down to a long training. So, for the present, the £5,000 the Society is longing to loan goes on being the money that nobody wants.

Predictably, such a tempting article brought forth an enormous increase in the number of applications received by the Committee and the Society was inundated with new requests for assistance, including many from older women, so the Loan Fund was once again quickly depleted. Ms Carr followed up with a further piece in the paper on 31 July, headlined '*Money Everybody Wants*'. The newspaper's second article said:

The £5,000 that nobody wanted a few weeks ago has become the money paying for the business and professional training of a dozen women. As a result of a story in this feature about the funds that the Society for Promoting the Training of Women had lying idle through lack of applicants, 300 women wrote to the Society. They were young students needing to augment State grants; daughters of professional men whose fathers' incomes barred them from getting a State grant; and older women who have never before qualified for a career. There were also women already trained in a profession but wanting to take higher qualifications.

So far, 12 of these women have embarked on training to be teachers, a doctor, a matron of an old people's home, a personnel manager and a child psychotherapist. So now the Society which only two months ago was worried because it couldn't find any takers for its money has approved loans totalling £3,648 and is still considering more applications. (Winifred Carr *Daily Telegraph* 21 June 1956 and 31.07.1956)

THE CENTENARY YEAR

Three years later, during the Society's Centenary year, it again proved difficult to get any national publicity. In an attempt to do so Mrs Golding collected together all the previous 'statements' which had been prepared over time by Committee members, as well as relevant Annual Reports, and on 21 May 1959 sent them to Daphne Sidebottom hoping that she would be able to prepare a summary of those one hundred years. The anniversary was due to fall on 19 June that year[22]. Miss Sidebottom found the timescale a problem: in a letter dated 22 June 1959 she wrote to Mrs Golding apologizing for not having made much progress with the publicity statement, adding that she "seemed only able to write something that sounded like a propaganda leaflet." So the date of the anniversary came and went; and it was not until late in 1959 that replies were received from some of the newspapers, none of which was prepared to use the story (*CF* May 1959-February 1966). There were various excuses: some said the appropriate members of staff were away on holiday or were ill and no-one else could make a decision on the matter; there was a printers' dispute; and so on.

In spite of the failure to use the national press to publicise the centenary, the exercise did result in the preparation of a comprehensive summary of the achievements of the first hundred years and Miss Sidebottom later used her notes as the basis for an address she gave to the Annual Conference of the Society of Women Engineers in 1963. She told her audience: "As one reads the records of these first years, it becomes very clear that this was not the ordinary Victorian charity – in the most commonly envisaged way it was not a charity at all, extremely little money was ever given away by the Society, and the whole basis of its work was to enable women to earn money themselves." She ended her address with these words:

> Miss Boucherett … died in 1905. I personally feel a sense of satisfaction that she lived long enough to know the Society's work in its present form, and signified her approval of it in the legacy she left us of £2,000. To me there is a sense of historical fulfilment in recounting to an audience such as yours the story of Miss Boucherett and the Society she founded. Even her agile mind, I do not think, could possibly have envisaged at that time a conference of women engineers – of women both qualified and working on an equal footing with men in a profession that for longer than many must have seemed a masculine preserve. With what satisfaction she would have viewed your Conference! And the contrast it provides does perhaps epitomize the whole great overturn in the position of women that has taken place since she met with her circle of friends in Great Castle Street a little over a hundred years ago, and planned the first tentative steps for her Society. (Daphne Sidebottom 5.9. 1963)[23]

The centenary was of course the subject of a special mention in the Annual Report:

> The year under review is an historical one in the history of the Society, for it marked a hundred years of work to improve conditions for women in the fields of education and employment. When the Society was founded in 1859 its first task was to campaign, by various forms of publicity and other means, for women to receive a better education, thus fitting them to be trained and eventually suitably employed in the many and varied occupations which were slowly to become within their scope. The pioneer work having been achieved, the Society started to help individuals by means of interest-free training loans. Proof of the success and necessity for this work is that – through the Loan Training Funds – 1,750 educated girls and women have been able to train for professional and technical work during the past sixty-one years.[24] The total amount which has been granted in loans is now £82,083. (*AR* 1959)

The *General* Fund often struggled to maintain a sufficient balance to meet its commitments. In 1955 it had an estimated deficit of £320 and the Annual Report drew attention to this, blaming that "serious deficit" on the loss of investment dividends (the Stock Market was in a particularly volatile period). Luckily, however, towards the end of the year the Committee received additional donations, and the Report added that they wished "to express their appreciation and gratitude to the Public Trustee and The Thomas Wall Trust who responded so promptly and generously to the Society's appeal for financial help". (*AR* 1956)

The brief surplus in the Loan Fund accounts experienced in 1956 disappeared quite quickly. A subsequent Report noted that "a considerable proportion of the Society's loan fund capital was being utilized by grantees still in training ... [so that the Committee was] ... only able to consider new applications as and when adequate repayments accumulated" (*AR* 1958). In general, grants could be offered from most of the different loan funds; but if the terms of a bequest restricted the use of a particular fund, Public Trustees' regulations had to be observed. However, correspondence during 1981 indicates that the Pioneer Loan Training Fund's (PLTF) early rules[25] (i.e. that its candidates should be "of gentle birth") had been allowed to lapse by the time that Fund was transferred to SPTW in January 1946 (*CF* 6.8.1981); and the Central Bureau's requirement that beneficiaries had to be "of British birth on both sides" was also taken for granted, since "there could never be any question of the total combined Loan Training Funds being used exclusively to assist foreign students" (*CF* 21.9.1981).

Amalgamations such as the one with the PLTF led to the need to make fresh changes to the Society's letter headings. The Society's printed headings had included 'Founded in 1859 as the Society for Promoting the Employment of Women' (see illustration in Chapter 4); after 1939 the words 'Incorporated in 1879' were dropped from the heading – presumably part of the wartime printing economies. Another change at that point was announced in the next Annual Report, which said that "owing to the need for economy, it has been decided to issue the Report this year in the form of a leaflet instead of the usual booklet, and for this reason the Committee regret that no list of subscribers can be included" (*AR* 1940). The heading was further reduced from the 1950s.

Covers for Annual Reports, 1930s (top) and 1950s

GOVERNESS TO TEACHER: A CENTURY OF CHANGE

As teaching has accounted for such a large proportion of the Society's grants during its history, it is perhaps worth reflecting on some of the changes which the profession experienced during the life of this Society. Jessie Boucherett's motivation in founding SPEW had centred on the plight of the untrained, underpaid "distressed governess". In due course, over the next century, the untrained governesses disappeared and a wide range of qualified teachers emerged. The teaching profession was the focus of official interventions, encompassing legislation on equal opportunities as well as regulations regarding the qualifications of teachers. Inequalities such as those relating to pay, or bars on married women teaching, were gradually removed, sometimes as the result of expediency: the removal of the marriage bar took place as an outcome of the need to employ more women during the Second World War.[26] In spite of advances within this field of employment, the Society continued to receive requests for financial assistance well into the 1950s. The difficulties experienced by some older applicants are illustrated by the summaries of their stories contained in the archives, for example:

Aged 38. Applicant's father was killed whilst fire watching during the war and his widow was left with an income of less than £400 per annum. At that time applicant was at a University, but abandoned this course to earn her living. She worked as an uncertificated teacher for some years and then obtained a College Scholarship for tuition fees only for an Honours Degree course in History. She was ineligible for a State Scholarship as she was already a University student before October 1946 so that her case did not lie within the Ministry of Education regulations. The Society granted this applicant a loan of £200 for maintenance during the University course. Applicant has now obtained a Degree and qualified as a teacher and is repaying her loan from her salary of £690 per annum as a teacher.

Aged 37. Before her marriage applicant was a shorthand typist. She had to divorce her husband when her only child was three because of cruelty and obtained custody of the child. The husband successfully managed to evade contributing financially to their support, to the point of going to prison for a spell. Applicant decided to take a teacher's training which would enable her to support herself and her son and would give her adequate time to look after the boy. She obtained a Local Education Grant but this was not sufficient to see her through the two years' training and the Society made her a loan of £80 to help towards the cost. Applicant is now qualified and is repaying her loan from her salary as a teacher. (*GCIP 3/35*)

Many girls found that a teaching career became more accessible as a result of periodic legislation covering the raising of the school-leaving age, the advent of the National Curriculum, and an upsurge in the number of girls achieving good examination results. Only about seven per cent of the population stayed at school beyond the age of 15 until 1972 when the statutory age was increased to 16. A similar proportion of school leavers, ie seven per cent, continued into higher education, of whom a mere quarter were girls.[27] As office work was still so popular, it was natural that many of them would wish to qualify as teachers of commercial subjects themselves. The first mention of an SPTW grant for training as a 'commercial teacher' appeared in the Annual Report for 1956.

Despite periodic drops in the demand for teachers (notably the 1930s and then the 1980s)[28] teaching has remained a popular destination particularly as it is looked upon as work which is compatible with marriage and motherhood (working hours can simplify problems associated with child-care arrangements).

The end of the 1980s marked a time when the educational environment and the employment market were again in the midst of major changes: the National Curriculum ensured that the remaining gender divisions in 'option subjects' no longer applied, and the advent of the widespread use of computers was revolutionizing the workplace.

THE END OF AN ERA: DEATH OF MRS GOLDING

Mrs Golding's illness and eventual death left a void felt not only on the personal level for the Committee: it also resulted in a period when the Society was without a full-time employee, so that day-to-day affairs had to be conducted by the Chairman Mrs Thom and the Vice-Chairman Mrs Gillis Burgess. It was to be almost six months before a new Secretary was appointed (which created an opportunity to introduce computers to the office equipment, paving the way for a fresh approach to record-keeping). As will be seen in the next Chapter, these events led to a major decision being taken: to find an appropriate resting-place for the Society's historic archive and to seek ways of making that more accessible to the public. As the twentieth century drew to a close, society was already more noticeably egalitarian; the old formalities in social relationships had given way to more relaxed interaction, and the Society for Promoting the Training of Women was ready to face the challenges of the new millennium.

After more than fifty years in office, Mrs Golding's death in November 1988 was a great blow to the Committee. The Chairman, Mrs Maitland-Warne, wrote a letter to members in which she said in part:

Some of you may have seen the sad notice of the death of Winnie Golding in *The Times* and *The Telegraph* last week, but I am writing to you all on the Committee in case you missed this.

Mrs Golding had been desperately ill ... for a year or so, but was determined to carry on with the job she loved. More latterly she was also found to have [a further serious medical condition]. She treated all these afflictions with indomitable courage and optimism. It will be no surprise to us who knew her that her thoughts were to the end upon the welfare of the students we help and on the future of the Society. She died very peacefully on 24 November 1988.

I believe we may all want to think how we, ourselves, might like to tangibly commemorate Mrs Golding and when a Committee meeting is called, probably in late January (date not fixed yet) this will surely be an item for the agenda.

Of course, her greatest memorial will be through the many hundreds of students she has caused us to help over more than fifty years of her wise and caring stewardship of the Society; the majority of these students treated her as a personal friend and mentor during their university and training period and sometimes for years after.

To us, she is irreplaceable.
Yours sincerely,
Colette Maitland-Warne

In the words of a Committee member who knew her during those years, Winnie Golding *was* the Society. A second, who knew her for forty years, remarked that the Secretary was "Kingpin. She was very human and efficient, and good on finance." Another said: "One of my early memories of the Society was Mrs Golding's great sense of appropriateness of candidates for interview; she saw through the paper to the person" adding that "the Society was her life, her baby, especially after her husband died".

---

1   Chapter 4 refers to the move to Brompton Road.
2   This organization has been absorbed into the Mary Feilding Guild which provides residential accommodation for 'working ladies'. Lady Plowden, Jessie Boucherett and Lady Knightley were also very involved with both organisations. (See Chapter 3).
3   Years later, in 1956, Mrs Winifred Golding asked the solicitors if they knew the whereabouts of "the Society's seal", but the solicitor replied that he imagined "it was lost when your London office was damaged by enemy action. I think that the Society should have a Seal and suggest that you communicate with the Solicitors' Law Stationery Society Ltd... who would submit a design to you for approval if asked to do so" (CF 8.5.1956). Searches by secretaries in more recent years have also failed to trace it.
4   Miss Vansittart was the Society's Hon. Treasurer until 1938, then Vice Chairman. She was Acting Chairman for a few months between 1940 and early 1941.
5   Nowadays, of course, the Data Protection Act would preclude any such personal information being available to researchers.

6   Her husband Sir Frederick Ogilvie – a former Director-General of the BBC and the Principal of Jesus College, Oxford - had died in 1949 at the age of 49 only a year after the tragic death of their eldest son in a climbing accident in Switzerland.

7   Mary Macauley was awarded a BA in Modern History in 1922, and an MA in 1936.

8   Her committee carried out a major study of primary education in this country, culminating in The Plowden Report *Children and Their Primary Schools* (HMSO 1967). This influential Report made a strong case for child-centred learning; but she was also renowned for her interest in, and efforts on behalf of, the rights of gypsies, whose children she considered probably the most severely deprived in the country. As a result of this interest she agreed to become the chairwoman of the Advisory Council for the Education of Romany and Other Travellers.

9   The 1959 Crowther Report recommended raising the school leaving age to 16 years, the introduction of comprehensive schools and a new examination below GCE level - moves towards equal opportunities which were accepted by the Government but not completed until the 1970s.

10 These now form part of the archive at Girton.

11 Mrs Golding's efforts in this connection were recognized in the Annual Report: "We are grateful indeed to our Secretary Mrs Golding for undertaking and bringing to fruition with Mr Chandler the very complicated and protracted negotiations outlined at the beginning of this Report and which now make our affairs so much more streamlined and efficient. In more than fifty years as our Secretary, this piece of work will certainly stand out as a major achievement in her long and wise stewardship." (*AR* 1986).

12 The attendance lists in the Minutes refer to Miss Sidebottom as Mrs (Lionel) Buckney after her marriage in 1976. *The Times* 16 June 1976 reported that she married "quietly" at St Stephen's Church, Rochester Row, London SW1.

13 Mrs Thom epitomizes the qualities which characterize the Society's Committee members: public-spirited, well educated and with a wealth of life experiences. Patience was educated at St George's Harpenden, and then read French and German at St Andrew's. Marriage to Kenneth who was in the Foreign Office meant long stints abroad with intervals in London but when she and her husband were home on leave she was kept busy by teaching immigrants in Brent in the 1970s, was a Juvenile Magistrate, organized country holidays for city children, took an Advanced Diploma at Roehampton, as well as teaching dyslexic children at a London hospital. Following their permanent return to Somerset, Patience Thom spent a further ten years teaching dyslexic children. She has always enjoyed singing, and when in London sang with the Philharmonic Choir. Quite late in life she took up painting and now exhibits regularly. She has also written six books – some fiction and some on rural science.

14 Anne Bridger: *A Century of Women's Employment in Clerical Occupations: 1850-1950, with particular reference to the role of the Society for Promoting the Employment of Women* (2003).

15 As an economy during the War, and until the 1950s. the much briefer Annual Reports were printed every two years.

16 The Parents' National Education Union was established in the 1890s by Charlotte Mason who lived at Ambleside in the Lake District, where she trained young women to become governesses and teachers.

17 Competition between the many establishments now offering secretarial courses was quite fierce, and newspapers such as *The Times* and the *Daily Telegraph* contained a great many notices offering secretarial training during this period, which is perhaps why the Pitman organization included the following incentive in one of their advertisements for courses at their Bayswater Road, W.2 premises: "…Comprehensive training is offered for high-grade Secretarial appointments. Adequate air-raid shelter." (*The Times* p.10, 8.1.1943).

18 The Annual Report for 1940 mentions the death of Mrs Oliver Strachey, "Organising Secretary of the Women's Employment Federation ... which organization has always been in close touch with the Society".

19 It is perhaps worth commenting that a couple of decades earlier if faced with an enquiry about secretarial training, the Society's secretary would have been likely to refer the enquirer to Mrs Hoster; but by this date she was no longer alive and no similarly close links had been established with other individuals.

20 Labovitch, P & Simon, R *Late Start: Careers for Wives* (1969) Cornmarket Press.

21 After the War the Committee agreed that advances could also be made towards maintenance expenses (*AM* 1947).

22 This date marked the first meeting of Jessie Boucherett's supporters in 1859. The first *committee* meeting took place on 7th July 1859.

23 The speech was reproduced in the journal *The Woman Engineer,* vol.9, No.12, Spring 1964, pp.14-17.

24 That is, since 1898, about the time that the Society was moving towards offering loans, not trainings.

25 The PLTF was amalgamated with the Society after 1945. It had been founded in 1901 "to train one or more necessitous gentlewomen every year for some profession or employment for which they would otherwise be unable to qualify". In 1945 its Hon. Secretary "had to resign her post" and their committee decided it would be "wiser to hand over the administration of the Fund to some other organization with similar policy and ideals" so they approached SPTW. It was agreed that the PLTF would retain its separate identity under the name of the Pioneer Fund. Their committee agreed unanimously to amalgamate with SPTW and legal formalities were completed on 15 January 1946 (*AR* 1948-49).

26 It was not officially removed from the national teaching profession until after 1947, when the 1944 (Butler) Education Act was fully implemented. However, the London County Council ceased to apply the marriage bar in their schools from 1935.

27 McCarthy, H. "Gender Equality" in E*qualities in Britain, 1946-2006,* Centre for Contemporary British History: a Research Project and Report commissioned by the Equalities Review, March 2007.

28 The Society's Annual Report for 1982 drew attention to this, saying that teaching was one of the hardest hit professions as far as employment was concerned. "This is borne out by the fact that a large number of qualified teachers are seeking financial help to enable them to train for another profession, or to obtain a further specialized teaching qualification which will broaden the chance of success in that field of employment." (*AR* 1982).

CHAPTER 6

"Our dear old society": 1989-2009

This "dear old Society" as Gertrude King referred to it in 1926 has continued its valuable contribution to furthering women's opportunities for employment for the last 150 years: a cause for celebration especially in 2009 not only for its dedicated membership but also for the thousands of women who have benefited directly from its activities during those years. Many organisations have faltered but some, such as ours, have continued. In this book we have tried to show how the Society was able to transform itself to changing circumstances, enabling us to come through to the 21st century with its changing demands.

Over the centuries there have been occasions when some on the Committee disagreed with or even disapproved of aspects of policy, practice or the backing of other causes, and sometimes this led to resignations; yet the Society has survived. Despite changes it has stuck to its heritage and extended help to any woman, without racial, religious or political bias.

The composition of the Committee has evolved from a time when members were almost invariably recruited from the aristocracy and the upper middle classes - people who were able to use their familial and social networks to further the Society's aims – to a time when it attracts women to the Committee who have or have had successful careers themselves, and who often wield influence through their additional voluntary work. The members of the Committee are now known as Trustees of the Society, in line with the recent Good Governance requirements which apply to charitable organisations.

THE TRUSTEES

During this anniversary year the Trustees represent a range of experience in education, Women's issues and in the voluntary organisations and grant making. Within the educational field, Dr Carolyn Boulter the present Chairman and a member since 1984, is a retired academic and has been a lecturer and researcher in Initial Teacher Training especially science education, and has managed research in the Social Sciences at Reading University. Mrs Stella Harcourt is a lecturer in Tertiary Education at Southend and has recently taken a Masters in Social Sciences with the Open University. Professor Janet

Some Trustees (2008) and Secretary Mrs Thompson

Dine, a member since 2005, is professor of International Development Law at Queen Mary's College, where her current research concern is the interaction of human rights law and international trade law. Mrs Elspeth Richards, who joined the Committee in 2000, has extensive experience of teaching English and Drama at secondary school level and remains a secondary school governor. Mrs Ruth McCallum joined the Committee in 1993 and brings experience of teaching in schools overseas whilst accompanying her husband who worked with the British Council. Dr Karen Jardine Brown, a member of the Committee from the mid 1990s, is qualified in medicine and works in the field of dyslexia and hearing impairment.

Other recent members include Lady Julia Carter, whose wide experience of teaching, especially in higher education and with women from ethnic minorities, proved of great value to the Committee. Lady Carter is also a JP in Inner London and Chair of the charity School-Home Support. Miss Patricia Bayliss joined in 2001 and retired from the Committee in 2008. Her experience of careers in girls' education in Rhodesia, the United States and New Zealand has also been of considerable benefit to the Society. Mrs Geraldine Baker left the Committee after more than ten years' service. From her experience as head of a GDST school in London she brought empathy and care for the applicants and a realistic awareness of the challenges they faced.

The Trustees also owe a particular debt of gratitude in this anniversary year to the immediate past Vice Chairman, Mrs Sandra Lello. She retired in 2007, having served on the Committee for seventeen years, where her experiences as teacher and lecturer, and also as Warden of William Goodenough House (a post-graduate Hall of Residence at the University of London) were of great benefit to the Committee.

Other Trustees, representing the voluntary and grant-giving area, include Lady Ruth Hawley who has been associated with the Society since 1977 and brought with her a wealth of understanding of the voluntary sector and of other charities. Ruth began her own working life in the Diplomatic Service but after her marriage the family then spent many years in "Pay, Pack and Follow" mode as her husband's career took them to a number of different countries.[1] Lady Hawley is a past High Sheriff of Wiltshire and has held a number of other roles including chairman of her Parish Council, Commander of the St John Ambulance organisation, patron of a number of charities, lay canon of Salisbury Cathedral and a member of the Swindon Health Authority. Ms Nerina Inkson in addition to having previously been employed in the publishing industry, is the Executive Secretary of the PCAC. She has been a member of SPTW's Committee since 1997, where her extensive experience in managing the work of such a similar organisation is particularly valuable to the Society. She possesses a wide knowledge of current courses and the spectrum of other educational trusts. Mrs Gillis Burgess who joined the Committee in 1973 and was the previous Chairman (see page 160), is a past Secretary of the PCAC and this experience is enhanced by knowledge of the book trade and of archives. The Vice Chairman, Ms Joanna Murray, is a past grantee who is employed as a commercial pilot.

The Trustees have been fortunate to retain Ms Lindsay Mann as an increasingly important financial advisor. Financial expertise together with a marketing knowledge are areas in which the Society continue to seek experienced new membership of the Trustees.

Committee members give their time and expertise generously in pursuit of this "small but significant" Society's activities.[2] They possess independent spirits, are dedicated, interested and exhibit abundant common sense: and all have a genuine interest in helping to further other women's ambitions. It is, of course, impossible for a book such as this to include the stories of all those officers, members or grantees who have been associated with the Society, even during the last twenty years. There are, however, such stories to tell. Two recently retired personalities have been selected for more detailed profiles: past President Baroness Park of Monmouth, and Committee member Mrs Joan Jardine Brown.

PRESIDENTS

Past President Baroness Park of Monmouth, CMG, OBE, MA (Oxon) (b.1921)

Quite the most remarkable of the Society's recent past Presidents is Baroness Daphne Park, and although much has been written elsewhere about her, she merits a lengthy profile here as her life story is not only full of interest, but offers an inspiring example of what women are capable of achieving. In spite of leading a very busy public life, she gave her time and active support to this small Society for more than fifteen years, consistently demonstrating her genuine interest in the careers of its grantees and its members. She was President from 1992 until October 2005 and has continued her association with the Society since that date. Questioned about the motivation for her involvement, Lady Park said that she was initially attracted to it because of its illustrious benefactors, including Queen Victoria and the former Prime Minister William Gladstone; in addition she was especially interested in its role in supporting mature women through higher education. Moreover, the aims of the SPTW were in the tradition of Eleanor Rathbone, an old Somervillian and a very distinguished Independent MP whom she much admired.[3]

Daphne Margaret Sybil Désirée Park was created a Life Baroness in 1990 after a long career as a diplomat, membership of MI6 and a distinguished academic life. Having been educated in the years leading up to the Second World War, she was aware that higher education, in particular, was not a universal right or entitlement for women, no matter how 'bright' they might be (she maintains that her own achievements were "a combination of good luck and arbitrariness"). She brought this awareness to her dealings with the Society's applicants, as many of the young women who apply for SPTW's help struggle against heavy odds in order to fulfil their ambitions.

Born and brought up in Tanganyika (now Tanzania) where her father was a coffee grower and gold prospector, she was educated at home by her mother and through a 'correspondence course' with a bishop's daughter living in Dar-es-Salaam. The family home was a mud house in the jungle, with the nearest village a day's walk away. An early reader, with stories from the Iliad amongst her favourite books, by the time she was eight the seeds of her later career were sown when she read Rudyard Kipling and John Buchan: their novels convinced her that she wanted to be a spy. When she was eleven she was sent to school in England which meant first a day's walk from her home to the nearest road, accompanied by her parents, a three-day lorry and then train journey to Dar-es-Salaam, then sailing to Britain under the care of a family returning on leave.

It was to be another fifteen years before she saw her parents again: in the meantime her only brother had died in Africa aged 14. In England she lived with her grandmother and attended "a remarkable State school": a Dalton's

Baroness Park of Monmouth

school in Streatham. The grandmother's London home was bombed during the early years of the Second World War, which meant a move to the country. This initially affected her plans to go up to Oxford having just been given a major financial award from London County Council. However, Surrey County Council offered her a scholarship on condition that she taught in their schools for five years after graduating. Daphne Park refused that offer as her heart was set on a career in the Diplomatic Service; happily the education authorities were sufficiently impressed to grant her an award so that after all she was able to go up to Somerville where she read Modern Languages (1940-1943).

After Oxford she volunteered for war service, working between 1943 and 1945 as a FANY for the Special Operations Executive training Resistance fighters, who were to be parachuted into France in the run-up to D-Day. When the war was over she eventually caught the eye of MI6 and "leapt at the chance" to fulfil her childhood ambition. Three years later she was sent off to Cambridge to study Russian. She was posted to the British Intelligence Objective Sub-Committee in Berlin in 1945, then to Austria until 1948.

From then onwards, in every posting – Moscow, Hanoi, the Congo and Northern Rhodesia - Daphne Park had two roles: as a diplomat who was answerable to the Foreign Office and also in her MI6 role to that service. She remained with MI6 until 1979. As she put it: "You do an ordinary job with an extra dimension." To a twenty-first century reader, her jobs do not seem too ordinary!

Daphne Park's experiences in these countries will never be fully told as she is adamant that she will not publish her memoirs: she believes that the trust of friends and contacts would be jeopardised if such information became public knowledge. Nevertheless, she was prepared to share a few incidents, as a result of being asked by her former Service to appear on a BBC Panorama programme. When serving as H.M. Consul-General in Hanoi during the Vietnam war she had to fly from time to time in the International Control Commission aircraft, a Dakota. "We were sometimes shot at, so it was rather a dicey trip" was her under-stated description.

She tells of an occasion when in order to save the life of the Congolese Prime Minister's secretary she had to smuggle him out of a hospital in the boot of her little Citroën 2CV car – he then escaped across the river. On another occasion in the Congo she used a similar method to rescue a Zanu member whom she transported to Zambia in the vehicle's luggage compartment (at that stage her car was a small Volkswagen).

Daphne Park's academic life after these postings offered an opportunity to champion women's education at Somerville, then a single-sex College. In particular she supported girls from overseas, whose parents may have been reluctant to let them follow an independent academic career. Daphne Park always wanted her students to feel that Oxford was "an extension of their life", not something that excluded their families and friends. Whilst celebrating the many women students who had achieved academic or other professional success after leaving Oxford, she also valued those who made a success of marriage.

Lady Park's personal achievements are outstanding. In addition to being a past Principal of Somerville College, pro-Vice-Chancellor of Oxford University, a Governor of the BBC (1982-1987) and chairman of a Royal Commission and of the Legal Aid Advisory Committee, she has also served as a member of the boards of the British Library and of Voluntary Service Overseas. Now a well-respected and vocal member of the House of Lords, having been elevated to the peerage following her retirement from Somerville, Daphne Park can also look back on more than thirty years of leading the "double life" of a diplomat within the Foreign Office and membership of the Secret Service ("a spy" as press coverage has referred to her). Her postings to Moscow, Hanoi, the Congo and Northern Rhodesia all contained fascinating experiences, even though her life was in danger on more than one occasion.

In 2008 Lady Park raised the money to found a charity, Phoenix Zimbabwe, which assists Zimbabwean asylum seekers who may not work to train on courses as diverse as brick-making, founding a housing association, or taking up a new course in nursing.[4]

In 2002 Lady Park recruited another member of the House of Lords, Lady Judith Wilcox, as a Vice President of SPTW. However, as Lady Wilcox's many other duties as a member of the Lords mean that she is frequently abroad, she had to resign the post in March 2006; but she remains a member of the Society.

Lady Appleyard

President Lady Joan Appleyard

After Lady Park's retirement in 2005, the Society was once more without a President, and the Trustees were honoured when Lady Joan Appleyard agreed in 2006 to take on the role, chairing her first Annual General Meeting in 2007. Her earlier career as past headmistress of St Swithun's School, Winchester (1986-1994), as well as her experience as President of the Girls' Schools' Association (1992-93) means that she has brought to the Society a very wide knowledge of the educational and professional opportunities available to women.

Amongst Lady Appleyard's many other interests is her involvement with the English Speaking Union (ESU). When Joan's husband, Sir Leonard Appleyard, was Britain's Ambassador to China she had been persuaded by Baroness Heather Brigstocke (1929-2004) to set up a new branch of the ESU in Beijing, which achieved much success. On return to this country Lady Appleyard was appointed Vice Chairman of the English Speaking Union. Some of her other interests have led to her also chairing the Executive Committee of the Hants & Islands Historic Churches Trust.

Vice Presidents

There are currently two Vice-Presidents serving the Society. _Her Honour Suzanne Stewart_ accepted the Society's invitation in 1995. She has had a distinguished career at the Bar, having begun her training at a time when there were no women judges, nor even female ushers. She was appointed a Crown Court Judge in 1973, remaining in the post for twenty-two years before retiring. Judge Stewart's interest in the Society stemmed from her friendship with Mrs Thom (see Chapter 5), whom she had met when they were both students at St Andrew's University. She remarked that her family had always been involved with women's causes, as she came from "a long line of Suffragists".

Dame Tamsyn Imison DBE, MA, FRSA who became Vice President in 2002 is a distinguished academic and educational strategist. Her interest in zoology led to a teaching career, and her lifelong involvement in learning resulted in her becoming the headteacher of a prestigious school. She has received degrees from Somerville College Oxford (for which she is an honorary Fellow), Queen Mary College London, the Ruskin School of Drawing and Fine Art and the Open University, and heads a range of committees, including equal opportunities and the National Teaching Awards Panel. She was made a Dame Commander of the British Empire in 1998.

CHAIRMEN AND OTHER OFFICERS

Mrs Gillis Burgess (Chairman 1993-2003)

After joining the Committee in 1973 Gillis was able to bring her considerable experience with the Professional Classes Aid Council (PCAC), as well as with the National Book League and in the antiquarian book trade, to the work of the Society. Gillis was elected Vice Chairman of Committee in 1989 then Chairman in 1993, when Mrs Thom retired. As Chairman, one of her most important duties was to organise the preservation of the Society's rich historical archive – which in due course would come to be housed at Girton College Cambridge. When Mrs Golding died, Gillis Burgess had personally collected all the records and files from Buckinghamshire, and arranged to have them stored at PCAC's premises, where the Society's Committee meetings were now being held. As Chairman she then led the negotiations for the long-term preservation of the archive, and oversaw the arrangements for a research student to be offered a bursary in order to make use of that historical archive.

Asked to summarise memories of her years on the Committee she commented that its composition changed from being made up at first of "concerned amateurs", albeit from professional backgrounds, to a group where nowadays the majority of Trustees are able to bring their widespread

Mrs Gillis Burgess   *Dr Carolyn Boulter*

first-hand knowledge and experience to benefit the Society. She has always found meeting candidates at interviews very rewarding: from a middle-aged woman hoping to enhance her employment prospects through training to ice celebration cakes, to a postgraduate student who had applied to train in underwater archaeology.

Gillis stepped down from the Chairmanship in 2003, after ten years' effective leadership, and she continues to be a well-informed and dedicated member of the Committee. More recently, she has also proved to be an invaluable 'editorial assistant' in the preparation of the last three chapters of this book.

Dr Carolyn Boulter (Chairman from 2003)

The present Chairman of Committee is Dr Carolyn Boulter (née Blatch) who succeeded Mrs Burgess in 2003. Carolyn was recruited to the Committee by Joan Jardine Brown, a near neighbour. Carolyn has had a career in teaching and research in science education; she retired from her lectureship at Reading University in 2001. Her recent voluntary activities include chairing in the adult Magistrate's Court in Reading; and she was appointed to the Court of the Clothworkers' Company in 2005, after having been a Liverywoman since 1995.[5] Carolyn was appointed High Sheriff of Berkshire for 2008-2009 – a position which only three or four women have held since the beginning of the thirteenth century. As a reflection of some of her central concerns, Carolyn chose as themes during her busy year in that office 'Women defendants in the Criminal Justice System', 'Environmental Education for Sustainability' and

'Interfaith Dialogue'.

Carolyn's membership of the Society reflects her abiding interest in charitable work in general. A quarter of a century after she joined the Society she is still passionately keen to assist it to continue its traditions into the future, by adapting to contemporary needs. She is proud of the way the Society's projects have developed over time and is actively involved in expanding its ever-present need for fund-raising. She has also led the Committee into its present compliance with Good Governance regulations, through annual Development Days and the 2009 Conference 'Transforming Charities', as well as playing a major part in the ongoing programme to publicise the existence of the archives.

Vice Chairman, Ms Joanna Murray, is a commercial pilot who manages to fit virtually all Committee meetings into her busy working schedule as well as her family life. Joanna became a member of the Committee in 1995 and has the distinction of being the only Trustee who is a former grantee of the Society, so she is well placed to understand the issues facing today's applicants. She was responsible with Tim Robson, her partner, for setting up the Society's website in 2005 which has proved of great benefit to potential applicants as well as providing wider publicity for SPTW.

Past Committee Member Mrs Joan Jardine Brown (née Butler b.1917)

The second personality to be accorded more substantial space in this chapter is Mrs Joan Jardine Brown, who illustrates the long-serving commitment of so many members of this Society. Joan was a member of the Committee from February 1964 until her retirement in September 2005, but she continues to retain an interest in its affairs to the present day. She recalls attending her first Committee meeting: "A table-full of white-haired old women is what I first remember. Now I am one of them!" Joan remarked that "at first the meetings were quite formal. People were never addressed by their full names; and hats were worn to meetings." She added that these days meetings were much more relaxed than in the sixties and seventies – "more fun. It's always been interesting but now it's fun." When Joan joined the Committee her children were still at school, and she was working as a physiotherapist at the Chelsea Hospital for Women. Her early courses of training in the 1930s were at that time known as "Massage and Medical Gymnastics" and "Medical Electricity and Light and Electrotherapy". The information regarding choice of career of some of the Society's earlier grantees (mentioned in Chapter 4) indicates that her chosen profession was growing in popularity during the 1930s. At that time the title Physiotherapist was not applied to this specialism, but during World War II she automatically became a member of what was by then the Chartered Society of Physiotherapists.

Joan Butler was educated at Edgbaston High School in Birmingham then

Mrs Joan Jardine Brown
and her 'Prima' yacht design

at age fourteen transferred to an independent boarding school (St Felix's) in Southwold, Suffolk. Joan later became chairman of the Old Felixians during the years between being a mother and a grandmother. She admitted that she had "drifted into" physiotherapy; and that her career choice was "not influenced in the least" by her school as she "knew exactly what she wanted to do when she left ... which was to get married". She married her first husband, Robert in 1958; he died in 1972.[6]

Joan's father, Dr Thomas Harrison Butler[7], an honorary ophthalmic surgeon, sailed and designed yachts as a hobby, an interest which his daughter shared. His boats are now built all over the world. At the age of nineteen, Joan herself designed a yacht which she named *Prima*; this was at the same time that she was working for her professional examinations. That design has been built abroad at least five times, but until 2002 when two students at Lyme Regis Boat-Building College used her lines for a course project, Joan had never seen her in three-dimensional form (see photograph). There is now a Harrison-Butler Association originally formed by six founding members who all owned HJB yachts. After her second husband's death in 1976 (after only thirteen months of marriage) Joan found the running of this Association as President, very therapeutic. There are now over 200 members.

Joan Jardine Brown represents an era which is now almost forgotten in twenty-first century Britain. Her parents' children were born in a number of different countries: at the time of their marriage her father was a Plague Officer in South Africa. His fiancée went out to Cape Town for their wedding in 1900, which was held in Cape Town Cathedral. The bride wore her petticoat for the ceremony, as she had left her skirt hanging in the cupboard in her state-room on the boat! Later the family lived in Jerusalem, but returned to England where Dr Butler later became a distinguished ophthalmologist.[8]

Asked to recall any particular cases from her Committee days which have stayed in her memory, Joan mentioned one from the 1960s: a divorced mother of a seven-year-old son, training to be a solicitor. This woman seemed to be "a rather difficult character". However, the Committee members felt that they must not let their personal feelings affect their decisions and so they agreed a grant to enable the applicant to complete her training. Sadly though, "she ratted on us and finally we had to send in the bailiffs; but she had learned enough law to have made everything over to her son". Happily, such incidents are rare. When the time came for Joan to retire from the Committee in 2005, she admitted that she would miss the meetings: "One used not to know other members apart from at meetings, but it is different now". Social events, Development Days and plans for the 2009 celebrations have helped to cement friendships between Committee members.

SECRETARIES 1989 TO THE PRESENT

The Rev. Brian Harris

The closing years of the 20th Century were marked by another 'first' for the Society: the appointment of a male Secretary. After Mrs Golding's death in December 1988 there was a brief period when no salaried employee held the post. Instead, the Chairman and Vice Chairman had to oversee the administration, management of meetings and personal interaction with the grantees.

In due course, the process of advertising for and selecting a new Secretary got under way, and during the summer of 1989 a recently-retired Church of England Minister was appointed. This was the Rev. Brian Harris. It was the great good luck of the Society that Brian's wife Shirley was not only interested in the work he then took on, but was willing to give freely of her own time and expertise in carrying out many additional activities. For the next 13 years the Society benefited from this couple's dedication to its affairs. Brian retired as Secretary in December 2002.

Having started his working life in teaching, Brian had left his headteacher post at the age of 48 to attend theological college, where he was ordained. He later returned to the world of education, accepting a headship in a comprehensive school in Manchester, where he remained until officially retiring: at which point he returned to the Ministry. It was after a second retirement, from his Ministry in Warburton, that he decided to apply for SPTW's secretaryship.

On appointment, Brian's first task was to re-establish close contact with the grantees, as to some extent they had been left alone during Mrs Golding's lengthy final illness. It was necessary to get in touch with many of the grantees as he found that a number of repayments had lapsed, and some grantees had failed to take out the debt-guarantee insurance which was normally required if applicants were unable to provide appropriate guarantors. Brian arranged that the missing premiums would be paid, in order to keep the policies active. He rekindled the tradition of regular sympathetic contact with all the grantees which had always been a feature of previous secretaries' practices.

Although the majority of such contacts were friendly and productive, he recalls that one young woman who had been helped with the costs of her PhD course actually "laughed in his face" when he asked her to pay up! Another difficulty he had to overcome related to the conditions surrounding the large bequest from Ms Walters – now known as the Celtic Fund – as grantees wishing to benefit from this fund were, according to the conditions

The Reverend Brian Harris

of the benefactor, to be practising Christians but should also be of 'Celtic origin'. The Charity Commissioners had frozen the fund's account until they could be satisfied regarding the uses to which it was being put. Brian Harris was able to supply the appropriate reassurances to them and access to the bank account was restored, to the relief of the Committee.

Mrs Morgan Thompson

After Mr Harris's retirement the Society was again most fortunate in the appointment of his replacement, Morgan Thompson.[9] Her employment, from January 2003 until she left in 2007 to live abroad with her family, followed successful careers in administration and as a lecturer in higher education.[10] Morgan has served as a Magistrate, as a member of voluntary committees, and finds time to pursue a wide range of other activities. She brought to the Society a very deep and personal concern for the applicants, which is apparent from the many letters from grantees attesting to the support she gave them. During her five years with SPTW changes in student funding meant much anxiety for many; and her wise and efficient administration also assisted the Society to implement financial changes and to stabilise the capital fund. She did much to expand the membership; created a Newsletter for members; and oversaw the development of the website. Morgan was also keen to expand connections with other charities and made many new contacts. The Trustees were very sorry to lose Morgan's services, but said goodbye in style by giving her a tea party, held at the Women's Library in March 2008.

Mrs Michelle Bennett

Faced with the task of replacing such an excellent Secretary, the Trustees feel very fortunate that after national press and on-line advertisements, a very strong field of applicants emerged, and they are privileged to have attracted Michelle Bennett to the post. Michelle started work with SPTW in November 2007 and in the best traditions of her predecessors she carries out her duties with great enthusiasm and expertise. Her previous experience over seventeen years as a higher education manager and administrator at the Royal College of Nursing, as well as experience as a teaching assistant, is now being used to SPTW's advantage. Her priorities for the future include organising the records from the last twenty years, which have yet to be added to the Girton archive (a task which is made more exacting as such records must comply with the Data Protection Act), and to continue the improvements in the ways that students are now contacted, through further development of electronic communication and computerisation of the Society's work.

STORING THE ARCHIVE: FIRST STEPS

The second major task facing Brian Harris when he was appointed Secretary was to take control of the considerable quantity of papers which had accumulated over more than a hundred years, and which, for many decades since 1940, had been stored at Mrs Golding's home in Buckinghamshire. Much of the material was kept in tea chests and cardboard boxes – these had been transported to London by Mrs Gillis Burgess after Mrs Golding's death – and were now to be transferred to Brian's garage. The arrangement was meant to be 'temporary', but there they stayed for almost eight years.

The Committee had long been considering how to make its rich archive accessible to a wider readership, and the idea arose that it should be placed in a suitable library so that researchers of women's history could make use of it. Negotiations with some institutions had failed; but a successful approach to the Mistress of Girton College was made through Mrs Thom, a previous Chairman of Committee, and in due course the boxes were transferred there and put under the care of its archivist, Mrs Kate Perry. This took place early in 1997, with the Society making a donation of £200 to the college library "for storage".[11]

Having the Society's archive housed in such a prestigious library did not, at first, produce the wider awareness of its existence which had been hoped for. However, a Fulbright Travel Scholar from the USA, Michelle Tusan, enquired at Girton if any archives were available which would augment the materials about SPEW which she already knew about. She wrote: "As it turned out, the Society had recently offered its archival records to Girton College. They arrived in three tea chests and several cartons on 30 January 1997, having been stored for a number of years in a basement belonging to

Mrs Kate Perry (standing) at the Girton College archives
assisting the researcher

the current secretary of the association." Tusan's article went on to describe the content of the archive, which at that time was uncatalogued.[12] More importantly, the Australian social historian Dr Ellen Jordan[13] (co-author of this book) who had been writing about the Society for many years using sources such as the *English Woman's Journal*, paid a visit to Girton for the first time in June 1999, two years after the SPEW files had been transferred there. Since then, she has used the files as a basis for three academic publications (see References 2001; 2002; 2006) and has also made mention of them in a number of conference papers.

EXTENDING AWARENESS OF THE ARCHIVE'S EXISTENCE

The archive had been at the Girton library since January 1997; yet two years later there was still little public awareness of its existence, and the Committee felt it was time to consider additional means of bringing this about. The suggestion arose that some of the Society's precious capital should be used in offering a bursary to a researcher who would in return make use of its content. Negotiations with a number of universities and institutes of higher education followed, in an attempt to find one who was prepared to link their own plans for a research studentship to the Society's wish to have their archive used as part of the topic. A successful conclusion was reached with the Cheltenham and Gloucester College of Higher Education (now the University of Gloucestershire) who planned to offer a three-year research studentship as part of its own expansion programme. The College's Faculty of Education and Social Science agreed to include in its advertisement an option for the successful applicant to select from three possible areas of interest, which it was felt the Society's archive could support. In addition to the student being supervised by the Faculty's Professor, Dr Mary Fuller[14], the historiographic aspects of the study would be under the guidance of a member of Cambridge University's staff, Dr Pam Hirsch[15].

In due course, the selection process resulted in Anne Bridger being enrolled on the University's Ph.D programme, with her three-year appointment dating from 1 January 2000. Her chosen topic, from amongst those offered within the archive's contents, was the Society's role in opening up commercial occupations to women. She was awarded her degree at the end of three years for a thesis entitled "A Century of Women's Employment in Clerical Occupations 1850-1950, with particular reference to the role of the Society for Promoting the Employment of Women".[16] This topic covers only a small part of the rich historical evidence the archive contains, and it is hoped that many other researchers will continue to explore its content in order to ensure that the Society does not lose its heritage. Girton College's archivist, Mrs Kate Perry, is an invaluable source of knowledge, help and advice, and without her this book, and Anne's thesis, would be the poorer.

LETTERS FROM GRANTEES

For many years Annual Reports carried extracts from the letters received from grateful grantees, which frequently praised the Secretary personally for her care and kindness, and detailing the ways in which the Society's loan had enabled a grantee to fulfil an ambition. Earlier chapters have offered brief examples of such letters, and the additional extracts which are included here indicate that what has not changed over the centuries is the heartfelt gratitude of the recipients of loans, as well as the need for a Society such as this to continue to exist. The Annual Report for 2001 included a number of such extracts, of which these are two examples:

> From a newspaper journalist: I enclose the final repayment of my £1000 loan from the SPTW. Let me take the opportunity to thank the SPTW for their generous loan and repayment procedure. The money was vitally

important in enabling me to complete my journalism training course. I would very much like to keep in touch with the SPTW. Some day I hope to be in a position to fund future loans for young women.

<u>From a Student Osteopath</u>: It was great to receive your letter for obvious reasons. I would just like to take the opportunity to say how warm and encouraging everyone was in my interview, and if that could be passed on to relevant persons I would be most grateful.

Many former grantees have subsequently become subscribing members of the Society, as these two examples bear witness: "Please find enclosed a donation to continue supporting the Society's work in helping women in training. I would be interested in finding out about becoming a subscribing member of the Society. Without the help of the Society when needed, I would not be a Veterinary Surgeon now." And from a Psychologist: "Please find enclosed cheque as my subscription... . Thank you for the Annual Report. It is good to read about how the Society functions, and continues its very supportive work."

In 2009 a long letter was received from a Research Fellow, part of which is reproduced here:

Luck nearly always seems to be on my side. ... When I didn't have enough money to complete my [MSc] year I was lucky enough to receive a loan from SPTW.

Obtaining my [postgraduate degree] in London opened many a door not only the opportunity to study malaria and receive my PhD ... but also collaborations in Tanzania, USA and Oxford. Following my studies in Tanzania I was asked to return as a research assistant after being awarded a grant from the Bill and Melinda Gates Malaria Foundation. Working and living in Africa was a life-long ambition which I relished and still miss every day. Currently I am now a research fellow ... where if awarded further grants I may have the opportunity to continue my research of trypanosomiasis and travel to Uganda. ... Working in Tanzania I saw the effect of poverty on people and their communities which made me passionate about helping people; be it through my science research in understanding how to prevent and treat tropical diseases or having more hands-on approach as in my [earlier] charity work in India.

I have to thank SPTW for their generous support of my education without which I would not be who and where I am today. I would not have achieved so many of my goals and be lucky enough to be doing a job that is interesting and challenging. Thank you.

INTO THE FUTURE

Throughout its 150 years the SPTW has helped women to achieve their professional ambitions. Society continues to change as do the experiences of the women who apply for loans, and their access to funding. The years since the Dearing Report[17] have seen the introduction of student loans and increased financial burdens for those embarking on further education, with the average debt at the end of a first degree now well in excess of £20,000. The Society continues to be sought out by students as SPTW's awards, unlike commercial loans, remain interest free. Nevertheless, the Society has had to make more stringent conditions for repayment to avoid being at the end of the queue for settlement. Efforts are made to link the students more closely to the aims and work of the Society in order that they may wish to repay it more quickly;[18] but Trustees will need to engage grantees even more closely with the work SPTW does, as greater proportions of young people are to be encouraged by the Government to attend university.

Another issue which continues to be debated is the reason the Society remains focussed on loans for women. Sometimes this stance is questioned by those who are concerned about equal opportunities for men: they see men's clubs opening their doors to women; and many consider that the battle for equal opportunities for women has been won. Trustees are aware, however, that although huge strides have been made in women's access to the professions, the same cannot be said about the promotion of women to the top positions: society still penalises women for trying to raise children, care for dependent relatives and manage a substantial full-time job at the same time, a problem which could grow as recession bites.[19] There is in the Trustees' view still much work to do in helping women to enter the professions and reach the highest levels and this is best done by helping to encourage women to be major contributors to the country's economy.

The roots of the Society for Promoting the Employment of Women were embedded in the attitudes, times and people of the Women's Suffrage Movement, with its insistence on the right of women to equality of opportunity – to vote, to own property, and to work. The hope for the future might be that this voice might be reclaimed and used in a society where the case for change has to be made with greater subtlety in what is seen by some as a post-feminist age.

The Society's main function today relies on a circulating capital fund which is dependent on regular repayment from grantees as well as a good return on investments. When, as at present, demands for loans increase and interest returns are uncertain, this sum needs to be more substantial and a firm hope for the future is that the Society will continue to attract capital not only from donations and bequests but also from businesses. In recent years SPTW has shortened the loan repayment time and the level of repayments has improved, largely as a result of the hard work of the Committee and

Secretaries in cementing good relationships with grantees. That has been a constant theme over the centuries, and one that is seen as vital to the Trustees' present work. Forging long-standing relationships with grantees is clearly vital to a healthy future for the Society, as is the development of networks between the grantees themselves, which could encourage their commitment to future applicants.

This Society has always been in touch with other like-minded charities and, as earlier chapters have shown, some have already been amalgamated into it. Networking with other charities is a primary concern for the present Chairman and Trustees, as the belief that there are lessons to be learnt from and with others in the field, about the ways in which small charities such as this transform to meet changing needs is central to SPTW's future. This belief formed the motivation for the mounting of the 2009 Conference, "Transforming Charities", in July of the 150th anniversary year.

Finally, it is perhaps worth while repeating the fervent wish which had been expressed by Gertrude King in April 1926 (see Chapter 4), that the Society's name will live on, whatever changes are likely to befall it in the future:

> It is difficult to change the name of anything and yet retain the prestige of that which had the original name. If the Society has a new name in alluding to its early days and early supporters it will be necessary to say that it was founded in 1859 under the name of the Society for Promoting the Employment of Women etc. ... You must guard against the idea of its being a new Society just started; [others would then] get the credit for all our dear old Society has done and all those dear people who signed the Articles of Association will be quite forgotten. ... it is very difficult to find [a name that suits the present work] ... and yet retains the high tone of self-respect and self-help which was the characteristic of the Society in the old days.

---

1   Sir Donald Hawley, KCMG, MBE died in January 2008.

2   Although Committee meetings are now held quarterly, there are many other occasions when members need to attend to Society business.

3   Eleanor Rathbone (1872-1946) stood for Parliament as an Independent candidate, and was elected as the first woman MP of the Combined English Universities (from 1929 until her death). She was a good friend of Daphne Park's headmistress Muriel Davies. The two women travelled to Germany and Spain in the late 1930s and brought back Jewish children from Germany, and Basque children from Spain, where they were then educated at Dalton's School.
   Whilst she was SPTW President, Lady Park succeeded in getting some welcome financial support for the Society from the Eleanor Rathbone Trust.

4   The students do not work in Britain: they are here to learn, and when trained, will eventually return to their own country and disseminate the broad range of skills which the charity is helping them to acquire.

5   By coincidence, the Clothworkers was one of the earliest City Companies to make regular financial donations to the Society during the nineteenth century: indeed, Sir Owen Roberts (and his wife, featured in Chapter 3) played an important part in SPEW's affairs.

6   Robert Jardine Brown, MA, LL.D, D.Litt. created the BBC's legal department and ran it for 17 years under Lord Reith. Many years later he became Principal of the College of Estate Management, and the first Dean of that Faculty of Urban and Regional Studies when it was absorbed into Reading University.

7   Thomas Harrison Butler, MA, DM (Oxon), FRCS (Hon.), ARINA (Hon), was the author of a book *Cruising Yachts: Design and Performance* published by Excellent Press, London, 4th ed. 1995.

8   Other well-known relatives of the Butlers include the nineteenth-century social reformer (and friend of the Society's founder Jessie Boucherett) Josephine Butler (1828-1906); and the architect of the ground-breaking 1944 Education Act, the Rt.Hon. Richard Austen (Rab) Butler, MP (1902-1982).

9   Morgan is depicted in the photograph on page 154. She is far right on the back row.

10   As part of Mrs Thompson's work as course tutor during the 1980s she designed a module on "The Changing Role of Women" – an innovative topic at that time - which demonstrates her "long standing interest and commitment to the promotion and facilitation of learning for women".

11   The Society's link with Girton is historic, since the college's founders, Emily Davies and Barbara Bodichon, were both closely associated with SPEW's origins; Davies served on SPEW's Committee, even acting as Hon. Secretary for a time; and Jessie Boucherett was also one of the first to contribute towards the Girton fund-raising.

12   M E Tusan 2000 'Not the Ordinary Victorian Charity': The Society for Promoting the Employment of Women Archive' in *History Workshop Journal* No.49, 221-29.

13   See Jordan 1998.

14   Professor Mary Fuller, Department of Education, Faculty of Education, Natural and Social Sciences, University of Gloucestershire.

15   Dr Pam Hirsch, University Lecturer in English Literature and Film Theory, Faculty of Education, University of Cambridge; Graduate Tutor, Newnham College, Cambridge.

16   The thesis was subsequently selected by the British Library to be included in its first selection of doctoral theses to be digitalised, chosen on the basis of being one of the most frequently-requested items. Drs Jordan and Bridger also published an article in *Women's History Review*, as a result of which enquiries from other researchers have been received, so we feel that SPTW's hope of disseminating its story is at last being realised. (See Reference Jordan and Bridger 2006).

17   The Dearing Report (1997) identified the gap in funding for universities who were being encouraged to take an increasing proportion of the post-18 age group.

18   The archives contain many letters from grantees indicating their awareness of such a responsibility as well as their gratitude. The most recent of these, received in 2009 from a 47-year old married woman in the third year of her Honours degree course, notes that the Society "was the only one to offer any financial help and even though it is a loan I am truly grateful; and it is my duty to pay it back so someone else can benefit, just as I have."

19   In 2009 this attitude has become more apparent as women's jobs are declining at about twice the rate of men's.

REFERENCES

Bakewell, Joan. 2003. *The Centre of the Bed*. London: Hodder & Stoughton.

Beale, Anne. 1889. "Finding Employment for women." *The Quiver*, 113-6.

Blackburn, Helen. 1902. *Women's Suffrage*. London: Williams & Norgate.

Boucherett, Jessie. 1864. "Adelaide Anne Procter." *English Woman's Journal*, 13 (72): 17-21.

Boucherett, Jessie. 1884. "The Industrial Movement." In Theodore Stanton (Ed.), *The Woman Question in Europe*. London: Sampson Low.

Bridger, Anne. 2003. *A Century of Women's Employment in Clerical Occupations: 1850–1950, with particular reference to the role of the Society for Promoting the Employment of Women*. Thesis submitted to the University of Gloucestershire in accordance with requirements of degree of Doctor of Philosophy in the Faculty of Education and Social Sciences.

Chalmers, F. Graeme, 1998. *Women in the Nineteenth-century Art World: Schools of Art and Design for Women in London and Philadelphia*. London : Greenwood Press.

Cockburn, Cynthia. 1991. *In the Way of Women: Men's Resistance to Sex Equality in Organizations*. London: Macmillan.

Cohn, Samuel. 1985. *The Process of Occupational Sex-Typing: The Feminization of Clerical Labor in Great Britain*. Philadelphia: Temple University Press.

Crawford, Elizabeth. 1999. *The Women's Suffrage Movement: A Reference Guide 1866-1928*. London: UCL Press.

Crompton, Rosemary, and Gareth Jones. 1984. *White Collar Proletariat: Deskilling and Gender in the Clerical Labour Process*. London: Macmillan.

Cuffe, Ellen Odette and Constance Hoster. 1924. *Style and Title. A complete guide to social forms of address*. London: Christophers.

Cundall, Joseph. 1895. *A Brief History of Wood-Engraving from its Invention*. London: Sampson Low, Marston and Company.

Davies, Emily. 2004. *Emily Davies: Collected Letters 1861-1875*. Ann B. Murphy and Deirdre Raftery (Eds), Charlottesville and London: University of Virgina Press.

Davies, M. 1982. *Woman's Place Is at the Typewriter: Office Work and Office Workers 1870-1930*. Philadelphia: Temple University Press.

Diamond, Marion. 1999. *Emigration and Empire : The Life of Maria S. Rye*. New York: Garland Pub.

Donnison, Jean. 1977. *Midwives and Medical Men: A History of Inter-Professional Rivalries and Women's Rights*. New York: Schoken Books.

Drake, Barbara. 1984. *Women in Trade Unions*. London: Virago.

E. 1864. "Law-Copying as an Employment for Women". *The Alexandra Magazine & Englishwoman's Journal*, 5: 305-310.

Faithfull, Emily. 1871. "Women's Work, with Special Reference to Industrial Employment." *Journal of the Society of Arts*, 1871: 378-383.

Gordon, Peter. 1999. "Introduction." Knightley, Louisa M. *Politics and Society: The Journals of Lady Knightley of Fawsley 1885 to 1913*. Northampton: NRS.

Grogan, Mercy. 1880. *How Women may Earn a Living*. London: Cassell, Petter, Galpin.

Harrison, John. 1888. "Type-Writers and Type-Writing." *Journal of the Royal Society of Arts*, 17: 345-55.

Hinings, Jessica. 2004. "Pfeiffer, Emily Jane (1827–1890)". *Oxford Dictionary of National Biography*, Oxford University Press.

Hirsch, Pam. 1998. *Barbara Leigh Smith Bodichon 1827-1891: Feminist, Author and Rebel*. London: Chatto & Windus.

Howes, Bea. 1967. *Arbiter of Elegance*. London. The Harvill Press Limited.

Jameson, Anna. 1846. *Memoirs and Essays Illustrative of Art, Literature and Social Morals*. London: Bentley.

Jameson, Anna. 1855. *Sisters of Charity: Catholic and Protestant, Abroad and at Home*. London: Longman, Brown, Green, & Longmans.

Jameson, Anna. 1856. *The Communion of Labour*. London: Bentley.

Jordan, Ellen. 1998. "'The great principle of English fair-play': The admission of women to the Pharmaceutical Society of Great Britain." *Women's History Review*, 7 (3):381-409.

Jordan, Ellen. 1999a."'Women's work in the world': The birth of a discourse, London 1858." *Nineteenth Century Feminisms*, 1 (1):12-38.

Jordan, Ellen. 1999b *The Women's Movement and Women's Employment in Nineteenth Century Britain*. London: Routledge.

Jordan, Ellen. 2001. "'Admitting . . . a dozen women into the Society": The first women members of the British Pharmaceutical Society.' *Pharmaceutical Historian*, 31 (2): 18-26.

Jordan, Ellen. 2002. "'Suitable and Remunerative Employment': the Feminisation of Hospital Dispensing in Late Nineteenth Century England." *Social History of Medicine*, 15 (3): 429-456.

Jordan, Ellen and Anne Bridger. 2006. "'An unexpected recruit to feminism': Jessie Boucherett, the Society for Promoting the Employment of Women, and the importance of being wealthy." *Women's History Review*, 15(3): 385-412.

Keep, Christopher. 1997. "The Cultural Work of the Type-Writer Girl." *Victorian Studies* 40 (3): 401-26.

Levine, Philippa. 1987. *Victorian Feminism 1850-1900*. London: Hutchinson.

Manners, Janetta. 1881. "The Employment of Women in the Public Service." *Quarterly Review*, 151:181-200.

Manton, Jo. 1965. *Elizabeth Garrett Anderson*. London: Methuen.

Martindale, Hilda. 1938. *Women Servants of the State 1870-1938. A History of Women in the Civil Service*. London: Geo Allen & Unwin Ltd.

Martindale, Hilda. 1944. *From One Generation to the Other*. London: Geo Allen & Unwin Ltd.

Martineau, Harriet. 1859. "Female Industry." *Edinburgh Review*, 109: 293-336.

Parkes, Bessie Rayner. 1860. "A Year's Experience in Woman's Work." T.N.A.P.S.S., 1860: 811-819.

Parliamentary Papers. 1875. Appendix to First Report of the Civil Service Inquiry Commission, 23: 218-9.

Pinchbeck, Ivy. 1969. *Women Workers and the Industrial Revolution 1750-1850*. London: Frank Cass.

Scudamore, F. 1871. Report by Mr Scudamore on the Re-organization of the Telegraph System of the United Kingdom. London: H.M.S.O.

Sidebottom, Daphne. 1964. "Some Aspects of the Training and Employment of Women During the Last Hundred Years". *The Woman Engineer*, vol.9, No.12. Spring (14-17).

Smith, Barbara Leigh. 1857. *Women and Work*. London: Bosworth & Harrison.

Spring-Rice, Margery. 1939. *Working-Class Wives. Their Health and Conditions*. Pelican

Stokes, Penelope. 1992. *Norland: The Story of the first one hundred years*. Norland College.

Stone, James S. 1994. *Emily Faithfull: Victorian Champion of Women's Rights*. Toronto: P.D. Meaney.

Sturrock, June. 1999. "Women, work and the *Monthly Packet*." *Nineteenth Century Feminisms*, 1 (1): 64-80.

Tusan, Michelle. 2004. "Performing Work: Gender, Class, and the Printing Trade in Victorian Britain." *Journal of Women's History* 16 (1): 103-126

Yonge, Charlotte M. 1865. *The Clever Woman of the Family*. London: Macmillan

Young, Michael. 1961. *The Rise of the Meritocracy, 1870-2033: an essay on education*. Penguin.

INDEX